Praise for
LOVE IS THE BEST MEDICINE

"Nick Trout is back with a follow-up to his bestselling *Tell Me Where It Hurts: A Day of Humor, Healing, and Hope in My Life as an Animal Surgeon.* It's filled with the same engaging writing readers now expect from Trout, who is often compared to James Herriot. And as lovers of dog stories know, that is a very good thing."

—*USA Today*

"Veterinarian Trout offers up a surefire comfort read for Animal Planet fans with this intimate look at the lives of two dogs and the people who loved them . . . Easily traversing the border between science and society, Trout's chronicle will appeal to readers from teens to grandparents."　　　　　　　　　　　　　—*Booklist*

"What he's really writing about, and teaching the rest of us, is how to truly live."　　　　　　　　　　　　　—*The Free Lance-Star*

"Trout, a surgeon at Boston's Angell Animal Medical Center and bestselling author of *Tell Me Where It Hurts,* delivers his heartfelt account with a humorous introspection that reaffirms the extraordinary level of caring veterinarians can have for their patients. Highly recommended for lovers of animals of all shapes and sizes."

—*Library Journal*

"A riveting emotional roller coaster into the behind-the-scenes life of a veterinarian."　　　　　　—**Temple Grandin,** author of
Animals in Translation and *Animals Make Us Human*

"I sat in my human mom's lap while she read *Love Is the Best Medicine*. She liked it a lot and said 'Everyone should read this book!' She laughed, and I had to lick the tears from her cheeks when she cried."

—**Bogie**, dog of *New York Times* bestselling author
Debbie Macomber

"Dr. Nick Trout's latest work is an unflinchingly honest journey through love, loss, and redemption. This is a book not only for anyone who has ever loved an animal, but for all who have loved. Dr. Trout allows us an intimate glimpse into the heart of a veterinary surgeon, and the souls of the patients he fights to save. There are many lessons here: of hope conquering fear, joy triumphing over grief, and family getting us through it all."

—**Dr. Louise Murray**, author of *Vet Confidential*

"This beautifully written book is from the heart and soul of Dr. Nick Trout; an extraordinary veterinary surgeon who has found that perfect balance of genuine compassion and dedicated skill. He eloquently reveals the undeniable importance of our relationship with animals and the rich rewards of having them in our lives. Utterly delightful and compelling, *Love Is the Best Medicine* is a must read."

—**Melanie Sue Bowles**, author of *The Horses of Proud Spirit*
and *Hoof Prints: More Stories from Proud Spirit*

LOVE IS THE
BEST MEDICINE

ALSO BY NICK TROUT

Tell Me Where It Hurts

LOVE IS THE
BEST MEDICINE

What Two Dogs Taught One Veterinarian
About Hope, Humility, and Everyday Miracles

DR. NICK TROUT

BROADWAY BOOKS

New York

Originally published in hardcover in slightly different form
by Broadway Books, an imprint of the Crown Publishing Group,
a division of Random House, Inc., New York, in 2010.

This book contains an excerpt from the forthcoming book *Ever By My Side*
by Dr. Nicholas Trout. This excerpt has been set for this edition only and may
not reflect the final content of the forthcoming edition.

Library of Congress Cataloging-in-Publication Data
Trout, Nick.
Love is the best medicine / by Nick Trout.
p. cm.
1. Dogs—Anecdotes. 2. Human-animal
relationships—Anecdotes. I. Title.
SF426.2.T76   2010
636.7—dc22   2009022423

ISBN 978-0-7679-3198-4

Printed in the United States of America

COVER DESIGN BY JEAN TRAINA

Photograph on cover and title page by GK Hart/Vikki Hart/Getty Images

2 4 6 8 10 9 7 5 3 1

First Paperback Edition

For Sandi and Cleo, Helen and Eileen

Experience is not what happens to a man; it is what a man does with what happens to him.

—ALDOUS HUXLEY

Contents

Author's Note

THIRTY years ago, as a wide-eyed, dumbstruck teenager, I helped resuscitate a lifeless newborn puppy, rudely dispatched into this world via cesarean section. For me it was a pivotal event, an awakening, igniting a dream and ultimately a career as a veterinarian. Decades later, I can still be floored by the surge of excitement that struck me back then. Sometimes it can be brazen like the fist-pumping thrill of deciphering a mysterious ailment. Sometimes it can be subtle, hidden behind a secret smile as you watch a reunion between an old man and his four-legged companion from afar. No matter what form it takes, veterinary medicine casts a spell and I was hooked long ago. I love that whenever I least expect it, I will feel the familiar buzz that reminds me there is something magical about healing sick animals.

In the twenty-first century, veterinarians can offer our pets advances in healthcare no less than, and, in some instances, more cutting edge than our own. Forget about your garden-variety joint replacements and kidney transplants, I'm talking about gene therapy, stem-cell treatment, and anti-cancer vaccines. This is happening right now and the scientific breakthroughs that make it all possible demand our understanding and respect.

At veterinary school we become indoctrinated in the church of the scientific method, accepting the gospel according to rational thought and proven data. There is always a logical explanation. Serendipity has no place in our daily skirmish between life and death. Like so many of my brethren, I drank the Kool-Aid, believed in this philosophy, but as soon as I graduated, I woke up in the real world of medical ambiguity, everyday miracles, everyday heartbreak, and the kind of life lessons that don't come with a lecture and a handout.

In my first book, *Tell Me Where It Hurts*, I tried to capture the pace, the rush, and the impact of all that is new in veterinary medicine, putting the reader on my side of the examination table, sharing the struggles and the joys of trying to heal animals. More importantly, I hoped to convey one simple and prevailing truth, that for all the fancy technology and medical advances, what endures and what will always matter most is the intensity of the relationship between human and animal. We can label the emotional connection between pet and owner with an inadequate and cold phrase like "bond," but for those of us humbled by the awesome responsibility of trying to keep the connection alive, perhaps we should call it as we see it. Fundamentally, our professional goal is to repair and sustain mutual love.

Most of what follows is my attempt to document the undeniable strength of this love, to discover what makes it tick, and to reveal everything you will *not* find in veterinary textbooks, through my encounters with some extraordinary humans and animals over a two-year period. These pet owners were kind enough to take me beyond the dispassionate detail of a pertinent clinical history and reveal another side to *their* stories, helping me comprehend the intensity of the relationship they want me to restore. Their insight serves as a reminder that, for the most part, pet and owner come as a package deal and the privilege of rendering care for animals has consequences far beyond the physical limitations of an ailing body covered in fur, feathers, or scales.

At the heart of this book are the true stories of two animals, Helen and Cleo, and their remarkable humans. Read on and you will appreciate that I am not playing favorites. There have been many easier cases to recount, tougher diseases sent packing, and successes that had me smiling for days. But I dare you to search your memories, filter for what really lingers, and come up with anything other than the highest highs and the lowest lows. These stories intersect at one point. From entirely different worlds their paths crossed because, independently, they sought medical attention from one veterinarian who happened to be me. Thankfully, though I may be integral to the plot, mine is at most a supporting role. The real stars of the show are easy to spot.

Where possible, I have tried to maintain the chronology of the major events, my memory supplemented by medical records, interviews with colleagues, e-mails, letters, telephone and face-to-face conversations with owners. In many instances I describe pertinent background and events surrounding these stories based upon facts and the emotional circumstances as they were conveyed to me. This was never meant to be a commissioned biography and as such it is influenced by *my* interpretation, taking the liberty to make inferences, to fill in the gaps with educated guesses, to envisage unrecorded conversations, all the while striving to build a story true to the essence and integrity of my characters, those on two legs and on four. In some cases, the names of pets, owners, and veterinarians and any particular identifiers have been changed to ensure anonymity. In others, real identities remain.

If life's journey is a continuous education and everything happens for a reason then this is my attempt to share some of what I have learned. Over the years I have come to appreciate how animals enter our lives prepared to teach and far from being burdened with an inability to speak, they have many different ways to communicate. It is up to us to *listen* more than *hear*, to look *into* more than *past*. What passes for understanding requires commitment, patience, and, granted, an occasional leap of faith, but every so often even the cynic can decipher our pets' messages and appreciate a simple yet indelible message. For me, these particular cases spoke loud and clear, giving me an unforgettable lesson in hope, generosity, and the incredible capacity for humans and animals to open their hearts to each other.

LOVE IS THE
BEST MEDICINE

1   HELEN

INSIDE the restaurant, they were just an ordinary couple, enjoying their dinner, comfortable with the lulls in conversation that define a successful relationship. Yet Ben was tuned in to everything unsaid, to the waves of distraction playing over Eileen's face, her refuge in the safety of neutral topics—his latest commission, an upcoming exhibition in California, the antics of their beloved Newfoundland dog, Didi, patiently waiting for them to come home. He knew what was really on Eileen's mind, but at this stage in their marriage he had learned his wife would talk about her troubles when the time was right.

Outside the restaurant, there was a creature waiting in the shadows. Historically, only certain humans—the kind with food—were of any interest to this animal and like most of her species, she relied heavily on olfactory guidance to pick her targets. But on this bitter, cloudless night, refrigerated air would have forced her to trust to visual cues, searching for victims with a friendly, receptive demeanor and preferably carrying a doggy bag.

An elderly husband and wife shuffled toward a frosty-white Cadillac like a couple of emperor penguins. By any standard they looked approachable, likely to be sympathetic, and there was that all-important polystyrene container in hand. Then the woman spoke, and the shrill and relentless pitch of her voice forced the creature to back off, the tirade fueled by an inattentive waitress, stale bread, and overpriced entrees, the woman's husband distracted and happy to grunt in agreement, his index finger working some meaty detritus trapped between difficult-to-reach molars.

Next up was a gaggle of twentysomething women, laughing and shouting, pitching back and forth, alcohol, high heels, and black ice adding to their amusement as they staggered across slippery asphalt arm in arm, five abreast. No doubt they were getting in practice for next month's office Christmas party. Only one of these Spice Girls kept a straight face and fortunately she was the one fumbling for a set of car keys.

There was a man overdressed in a suit and tie, out of place with an attractive woman in blue jeans, the two awkward together in the open raw darkness. She stood upright, feet together, hugging herself, drum tight, impervious to his forced small talk, his rehearsed prelude to plucking up his courage and leaning forward, hoping for a kiss, as she read the move and delivered a polite smile while extending a weak hand to shake. The moment said it all—thanks, but no thanks. Another blind date disaster, another phone number for her to screen on her caller ID.

The guy headed toward the pickup truck had encountered the creature before and perhaps it was recognition that had her edging out of the shadows until he opened the passenger side door and a stream of curses exploded in the frigid night air. The words were meaningless to her but their volume, clipped intonation, and vehemence packed a punch. His ice scraper was no longer in the glove compartment where he thought he had left it, forcing him to pull on the cuff of his lumberjack shirt and scour a hole through the gathering frost on his windshield.

And then there were Ben and Eileen, headed for a small SUV in the farthest corner of the lot. Despite the absence of a doggy bag, their body language sent all the right signals. They walked slowly, his arm around her shoulder, his head floating a foot above hers, angled down, a big hand visible and offering a reassuring squeeze.

"You've gone all quiet on me," said Ben. "You okay?"

Eileen looked up and worked on forcing a smile into her voice.

"I'm good," she said and added, "I was just thinking about Helen. I'm going to miss her, you know."

Ben nodded but kept quiet, watching her find the words.

"I mean, it's not as if she didn't have a wonderful life. Ninety-two years old—three children, nine grandchildren, twenty-one great-grandchildren. Independent, determined, and opinionated until the end *and* she gets to die peacefully in her sleep. What more could anyone ask for?"

Ben pursed his lips, keeping in step with her deliberate, short stride, surprised they had never gotten to this when he was eating his main course of homemade gnocchi. He had come prepared to discuss the death of Eileen's last living grandparent, Helen, to defend the inevitability and unpredictability of loss, the way it can summon injustice and anger as it clings to those left behind. But he could clearly see the only emotion welling up in his wife's big blue eyes was sadness.

"Your grandmother was a great lady and if 'Ma' taught me anything," Ben stretched out the *a* like a lifelong Red Sox fan from South Boston, "it would be not to go all mawkish over her passing. Let's not forget, Helen was the matriarch who nurtured three generations of unruly boys with the line 'Don't come crying to me when you're dead'!"

Eileen began to laugh, the uninhibited laughter of vulnerability and relief.

"You're absolutely right," she said, hearing Helen's familiar scratchy voice fade away inside her head. She looked up at her husband, loving him for his gift of always finding the right words and the satisfaction written all over his face for having done so.

"Thanks. And thanks again for dinner. It was great."

"You're very welcome," said Ben, pecking her on the cheek before breaking away and pressing the key fob, lights on the Toyota RAV 4 blinking in anticipation of their arrival.

Ever the gentleman, he came around to the passenger side and opened the door. He had time to squeeze in a theatrical bow and sweeping hand gesture before releasing a loud involuntary screech, as something small and black entered his peripheral vision from the left, moving at high speed and headed directly for his wife.

Some time later he would try to defend his shocked reaction, blaming the poor lighting, the moonless night, the absence of street-lamps, his myopia and need for a new contact prescription. He would reference his childhood fear of bears, his fleeting impression of a stealthy, possibly rabid beast, its velocity smacking of focus, target, and intent to harm. Finally he would claim that the controlled scream was his best attempt at offering his wife some kind of a warning, given all of these limitations.

"It's just a dog," said Eileen, squatting down to initiate a proper greeting without hesitation. "What did you think it was?"

Releasing a breathy "Jesus Christ," Ben disengaged his flattened body from the car's hood.

"I just saw this black thing, coming out of nowhere," he said, moving closer.

Eileen appeared not to hear him, focused on comforting the trembling ball of fur at her feet.

The dog had homed in like a heat-seeking missile, squirming around her shins in a tail-wagging, butt-wiggling frenzy of excitement, going turbocharged with the apparent ecstasy of human contact. As soon as Eileen bent down to pet her, she could feel the uneven curly knots of fur, clumps of matted, congealed hair hanging from her body, gritty, greasy dirt leaping onto Eileen's fingertips. The dog flipped over, onto her back, big front paws limp, back legs splayed, relaxed, praying for a belly rub or a scratch in a difficult-to-reach armpit, and as Eileen obliged, the dog's eyes closed and her teeth began to chatter, as if she were saying "thank you" in Morse code.

"What is he?" said Ben.

"He," said Eileen, "is a she, and she, if I am not mistaken, is an American cocker spaniel."

As Eileen spoke, the momentary shift in her attention had the dog back onto all four legs, frantically resuming the quest for a physical connection, rooting with its short snout like a veteran Provençal hound catching the scent of wild truffles.

Ben watched his wife pick up the little dog's head with two hands, gently cradling the weighty pendulous ears in her grasp, locking eyes, offering words of reassurance, and he saw the patent intensity in their connection, an electrical circuit being completed, and he knew he was in trouble. He had enough of a sense of Eileen's compassion and weakness when it came to animals to know exactly where this was headed.

Ben considered himself a bona fide animal lover having grown up with all manner of pets: birds and horses, cats and dogs. However, for the past five years, he had been devoted to 140 pounds of black female Newfoundland that went by the name of Didi. Larger than life, Didi was an Airbus of a dog, filling rooms with her presence and hearts with her easy joie de vivre. Ben relished the simple pleasures of living with this goofy-Newfy. Of all the dogs he had ever known, there was something about this giant, this temptress of the bear hug—reeling you in every time as her independent streak made you work to share her space, and not the other way round. Yet here, at his feet, suddenly and unsolicited, a very different kind of dog was igniting an unsettling little sparkle in his wife's eyes. By comparison, here was a creature that seemed, irrespective of size, somewhat agitated and particularly needy. Neither he nor Eileen had ever considered getting a second dog. Why would they? Didi provided all the canine presence anyone could possibly want or hope for. And besides, there were basic practicalities to consider—dog food and veterinary bills—and who knew how well this cocker spaniel might get on with other dogs? If only out of prudence and a sense of loyalty to his beloved Didi, it seemed appropriate to air some measure of reservation, though this would require diplomacy, if not caution.

"She must belong to someone," said Ben, more statement than question.

Eileen felt around the dog's neck.

"No collar, no tags."

She encouraged the dog to roll over, quickly rewarded once more with obedience and a desire to please.

"And I don't see any sign of a tattoo."

Ben squatted down and offered the dog a belly scratch while inspecting the bald skin patches of her groin for ink. Nothing but a coating of what felt like a thick lacquer of engine oil. He jiggled a sizable love handle on the dog's hips.

"Well, whoever owns her makes sure she is well fed. No shortage of insulation here."

"Thank God," said Eileen, a little defensively, surprised by her husband's lack of chivalry and decorum. "It's freezing out here."

She glanced over at Ben.

"Go see if she belongs to the restaurant."

Ben eased back into a standing position.

"What, now?" He sensed that the whine in his voice was not helping his cause. He opted for a different tack. "Look," he said, "she has to be a smart dog. She knew what she was doing when she found you. She'll find her way home, no problem."

Eileen ignored him and scooped the dog up and into her arms.

"Hand me the keys. I'll warm the truck up while you're gone. If she hangs out in this parking lot chances are someone who works here will know who she is."

She was smiling, enjoying this little drama, this chance to do good, knowing he would capitulate as she opened her hand, took the keys, and watched him head off the way they had come.

"Lock up until I get back," he said over his shoulder, without expecting a reply.

Ben saw that the lights inside the main entrance had been dimmed, warding off late arrivals, even before he pulled on the front door and found it locked. Mario's closed at ten, according to the white stenciled lettering behind the glass; his wristwatch said 9:57—justification enough for knocking, a sturdy rap that might summon the maitre d'. Then he heard a woman's laughter emanating from somewhere out back and headed toward the sound. Maybe the spaniel belonged to the owner or someone renting a room over the restaurant, someone who knew their dog would be smart enough to stay within the confines of the lot.

At the back of the restaurant Ben saw the stark outlines of two individuals in white cotton jackets. They were standing off to the side of a large Dumpster, in conversation—a goofy comedic male and a receptive giggly female—the red glow of their cigarettes bobbing in the darkness, arcing from mouth to waist and back to mouth again, and just before he reached them he had a bizarre flashback to a childhood memory. For a split second, on his mind's big screen, he could clearly see a performance of Disney's *Lady and the Tramp*, the scene with the two dogs sucking on the same strand of spaghetti, chewing their way toward their first awkward kiss, a swarthy heavily accented waiter serenading them with a booming rendition of "Bella Notte." Suddenly Ben was struck by the improbable notion of tracking down a wandering cocker spaniel at an Italian restaurant.

As Ben approached he saw the woman in a slash of light spilling from an open kitchen door. In addition to her chef outfit she wore a red bandanna to cover her hair. She punched her friend in the shoulder affectionately.

"Excuse me, I don't suppose you've lost a dog or know if one's gone missing."

The man was young, maybe nineteen or twenty, working on his goatee like it was his first, enjoying the novelty of its feel on his face, stroking its outline to make sure it was still there. He squeezed in another quick puff before asking, "What sort of a dog?"

"Cocker spaniel," said Ben. "Black. Female."

The kid appeared to ponder the question before taking his last drag like it was a joint, grimacing, holding on before flicking the butt into the night.

"No," he said, shaking his head. "I've not seen a single dog in all the time I've worked here."

"And how long have you been working here?" said Ben, thinking weeks, maybe months, but knowing the kid wasn't old enough for years.

"Since six o'clock this evening," said the kid, swatting his accomplice, who cracked up on command. "It's my first night on the job."

Ben managed a fey smile, wearily letting his head fall to one side.

"Maybe there's someone else in the restaurant I can ask."

Miss Bandanna finally got ahold of herself.

"No need," she said. "I know the dog you're talking about. Friendly, fat, likes to work her booty."

"The very same."

"She's a regular, always coming by, waiting by the back door, looking for scraps." She turned to the kid.

"If Chef ever catches you feeding her he'll threaten to fire you on the spot even though we've all caught him giving her leftovers."

Then back to Ben.

"Restaurants and stray dogs don't go well together, you know. And if you ask him, Chef will reckon you're a health inspector and deny ever knowing her."

"This explains the love handles," thought Ben before asking, "So where does she come from?"

"No idea. But this place is out in the boonies, on a busy highway. Nearest house is half a mile that way." She thumbed over her shoulder. "So if she's wandering that far, this often, she don't gotta be getting fed at home. Why else would she come here?"

WHEN Ben returned, the car was engulfed in exhaust smoke, idling, the windows fogged into frosty beer mugs. He tapped on the driver's door, heard the central lock mechanism release, and jumped into the rush of warm air.

As soon as he sat down he was assaulted by an intense aroma, fetid and pungent and normally restricted to wildlife. Ben noticed the absence of his wife in the passenger seat next to him. As he twisted around, she appeared over his shoulder, seated in the back with her new canine companion, the dog lying not on the tired cloth of the back seat, but instead strewn across a special plaid blanket, a blanket reserved for the loyal Newfoundland who would be there to greet them as soon as they got home.

Eileen might have imagined her husband was grasping for the right words, words of admonishment over the temporary betrayal of their darling Didi, as this little interloper, this furry hobo usurped a favorite travel rug. In fact he was gagging on the overpowering smell emanating from the backseat.

Like hot water leaching the full flavor from tea leaves, the warm air circulating in the SUV had ripened the poor creature's cornucopia of aromas into one foul, potent, and unremitting stench.

Ben brought his cold hands up to his face, covering his nose.

"Tell me you smell that," he said.

Eileen let her chin fold into her neck, rolled her eyes up.

"She just needs a bath, that's all."

He fanned a flat palm below his nose. The smell had a depth, a maturity, a bouquet combining the ripe pungency of a wild animal with the acerbic whiff of the foulest dog breath.

"You mean a Meryl Streep, *Silkwood*, nuclear-decontamination-type bath?"

Eileen knitted her brows and covered the dog's ears with her hands as though sparing her the embarrassment.

"We're ignoring you. What did they say?"

"They said she doesn't live here. But she comes round all the time looking for food. They don't know where she's from."

Eileen worked her lips into something between a pout and a frown, and the spaniel seemed to sense her concern and a need to reassert a presence, leaving the blanket and crawling into her lap.

Ben felt the "Now what?" moment hanging between the three of them, as he watched Eileen and the dog. It was getting late and he couldn't deny there was a small part of him that felt like the stinky, if affectionate, intruder in the car was becoming a bit like that uncle who overstays his welcome at the family Thanksgiving party and just as you think he is going to ask for his coat he troubles you for a double espresso!

But then he took in his wife and the dilemma written across her face. Once again Eileen had stepped up and taken action without having to decide or debate because the right thing to do would always be the right thing to do.

"What are you thinking?" said Ben, adding, with a smile, "Or should I say, what do you think *we* should do with the dog?"

Eileen read the beginnings of acquiescence in his eyes and nodded her appreciation.

"Well, we can't leave her here. She'll die of cold out there."

Eileen had a point, Ben thought, but according to his sources it wasn't as though the dog didn't make this run to her favorite food bank on a regular basis. She was old enough to have weathered at least a decade of harsh winters far tougher than tonight's. She would find her way home without difficulty. Then again, tossing her out to fend for herself after giving her this brush with warmth and affection felt all wrong.

"What if someone's looking for her?" he said.

She didn't hesitate.

"But what if they're not? What if they dumped her in the nearest parking lot who knows how long ago and kept driving. What if she's been left to fend for herself?"

Ben pensively bounced a clenched fist on his lower lip before turning in his seat to face forward, applying his seat belt, and sliding the truck into reverse.

"What are you doing?"

Ben stopped the SUV, slipped it into drive and said, "We need to make sure we're doing the right thing."

TAKING his directions from the sous chef, Ben drove the half mile down a deserted rural highway in search of the nearest neighborhood, and when the vast, impenetrable woodlands of central Massachusetts suddenly gave way to a modern development, Ben hung a right into a rolling barren landscape peppered with McMansions.

"This doesn't seem right," said Eileen.

The homes were set back behind large, rectangular lawns topped by a blanket of frost so neat it looked as though it might have been applied by hand, a white bedsheet with perfect hospital corners. Two- and three-car garages ensured the sidewalks and driveways were empty and there was no one in sight, the occasional floodlight bursting into life as their curb-crawling vehicle set off another motion detector.

"I agree," said Ben, scanning left and right, unable to find a single stray leaf to spoil the efforts of professional landscaping crews. "With no disrespect to your little friend, I don't see her making the annual holiday family photo for the kind of people living in these homes."

The road snaked through the neighborhood, ending at a stop sign where Ben elected to take a left in hopes of working his way back to the main highway. Eileen encouraged the spaniel to stand on her lap and look out the window, as though the dog might divine the correct route and signal it with her tail, like a tracking device.

In the passing gleam from a street lamp, Ben checked in his rearview mirror and caught a flash of the two of them. Eileen, indifferent to the little dog's smell and the horrors of what was decaying inside her mouth, was animated and encouraging, pointing out the passing sites as if they were touring a capital city.

As the road narrowed, the houses changed—small Capes and ranches emerged, closed above-ground pools, picket fences desperate for a coat of paint. Ben slowed down as he spied one particularly ramshackle Victorian Colonial.

A number of abandoned cars on blocks lay strewn across a front lawn more dirt than grass. The wraparound farmer's porch was collapsing at the corner, tilting the floor at a perilous Hitchcock camera angle. Bluish television light filled the gap between half-drawn curtains, and last year's unlit icicle Christmas lights still hung from dilapidated guttering. But what drew Ben's eye to this particular property was the bottom of a one-car garage. Over to one side, cut into the peeling paint on the aluminum siding, was a black rubber dog door.

Ben glanced over his shoulder at Eileen and the dog and wondered if the spaniel was the Goldilocks whose size fit the flap just right.

"This house might match this dog," he thought.

"What is it?" said Eileen.

She obviously hadn't seen the flap cut into the garage. Then again, Ben could have been completely wrong. The dog appeared to show no sign of recognition, no tell, unless her sudden stillness was meant to be a warning, urging him to drive on.

"Nothing," said Ben. "Let's go up a bit farther."

Two hundred yards farther down the road Ben caught sight of something moving in his high beams. He slowed down, believing it to be a wild animal, but the proverbial deer in his headlights was actually a woman bundled into a heavy winter coat and woolen ski hat, attached to a pair of snorting pugs on retractable leashes. He couldn't tell whether the woman was more embarrassed to be caught picking up "Tootsie Rolls" and secreting them inside her doggy poop bag or the fact that one of the dynamic duo had crapped on a neighbor's front lawn.

The SUV pulled up alongside her and Ben powered down the front passenger window only to find Eileen doing the same thing in the back.

"Excuse me," said Eileen. "I'm sorry to bother you so late at night but I was wondering if you know this dog."

Eileen didn't have to encourage the spaniel to show herself in the window space because as soon as the gap appeared she was standing on her back legs, sticking her head out into the night like a hungry kid ordering fast food at a drive-through. And then, for the first time in their presence, the spaniel barked. Whether it was prompted by recognition or a need to be territorial and defensive, aimed at the woman or aimed at the dogs, it was hard to say, but her quick double yap once more fired up her stubby tail and the rest of her enthusiastic derriere.

Both pugs stared back, the more demure of the two returning the greeting while his companion concentrated on scratching parallel grooves into the frost with his back feet.

The woman came up to the spaniel's window, instinctively petting the dog with her free hand.

"Where did you find her?" said the woman.

"Down at Mario's," said Ben. "She was wandering around their parking lot." All the while he was thinking, "You said *her*. Just a guess?"

"We thought she might have strayed, gone looking for food," said Eileen. "There's not too many other neighborhoods nearby. We thought someone might know who she belongs to."

The woman dipped down a little more, stepped in closer. She seemed to be taking her time and Ben felt as though she was checking him out—thick black hair, neatly trimmed beard, woolen jacket.

She probably had him pegged as a high school teacher rather than a respected local artist. Then the woman turned to Eileen—pretty, strawberry blond—and Ben knew she'd be struck by those big blue eyes that glowed with genuine concern for the little black dog happy to be on her lap.

Suddenly the Pug Lady seemed distracted by something else in the backseat and Ben followed her gaze to, of all things, the dog blanket. It was covered in Didi's black hairs, and based on their length it was obvious those hairs couldn't belong to the little black dog sniffing around her face.

Sucking hard on her teeth the Pug Lady said, "Nope," with an unequivocal finality. "Never seen that dog before." And then, as if it might be important, added, "Nobody round here owns a spaniel."

She gave the dog a quick pat on the head, smiled as she said "Sorry," and dragged her pugs into the darkness behind the truck.

NEITHER of them spoke, and in less than a minute they were back at the main highway having to decide which way to go next. Privately neither Eileen nor Ben believed the woman with the pugs, convinced they both heard the same message in her denial—that even if the dog did have a home, she might deserve a better one. For Ben there was nothing left to think about, while Eileen had just being going through the motions anyway.

He indicated left and accelerated, Eileen leaning forward in her seat to squeeze Ben's shoulder, knowing he was heading back, past the restaurant and toward home.

"You know, I'm still going to try and find out who she belongs to," she said.

Ben adjusted his position so their eyes could meet in the mirror, so she could read his smile.

She sat back in her seat, the dog virtually asleep in her lap.

"She really does possess some interesting qualities," said Eileen.

"Aside from a talent for clearing confined spaces."

She laughed.

"If she wanders the streets begging for food she has to be a fighter, right? A survivor, a go-getter, feisty and determined. I mean, don't you see it, something familiar about that close-cut fringe of hair over her eyes? Remind you of anyone?"

Ben checked the mirror, and the lights from a passing car let him see his wife passing her hand over the sleeping dog's body. He shook his head, pretending not to know, rewarded with a moment of delight before she disappeared into darkness and said, "I think we should name her Helen."

2   CLEO

THERE are many reaons why so many of us choose to share our lives with a pet—it's the perfect antidote for loneliness, providing an endless supply of smiles and the certainty of unwavering companionship, and many of us have seen the way a pet can make a family feel whole. Whatever the reason, something clicks, and evolves into a side effect called love. More often than not the time frame for this connection is brief, perhaps instantaneous. Maybe this was what made the relationship between Sandi Davies and a singular miniature pinscher named Cleo all the more special. For here was a love affair over forty years in the making.

Sandi grew up as a baby boomer in rural Ontario, Canada, a freckle-faced little girl with rust-colored hair, frequently branded by her mother as "the greatest disappointment of my life."

"You were meant to be a boy," her mother would say, almost affronted, as though she were the victim of some grievous miscommunication. "Not a girl. I never wanted a girl, let alone imagined a name for a girl. All I had was Michael Ashley. You were meant to be Michael Ashley. Michael Ashley was supposed to be my son."

Like so many woman of the June Cleaver era, Sandi's mom was determined to appear permanently elated by the joys of living a perfect life. Why perfection necessitated an offspring of the opposite sex, Sandi never knew. But perhaps this was why, in a misguided effort to appease her mother's preference for this hypothetical Michael Ashley, Sandi developed into a tomboy. If worms and dirt and an indelibly grass-stained pair of Levi's were all it took, her mother's wish had come true.

"What's wrong with you?" her mother would scream, trying to brush the snarls from her daughter's short hair, hair that defied barrettes and bows. "You're wearing that dress and I won't hear another word about it."

Such mixed signals only compounded Sandi's confusion. She was supposed to be a boy, yet her mother also wanted a doll, something malleable, preferably silent and amenable to dress-up and the application of makeup and jewelry. Fortunately for Sandi the nearest small town was more than a forty-five-minute drive away, and it was at least a two-hour drive to a respectable department store, which meant that her mother's efforts to mold a protégé took place in the home, where she dreamed of meeting a better class of people and agonized over the latest innovations at the Joneses'. Sandi grew used to being subjected to fantasies about new appliances and haute couture from magazine and newspaper advertising.

"Look at this, just look at this," Sandi's mother might say as she accosted the child clomping through the house and demanded an opinion on Dior or Maytag as a long pink nail lovingly pointed out a wool jacket or pearly white washer. And though Sandi tried to please, she failed to appreciate and crave these finer things in life, her indifference to material prizes counterbalanced by a longing for her mother's attention and affection, simple gifts that were always somehow unattainable.

Consequently, shunned as a misfit, even an embarrassment, Sandi learned how to be alone. Their home was surrounded by woodlands and fields of reforestation peppered by potato farms. There were no other kids in the neighborhood because there was no neighborhood. During those times when her mother had a job, Sandi might not see, let alone communicate with, another human being for twelve hours at a stretch. Little wonder this lonely child lost herself in a perfect playground where animal friends rescued her from her isolation and saved her through their companionship.

One afternoon, walking the road home from her two-room public school, Sandi came across a cluster of caterpillars, sprinkled like furry orange confetti across the hot blacktop. Passing cars were a rarity but when one blew by, highlighting their peril, she felt compelled to act. Pulling the bottom of her T-shirt out of her shorts, she fashioned a collecting pouch, squatted down, and hopped across the asphalt gathering the vulnerable grubs. On an ordinary day the walk home from school took fifteen minutes, door to door, but Sandi's rescue mission and the delivery of every single endangered and wayward caterpillar to the safety of a green leaf in a nearby tree took over two hours.

Triumphant, bursting through the back door, Sandi shouted, "Mom, mom, guess what I just—"

"How . . . dare . . . you!"

Sandi heard the words before she saw where they were coming from, heard each syllable crushed between clenched molars. Then her mother stepped into the kitchen, gloved hands on hips, dressed as though she were about to drive into town.

"You knew I had a hair appointment this afternoon. I specifically reminded you this morning, but once again you were only thinking about yourself. When are you going to wake up from that dream world you live in?"

The lambasting continued, extinguishing all the delight and sense of accomplishment in her daughter's eyes. At some point most parents would interject phrases like "worried sick" or "something might have happened to you," defending their anger with fear. Not so Sandi's mother. We could cut her some slack, after all this was the early sixties, a time when children were routinely turned out like horses, encouraged to use their imagination for play, a time before cell phones, when a holler out the back door was enough. Still, a belief that your child had to be safe seems like a poor excuse for not looking.

Later, exiled to her bedroom, Sandi tried to fathom why her mother would care more about a haircut than about helping innocent creatures. Standing at the window, imprisoned and crying, this little girl did not know how to articulate her feelings, but she was certain that looking right could never be as important as doing right, and that tears and isolation were no reward for offering nature a small but helpful hand.

Animals began plugging the holes in Sandi's life, giving her purpose and something to love. She wanted to love her mother, but the abandoned and hopeless cats and dogs she rescued were quick to teach her that love requires reciprocity. It is a game requiring a minimum of two players. You get back what you put in and if one side loses interest, there's not much point in playing on.

The lucky beneficiaries of her mother's affection were mostly, and always would be, men. There had been a father, somewhere along the way, but he had disappeared, along with all their family photos, robbing Sandi of the evidence and what few memories remained of his pathetic involvement in her childhood.

Replacement fathers came and went, and during the gaps in between her mother might seek refuge and affection from her daughter. At these times Sandi's mother absorbed love like a black hole absorbs light, insisting on being loved. She sought reassurances regarding the freshness of her physical appearance, berated herself and then justified all her weaknesses as a mother. As soon as the hiatus between men ended, Sandi knew this temporary vulnerability would vanish, forgotten, the frigid and detached relationship with her mother instantly restored.

Pets were never so fickle in their emotions. They were always there for her, reliable, trusted confidants, attentive to a whispered secret and sworn to a vow of silence. They shared her moments of happiness and licked away her tears of sadness or the pain of a scraped knee, hugged away her loneliness. They became her most important social outlet and she engaged them in conversation regarding all the events of the day. One of these pets was Rocco, a beagle that had belonged to a neighbor of Sandi's aunt, a dog on death row, guilty of competing for his family's time and affection after the arrival of a new baby. Sandi lobbied, pestered and eventually sprung the dog, rewarded by an affectionate and loyal hound. Unfortunately, in one memorable incident, the depth of Rocco's appreciation proved hazardous to his health. Losing out to a squirrel gifted in the art of street fighting, Rocco sustained a significant injury to his manhood, a vicious bite that necessitated a visit to the vet and a number of carefully placed stitches. Every day Sandi rushed home from school to attend to her latest patient but as the days passed, the wound refused to heal, the stitches repeatedly splitting, tearing through the delicate tissue.

"God damn it," shouted her mother, "I'm not spending another penny on that stupid dog, do you understand?"

Of course Sandi understood, but what she didn't understand was why little Rocco felt compelled to show her his injury, in a frenzy of excitement that blossomed into unintentional, full-blown, and damaging arousal, every time she returned home from a day at school.

Afraid of what might happen, Sandi returned to the vet, describing the ritual of their daily reunion.

"Here, try these," said the vet, keeping a straight face as he poured a handful of tranquilizer tablets into a labeled plastic container. "Tell your mom to give Rocco a pill about half an hour before you come home from school."

The panic in Sandi's face at the idea of asking her mother for a favor, let alone one involving an animal, must have radiated across the examination room.

The vet bit into his smile, squatting down to align his gaze with hers.

"Just tell her the medication will make sure Rocco doesn't cost her any more money."

So Sandi did, and Rocco took the drug, the antidote to his emotional Viagra, thereby giving him a chance to restore his delicate sensibilities to full health.

Then there was a rough-coated Saint Bernard that went by the name of Sony who was liable to demonstrate a powerful protective streak when it came to Sandi, contesting the teenage advances of male suitors by attacking the flesh of their buttocks with robust and drooling jowls. And there was a stray white short-haired tomcat who would become Sandi's constant companion for nineteen years. This cat became privy to some of the most important firsts of her life— first crush, first kiss, first boyfriend, first breakup. When Sandi realized she had met the man she was destined to marry, this cat was the first to know. When she was pregnant with her first child, the same cat received the news before her husband. Like any new addition to Sandi's menagerie, all domesticated recruits were subjected to intense scrutiny by her mother, their approval always in some doubt. However, from the first encounter with this particular tomcat, Sandi sensed there was something special between them and she was unwilling to chance his rejection. She thought long and hard about how to guarantee his acceptance and when the answer finally came, Sandi knew she would always derive a certain pleasure from turning a cruel recollection to her advantage.

"There's someone I'd like you to meet," she told her mother, producing the sleek blue-eyed cat, sweeping back his soft ears, turning him into a miniature seal pup with each stroke of her hand.

Sandi's mother said nothing—a good sign. And he was awfully cute.

"What's his name?" she said, and Sandi tried not to smile, knowing they would be together, knowing her choice of a peculiar yet precise moniker for this stray cat was guaranteed to secure his future.

"I haven't christened him yet," said Sandi, "but with your permission, I thought we might call him Michael Ashley."

FAST-FORWARD a decade or so and instead of welcoming a new pet into her life Sandi was welcoming a baby girl. Unlike her mother, Sandi was thrilled to have a daughter, Sonja (her second child would be a son named Jamie). The exact opposite of her own mother, Sandi worshipped her daughter, loved her to the point of physical pain, an ache of happiness to have this joy in her life. Still, there is a big difference between cherishing a stray cat and raising a baby girl, and the consequences of Sandi's years of emotional seclusion from humans who loved her back began to surface.

When you confide in pets for most of your life, unrestrained honesty becomes the norm. Pets don't stand in judgment. They don't criticize. They don't sweat the small stuff. For the most part their gestures and opinions are bold and clear and positive. Sandi was used to baring her heart, spilling her feelings knowing that she could vent the turmoil and always be rewarded by their gentle touch and even temperament. Their understated kindness would restore tranquility. They were never too busy. No rain checks, no bad days. Animals were predictable, reliable, and eager to share. Sandi had no reason to suppose that loving a child would be any different.

Sonja, however, was not a foundling pet. Despite all their shared DNA—the sun-kissed freckles and russet eyes, pale skin and flowing red hair—Sonja Rasmussen was the emotional antithesis of her mother. Perhaps Sonja felt she was loved too much, if such a thing was possible. Perhaps she rebelled against all the transparency of her mother's feelings. Perhaps she saw her mother's desire to talk problems out, to instantly address, resolve, and bury conflict, as a sign of weakness. Whatever the reason, Sonja shied away from acts of affection, kept her feelings in indefinite lockdown, and preferred not to confide. Though their love for each other was undeniable, an emotional mismatch evolved and, as the years went by, this specific disconnect between mother and daughter became palpable.

Husband Jan and the kids had come to accept Mom's many strays and rescues as a fundamental component of the Rasmussen family. Pets were an essential ingredient of everyday life, and along the way Jan and Sonja developed a soft spot for Dobermans, something about their stature, presence, loyalty, and eagerness to please. Now eighteen years old, with college around the corner, Sonja was about to get a pet of her very own, but she knew her canine companion of choice needed to contract in size. Using the logic of "Honey I Shrunk the Doberman," Sonja believed she had hit upon the perfect dog—a miniature pinscher.

Sandi's own subsequent fascination for Min Pins may have germinated from a chance to help her daughter when Sonja arranged a naive and hasty purchase from a so-called breeder who was really running a puppy mill. When they went to pick up the puppy, scenes from a hidden-camera exposé invaded their senses—the cacophonous barking of animals desperate for human contact and breeding bitches crushed inside converted chicken coops, the smell of the dog waste piling up beneath their caged feet, filtered for convenience through the wire floors on which their pads permanently splayed. This holocaust of factory-farmed dogs was more than Sandi could bear, but reading the embarrassment and shame contorting her daughter's face, she decided to help Sonja rescue one hostage, even if they had to deal with the guilt of not liberating more.

"He doesn't look much like a Min Pin," said Sonja.

And Sandi had to agree. Their misfit had the domed head of a Chihuahua. Not that it mattered. Bruno, as he was later named, may have sported a little Mexican fire in his blood, but deep down on the inside, where it counted, he was a miniature pinscher.

———

ONE by one Sandi parted company with her children, those on two legs and those on four. Sonja met Dave, married, and was about to start a new life on the island of Bermuda. Jamie headed off to college, and, coincidentally, Sandi's menagerie of canine and feline waifs began to dwindle until she and Jan were left with an empty nest.

For a while this arrangement made sense. She and Jan were busy, their respective jobs necessitating a good deal of time on the road. Nevertheless, the absence of animal companionship did not sit well with Sandi. She missed the comfort and art of canine and feline conversation. Rescuing strays was such an unremarkable yet vital part of her life. Simply put, it made her feel human. Perhaps the greatest gift an animal has to offer is a permanent reminder of who we really are. And strangely, for the first time in her life, an animal in need had failed to reach out to her. Sandi never set out to help sick or abandoned animals. There was never a plan. They just showed up.

Sandi began to wonder: If animals were not coming to her, did she need to go to them? And perhaps, more importantly, why had they stopped calling?

Even though she had parted with cash for little Bruno, she felt like she and Sonja had responded to *his* cry for help.

The desire for a new dog began to work itself in, starting to itch, and Sandi allowed herself to wish she could scratch it better. When Sonja finally acquired a genuine miniature pinscher, Odin (her father, Jan, was allowed to flex his Danish muscle when it came to naming pets), Sandi realized that although she was thrilled for her daughter, secretly she was jealous. She began to crave a Min Pin puppy of her own.

Sandi's fiftieth birthday celebration seemed like an obvious opportunity for her wish to be granted. In fact, many readers will be screaming for Sandi to take the reins, to buy a dog herself and be done with it. Not so fast. Bear in mind the stranglehold of her childhood. The scars may have faded but they remained difficult to conceal, constricting and impeding what you and I might take for granted. Sandi grew up accepting that she never deserved attention. She was much less than special. She had done nothing to deserve reward. Buying a puppy for herself would have been pure indulgence and she would always feel like she had done something wrong, something selfish. But if one were to come to her as a gift . . . Laying out a minefield of hints and suggestions was the only extravagance she could manage. In the months before her birthday her excitement took hold, with Sonja and Jan conniving through a volley of e-mails and whispered phone calls as the day approached.

On the eve of Sandi's birthday, Sonja called her mother.

"I'm picking you up first thing in the morning. It's all arranged."

"Where are we going?" Sandi's euphoria did not mix well with the pretense of ignorance.

"Someplace special" was all she got in return, the confidence in her daughter's tone a billboard that said this gift would be exactly what Sandi wanted.

Pretending to be excited on the way there would not be necessary. But feigning complete surprise when she was asked to close her eyes, open her hands, and receive a squeaky, squirming black and tan ball of love was another matter altogether. Sandi actually found herself practicing in the mirror, fanning away imaginary vapors like a starlet about to make an Oscar acceptance speech.

When she slid into the passenger seat of Sonja's car, maintaining the facade became insufferable, the agony of the wait dueling with her resolve not to spoil what her daughter had so carefully planned— until they headed toward downtown London, Ontario. This was unexpected. In her mind's eye Sandi had seen a drive to a country farm and a scrupulous breeder. By the time her daughter pulled over outside a pet store, Sandi was no longer pretending to be surprised. Ever since the incident with Bruno they had shared a mutual distrust of the source of pet-store dogs. So why change now?

Sandi emerged from the car, hesitated, and then began walking toward the fur and sawdust trapped behind the glass.

"Mom, where are you going?"

From across the street, Sonja waved her mother over. She was standing outside a different type of store altogether.

"Mom, you and I both know I have a hard time expressing myself, but you know I will always love you. I wanted to find a unique way for us to celebrate your big five-oh together and this was what I came up with."

Sandi hoped the fearful arch in her eyebrows, the incredulity paralyzing her lower jaw might be construed as surprise.

"I want us to get matching tattoos," said Sonja, putting it out there as a request and a question.

Sandi could have let the disappointment get to her. Instead, in a moment of confusion, with her daughter, her firstborn, searching her face for acceptance, she moved past her own desires and saw the gesture for what it was. For the better part of her life Sandi had been nurtured by the unconditional love of animals. Her daughter was independent, guarded, and emotionally restrained. Declarations of love in any shape or form were rare and Sandi grabbed this one while she could, hugging Sonja tight, their physical bond a chance to recover composure, to accept the loss and appreciate the gain.

"I'm so glad you want to do this with me," said Sonja, her eyes still probing for signs of unwillingness, offering a way out. "What kind of tattoo do you think we should get?"

Never in her wildest dreams did Sandi imagine she would be answering such a question, and though the obvious suggestion was an inky illustration of her coveted Min Pin puppy, she and Sonja eventually agreed upon tiny, matching yellow roses on the inside of their right ankles, which, to Sandi's surprise and pleasure, became a cherished expression of their friendship.

For twelve more months stray pets failed to cross paths with Sandi, and as her fifty-first birthday approached, she allowed herself to dream that this was her year. Once again Sonja and Jan began to scheme online and on the phone, but when the day arrived, instead of a Min Pin puppy her gift was a ceramic pot filled with yellow chrysanthemums. Sandi, the queen of internalization, finally lost it.

"Dear God, Jan, I'm fifty-one years old. I'm not dead. Mums are for grandmothers and unless you and Sonja are keeping something from me, I'm not a grandmother yet."

In the end it was her son, Jamie, who broke down her reserve, forced a confession, and took it to his father. It was decided: after decades of letting strays find her, Sandi's family would see to it that she would find a pet of her very own.

Though she did feel a bit like she was interfering with fate, Sandi was determined to do her homework and get it right. She purchased books on how to find the perfect breeder, on selecting the perfect companion. Her lifestyle involved air travel, but luckily, for the most part, her flights were direct and relatively short. According to ASPCA recommendations, having your dog travel under the seat in front of you was the safest way to go. Therefore, based on size restrictions alone, the Min Pin breed remained a strong contender for the perfect canine companion. However, to win the title, he or she would also require a calm demeanor, excellent social skills, and, most important of all, an aversion to excessive barking. Sandi was asking a lot, and she knew it, but after six weeks of extreme surfing and research, she came upon an unpretentious home breeder of miniature pinschers a thousand miles away in Doon, Iowa.

Sandi placed a call, and the phone was picked up by a young, polite child. Here was an opportunity too good to miss, a soft target for a delicate recon mission. The kid was happy to blab and Sandi was pleased to discover that the dogs were an integral part of a big and boisterous family. Adult conversation came next, a friendly, mutual inquisition. Sandi was encouraged to contact the breeder's other clients; she even spoke to the breeder's veterinarian, getting an objective take on the breeding facility, the breeder's philosophy, and, of critical importance, the parental health records. Every box was checked before succumbing to the laws of physical attraction as digital images of three black-and-rust female puppies flew across cyberspace to meet her.

The pups were only days old, their eyes still closed, and for most of us, no matter how you spun the pixels, the trio of furry cherubs in the center of each frame would have been cute and adorable, but essentially identical. Yet to Sandi, they could not have been more different. It is hard to imagine love at first sight leaping, or even squirming, from these silent, still images, beamed in from so far away, but Sandi would assert that in this lineup of unusual suspects, she instantly knew exactly where to look.

Weeks passed, the blind fur ball opened her eyes and began to grow, and the breeder's photographic updates confirmed that Sandi had chosen wisely. There remained, however, the matter of Jan's only bargaining tool from the original offer of a new puppy. At the time, heady and breathless, Sandi had agreed without hesitation. Now, as the arrival date drew closer, she began to regret her easy capitulation. How could she trust a man obsessed with his Danish heritage to name the new love of her life?

As is so often the case, a search on the Internet only fueled her reservations. The Norse gods appeared to be inept when it came to naming the fairer sex. Freya or Frigga, the best options she could find, still felt far too sturdy for the delicate creature on her screen saver.

"I have two names in mind," Jan announced one day.

Sandi held her breath and gave him a "let me have them" look.

"Well, I rather like the name Lulu."

Sandi studied him, stupefied, with a ventriloquist dummy smile. It could have been much worse and maybe she could get used it.

"What do you think?" Jan rushed to the back door, stuck his head out, and shouted, "Lu-lu, Lu-lu," trying out a different intonation with each cry.

Sandi winced and said, "What else have you got?"

Jan was enjoying himself, hiding his grin, sighing into a shrug as if disappointed to have to use his backup.

"You seem to be besotted by this breed, these Kings of the Toy, so I think your little dog deserves a strong female name, something self-assured, something regal."

Sandi locked on to the word *regal*, and under her breath she berated herself for failing to explore the daunting prospects from Denmark's royal family.

"Please Jan, don't tell me you're thinking about naming her after a Danish queen?"

Jan shook his head.

"How about Egyptian?" he asked.

And as soon as Sandi had the clue, she knew he had made the right choice.

"Cleopatra. My little girl is Cleo."

| 3 | **HOME AND SECURITY** |

T WAS only when they walked into their kitchen that the practicalities of Helen's sudden presence in their lives really hit home.

Eileen carried the dog in her arms, uncertain how a disoriented spaniel might respond when a gigantic black Newfoundland head completely filled her visual field. She need not have worried. Didi got up from the kitchen floor, sniffed the air, mulled over the unpleasant fragrance, and loped off to the living room to lie down.

"Perhaps she thinks we brought home a pet skunk," said Ben, somewhat surprised by the big girl's indifference.

As if needing to prove a common genetic ancestry with this snooty black monster, the little spaniel began to bark, a mix between a bark and a whine really, like a vocal prod, a low-level persistent nudge.

"You think she's trying to tell us something?" said Eileen, placing her under the kitchen counter and bunching the plaid travel blanket up around her to form a cozy nest.

"What sort of something?" said Ben. "Get me out of here?"

Eileen knelt down on the floor beside Helen, stroking her head, the cry becoming a little softer, a little less frequent.

"What if she has something contagious?" she asked.

"Contagious?" said Ben, wondering where this logic was when they were back at the parking lot.

"You know, rabies, distemper, the stuff you get a dog vaccinated against. She's got no collar and therefore no tags. I'd never forgive myself if she's carrying some sort of disease and by bringing her home I'm going to expose Didi to it."

Ben thought about this. Eileen raised a good point. In theory he could bank this statement, use it as ammunition at a later time. Then again, he only had to watch how his wife fawned over the tiny tramp who had wheedled her way into their kitchen to know such thoughts were laughable. Something was taking place between Eileen and the dog they had christened Helen. It was obvious, undeniable, a connection that required no explanation or justification. It just was. And for Ben the best part was bearing witness to the fact that that was all it took.

"I don't think we need to worry," said Ben. "I mean look at her. Her muzzle has more gray than salt and pepper. She has to have survived at least a decade of exposure to all kinds of disease living her vagabond lifestyle. Her nose may be wet but it's not snotty. And her eyes are bright and not crusty." He shook his head. "I seriously doubt she's an infectious Trojan horse."

Eileen seemed unconvinced.

"She might not be housebroken?" he said, trying to be more practical than defamatory.

"Oh, I'm not so worried about that," she said. "I can teach an old dog new tricks."

But suddenly Eileen stopped running her hand over Helen's neck and shoulders. Kneeling, moving closer, she parted hair and peered into the mangy coat.

"Yuck," she said. "I thought I was feeling little skin bumps and warts all over her body."

Ben dipped down to join her.

"Me too," he said.

Despite the camouflage of dark fur, the kitchen light picked out an engorged, purple-green appendage attached to the filthy skin. And then there was another, and another. Juicy fat ticks, ripe and bloated with blood, were all over her body. Not that there weren't warts and bumps as well, it was just that the warts and bumps were all Helen, and not a threat to Didi.

"That's it," said Eileen, sweeping the dog back into her arms. "I'm taking her for a bath. It's what she's probably been trying to tell me all along."

"Do you need a hand?" asked Ben, though the lack of conviction in his voice instantly prompted a raised brow from Eileen. "'Cause if it's okay with you, I thought I might do a little work in the barn."

"Go ahead," said Eileen. "I'm going to give Helen her makeover and then I'm thinking us three girls might do a little movie night together."

Ben watched them disappear up the stairs of their small two-story contemporary home and headed outside to a large salt-box-style barn sitting kitty-corner to the main house. The property was set back from the main road, surrounded by the solitude of seven acres of open fields and deciduous woodland. Ben was an artist, a painter. The barn was where he worked, and for him late-night sessions were often his most productive. Tempting as it might have been to join his wife for a tick-picking soiree and bear witness to the unimaginably defiled water sluicing from that wretched dog's body, he had dead-lines to meet on a number of commissioned paintings. Besides, this was Eileen's project. As her husband he had grown accustomed to his wife's spontaneity when it came to acts of kindness, generosity, and empathy, be it toward people or animals. It remained a huge part of her appeal. It was plain to see how both sides would benefit as her bond with the foundling blossomed. Eileen would relish the oppor-tunity to transform this furry pauper into a Westminster princess.

Pepe Le Pew did not relinquish her perfume without a fight. Rinse after rinse the water ran black as Eileen worked the doggy shampoo into an unruly lather. Throughout the careful, head-to-tail liberation of ticks in various stages of satiation, and all the suds and spray, Helen had stood silently in the tub, head outstretched, doleful eyes staring up at her, trembling like a cell phone in vibrate mode.

The wet fur revealed the real folds and contours hidden underneath and it was clear from the surfeit of body fat that Helen had been an accomplished scavenger for some time. What kind of a life had she been living? There were no obvious scars or bruises to suggest anything like physical abuse. A label of neglect seemed to be a better fit, or maybe forced independence, though it was hard to imagine this relatively small, pure-breed spaniel competing against coyotes and raccoons in the wilds of Massachusetts. Where did she get her street smarts? How had she survived the harsh New England winters? Based on what Eileen had experienced so far, not-so-little Helen had obviously learned to use charm and flirtation to her advantage. What she lacked in speed and savagery she more than made up for with feminine wiles.

As Eileen began to towel Helen dry, the dog remained quiet, maintaining a passive stare. Eileen carefully lifted up those heavy, pendulous ears, gently dabbing at the red, raw, and swollen interior, long since abandoned to the will of thriving bacteria and fungi. She maintained a soothing monologue as she worked, the white towel finally swaddling the dog's head and chest, a canine version of a shrouded E.T. staring back.

Eileen felt it then, a keen awareness of this animal's need for her. And it was the absence of sound that sealed her fate. Eileen studied this creature staring back and realized her silence was saying volumes. It felt as though the dog's silence was a pause, a moment between them in which Helen was waiting to be understood. Eileen read this telepathy as a plea that said "*Look at the state I am in. Do you really think anyone will miss me? When do you think was the last time anyone even acknowledged my existence?*" She tried to imagine how bizarre the last few hours must have been for this dog, but in that moment, kneeling beside the tub, with her and Helen's eyes locked, Eileen focused on trying to convey one simple message—*trust me.*

THAT first night, Helen ultimately squeezed into a tight space between two couches. Perhaps it was the closest approximation to a familiar sleeping arrangement. Only then did Didi make her move, going over to where this stranger lay and, with great deliberation and delicacy, sniffing this *Mini-Me* over her entire body without waking her up. Apparently satisfied, she trotted off to her own bed to retire for the night, leaving Eileen puzzled by this detached introduction. Didi was used to other dogs. She was well socialized, a popular player at the local dog park. It was true that they rarely entertained other canine guests in the house, but this interaction seemed so reserved, almost awkward, it was as if the big girl knew to give Helen some space. Perhaps something in the way Eileen handled this newcomer made Didi realize she should go slowly.

By the next morning the physicality of the relationship between Helen and Eileen became apparent. It was as if they were adjacent convicts in a chain gang. Everywhere Eileen went, Helen was sure to follow, at her heels, moving from one room to the next, a furry lady-in-waiting. If Eileen went to the bathroom, Helen would insist on joining her. Conversely, Eileen's efforts to encourage Helen to use their backyard for her toilet needs were met by hesitation and a look of abject fear.

"She won't go outside without me," said Eileen to Ben, who drifted into the kitchen, grabbing his first cup of coffee of the day. "I've tried a couple of times but she digs in at the door and stares at me. I think she thinks I'm getting rid of her, asking her to leave."

Ben eyed his wife over the rim of his mug, taking a swallow, noticing the spaniel tethered by some invisible thread to his wife's ankle. The painting had gone well the previous night and he had worked late. He had managed to miss the "canine reveal" after the midnight makeover, and to his disappointment, although the dog looked much improved, there remained more of her distinctive fragrance than he would have liked. The smell had been downgraded but it was still there, already acquiring a familiarity, like the odor on entering the home of an ailing grandparent, something you could endure and forgive, even tolerate out of kindness.

"She looks much better," he said, letting his eyes convey the unsaid remainder of his sentence.

"I know," said Eileen, dropping down to pet Helen. "It's her ears and her breath. Her teeth are awful. Not that it has affected her appetite. She's eating like she's headed for the chair."

Ben paused mid-sip, letting the sentence hang, wondering if his wife was feeling him out. But Eileen was elsewhere, stroking under Helen's chin and throat.

"I'm going to sort you out today," she said, speaking directly to the dog. "See what we can do for you."

Eileen smiled up at her husband, and Helen followed her gaze, and Ben's artistic eye instantly framed the shot, seeing the photo opportunity—the woman he loved and by her side a dog with an open heart, as though they had always had one another, as though they had already filled albums together.

IT WAS Eileen's mother, Clare, who provided some crucial information with regard to Helen's background. They had chatted early that morning about the dog lurking in the shadows of a restaurant parking lot, their failed attempt to find out where the dog came from, and how natural it had been to name her after Clare's recently deceased mother.

"You'll never guess who I just bumped into," said Clare, hardly pausing to provide the answer to her own question. "Our local animal control officer."

"You told him about Helen?" Eileen was unable to hide an element closer to panic than curiosity, as though her mother had inadvertently collaborated with the enemy.

"I did. But don't worry, I kept everything very vague. I made it sound like a friend of mine had seen an old black spaniel wandering around town."

"And?"

"And he knew all about Helen. Shaking his head, rolling his eyes. He looked exasperated."

"Did he tell you where she lives? Who's supposed to be looking after her?"

"He wouldn't say," said Clare, "but he told me he's fed up with picking up that poor dog. He says no matter how many warnings he gives them, the owners never take care of her or keep her on their property."

Eileen wondered whether she should give the officer a call herself.

"Did he say if anyone had reported a neighborhood spaniel as missing?"

She heard Clare huff a laugh into the phone.

"That was the first question I asked. He told me no, and when I described the dog he told me they never do. They simply don't care. In fact he went even further. I don't know whether he thought I was holding something back but he said, 'If you find her, don't call me, better to call MSPCA law enforcement.' "

Though Eileen appreciated this advice, due diligence necessitated she go online and track down the phone number for Cocker Spaniel Rescue of New England. Scrolling down their Web page she saw a dozen cockers up for adoption, and what struck her most was not the uniformly happy smiles on their furry faces, but their ages in the adjacent bios. With few exceptions these were young dogs in excellent health.

Eileen dialed the number as two quotes caught her eye.

"For every dog we can adopt out, five more are abandoned, abused, or given up." And then, transparently situated next to an image of a pleading dog, the highlighted line, "We need forever homes."

Eileen introduced herself to the energetic female volunteer on the other end of the line and quickly discovered that no one had contacted them to report a missing cocker spaniel fitting Helen's description.

"I'm afraid she already has a number of strikes against her," said the volunteer.

"You mean her age," said Eileen.

"Yes, there's her age. People are less likely to adopt an older dog. They worry about health problems, the cost of veterinary care. They worry about not being able to break them of bad habits. They worry about getting attached and getting their heart broken if the dog is only with them for a short time."

This explained the photographs of predominantly younger dogs.

"The other big issue is her color."

"Her what?"

"It's been called 'black dog syndrome,' " said the volunteer.

"Black dog what!" said Eileen. "You're telling me adopting a dog is influenced by color . . . by race?"

Eileen looked down at Helen. She had strayed a short distance from the computer desk, sitting with her back legs extended in front of her, front legs balanced in between, scooting along and wiping her bottom across the carpet in what appeared to be a well-practiced movement.

"No one knows exactly why, but it is a proven fact that black dogs are simply less adoptable."

"People discriminate based on a dog's hair color?"

"It's not just dogs," said the volunteer. "It happens in cat shelters too. Maybe there's something superstitious about it. Maybe people worry about seeing black hairs shed all over their light-colored furniture. The most popular theory seems to be that adopting a dog is all about love at first sight. Eye contact. Dark dogs can get lost in the shadows of dimly lit shelters. If you go unseen, you go unadopted and for the most part, wearing a shocking pink ribbon around your neck doesn't do much to improve your chances. Black dogs stick around three times longer than dogs of any other color."

"I didn't even mention that her ears are a mess, her teeth are not great, and she seems to have a problem with her anal sacs."

"Look," said the volunteer. "We will gladly take her off your hands. But I'll be honest with you, based on her age, color, and just those few health problems alone, the chances of a successful adoption are slim to none."

Eileen didn't want to ask what would happen if Helen wasn't adopted. She thanked the volunteer for her time and hung up.

LATER that day, when Eileen laid out the case for keeping Helen, she did so point by point merely to give Ben a chance to object or even to hesitate or provide a different perspective. Hope and trust found him in full agreement. And besides, they had pursued every reasonable lead to discover this dog's roots and found not only dead ends but barricades, off-the-record inferences whispering "give it up—she's so much better off with you." Eileen and Ben agreed that if at any time anyone came forward looking for her, they would do the right thing and she would go back to where she came from. If not or until then, they had a new dog and Didi had a new sister.

The first order of business for this impromptu adoption was a thorough health check by Didi's regular veterinarian, Dr. Judy, who was happy to make a house call a few days later.

"I can see why you fell for her," said Dr. J., contending with the effervescent creature at her feet, the stubby little tail swiping back and forth with the frenzy of windshield wipers in a downpour.

"I know," said Eileen, "she's got a wonderful personality and she's already so attached to me."

Eileen paused for a second, as if deciding whether to share a confidence.

"This morning, I bought her a little doggy bed with matching blanket so she could sleep next to me in our bedroom, and even when she is sound asleep, if I get up in the night to go to the bathroom, she'll wake up and start sniffing along some invisible trail until she finds me."

"Good thing she still has a decent sense of smell," said Dr. J., lifting up a weighty black ear and peering into the pink cauliflower folds within. "Because I can't imagine she hears very well. For all intents and purposes she has to be nearly deaf after a lifetime of neglect for a classic cocker spaniel ear problem. I'll leave you with some ear cleaner and topical and oral antibiotics. We'll see if they help her out."

Dr. J. lifted up on Helen's upper lip, inspecting the dental arcade below, and the dog took this as a cue to pant directly into the veterinarian's face.

"Whoa," she said, "that's impressive. Nothing personal, but I think I might pass on sharing some spaniel kissy-face."

"It's awful, isn't it? Sometimes I've seen the poor thing rubbing her face along the ground and pawing at her mouth as though something hurts inside."

Dr. J. placed a finger on Helen's lower incisors and gently induced her to "open wide." Chipped canines, stone-ground incisors, and molars caked in a lime green frosting of fetid plaques smiled back at her.

"She's going to need some serious dental work, I'm afraid. It's amazing that she eats as well as she does despite her bad teeth."

The history of tick infestation prompted a test for Lyme disease, Helen stoically accepting the needle in her jugular vein as the blood sample was obtained. More injections followed, in her neck and her right thigh, providing the vaccines that had either lapsed or were never given in the first place.

It was while Dr. J. was listening to Helen's chest with a stethoscope that the doctor had her first and only moment of hesitation during the entire examination. Gliding across the right side of Helen's chest, Dr. J. could detect the whisper of air drifting back and forth through healthy lungs. Off in the distance, she could hear the faint "lub-dub" of a strong heartbeat. However, when she switched sides, placing the diaphragm of her stethoscope behind Helen's left armpit—an optimal position to hear blood rushing through the heart's different chambers—her ears were greeted by relative silence.

Helen stood patiently, clearly unfazed by the apparent absence of a beating heart.

Dr. J. looked puzzled. She looked at her stethoscope, double-tapped the diaphragm with her finger, and heard two deafening thumps on a snare drum inside her head. There appeared to be no technical problem with her equipment.

She listened again, roving around an imaginary silhouette where Helen's heart might be inside this compact chest, looking like a safe cracker who can't quite dial up the correct sequence of numbers.

"Is something wrong?" asked Eileen.

Dr. J. raised her eyes, hearing the question but not daring to speak, as she finally picked up the heartbeat but somewhat more muffled and from slightly farther away than expected.

"Weird," she finally said. "I was having a problem hearing her heart on the left side of her chest."

"Is it something to worry about?"

"Hard to say," she said. "The heart itself sounds normal. I don't hear any dropped beats, murmurs, or abnormal rhythms. It's just a little dull and indistinct in that one area."

She gently patted the left side of Helen's chest.

"It's probably nothing. Overinterpreting any variation from normal in a dog with no history is easy. Who knows what might have happened in her medical past?"

THE severity of Helen's hearing impairment became increasingly apparent over the next few weeks. Both Ben and Eileen found themselves calling her name to no avail, inadvertently creeping up on her and making her startle with their touch. Only the loudest noise, like the screen door slamming shut on a whipping wind, penetrated her head and pointed her snout in the direction of the sound.

On Thanksgiving this deficiency took on a new urgency for Eileen. Helen was still transitioning from the status of lodger to family member, still glued to her mistress, though she had made allowances for visits to the mailbox at the end of the driveway, so long as constant visual contact could be maintained by sitting vigil at the front door. Then that Thursday morning, the kitchen suffused with the smells of oven-roasted turkey and freshly baked apple pie, Helen scrambled out the back door and began sprinting across the open fields, heading for the freedom of the distant forest.

She was halfway there by the time Eileen realized she was gone, little legs pumping, barking her head off as though she had caught the whiff of a deer or a solitary coyote staring back from the dense undergrowth.

"Helen! Helen!" Eileen cried, chasing after her as the dog continued on her course, either choosing to ignore the woman closing in over her shoulder or, more likely, not hearing a thing.

The fugitive was caught right at the equivalent of what would have been the barbed-wire perimeter fence, if this had been a prison break, looking surprised and pleased to see that Eileen had joined her, as though a human presence lent credibility to her belief that there had been a threat lurking on the outskirts of the property, a threat Helen was not afraid to subdue.

The incident prompted Eileen to purchase a small silver bell to attach to Helen's collar, its metallic tinkle offering the comfort of a poor man's canine LoJack. If she ever tried to repeat her great escape, at least they would hear her making a break for it.

Wɪᴛʜ Christmas came an appreciation of the relationship developing between Helen and Didi. What had started out like a mating ritual between desert scorpions had matured into understanding, respect, even codependence. Didi seemed so cognizant of her own proportions around her Lilliputian sister, so endearingly clumsy in her attempts to be gentle and tender. Though this lovable giant of a dog was so physically immense, it wasn't until Helen entered the picture that they realized something had been missing. Didi cherished and embraced her new companion so completely that Ben and Eileen came to believe a creature that took up enough space for three regular dogs had to have been lonely.

Come Christmas Day, the dogs wore matching red bows on their collars. Each dog had her own stocking hanging over the fireplace, with bones proportional to the size of the recipient—a carefully selected shank from the local butcher for Helen, something impossibly large for Didi that looked like it had been excavated by a paleontologist. Ironically, a mutually agreed-upon bone exchange took place early in the festivities, with Helen dwarfed by her enormous chew, dragging it through pine needles like an obstinate white log. Despite all her dental shortcomings, Helen happily whittled away at this project for weeks to come.

Early in the New Year Ben went through major periodontal surgery of his own, and the ensuing pain and difficulty eating opened up a whole new world of empathy for Helen's daily plight.

"I can't imagine what she's endured for so long," he said. "Here am I popping Percocet every couple of hours and it hurts drinking a glass of cold water. No wonder the poor dog is constantly rubbing at her muzzle. We really need to get her to a dentist."

And that was all the prompting Eileen needed to pick up the phone and place a call to trusty Dr. J.

"I can set Helen up with a veterinary dentist, but with dogs it's always a little more complicated than white knuckles and Novocain."

"What do you mean?" said Eileen.

"I mean Helen's an unknown commodity. I'm guessing she's twelve, thirteen years old but that's only a guess. Regardless, she needs some serious work on her mouth and that means general anesthesia. No dentist will want to touch her without blood work, chest X-rays, maybe even an ultrasound of her heart."

"Her heart?"

Eileen thought back to the house call, wondering if Dr. Judy had been holding back on her when she listened to Helen's chest. That difficulty hearing her heart with a stethoscope, was that indicative of heart disease?

"Eileen," said Dr. J., with the uncanny gift of a mind reader, "spaniels are a breed susceptible to heart valve disease. It's called endocarditis, and oral bacteria can be a major underlying cause of the problem. Anyone anesthetizing Helen would be crazy not to want to thoroughly check out her heart."

Eileen appreciated the explanation but was disappointed that there was one more hurdle standing in the way of relieving poor Helen's toothaches.

"Don't worry," said Dr. J. "I'll set it all up with a cardiologist I know. She's wonderful."

"Where does she practice?" said Eileen.

"She's at Angell. Angell Animal Medical Center in Boston."

Eileen looked down at the little black dog by her feet, wondering what secrets her body was trying to hide. Helen was an enigma, of indeterminate provenance. What mementos of her former life lay hidden beneath her fur, beyond the smiling eyes and twitching tail? What price had this innocent creature paid for her neglect?

One certainty struck Eileen powerfully—*nothing bad must happen to this dog.*

| 4 | **PARADISE INTERRUPTED** |

JANUARY in Bermuda can be iffy. Of course everything is relative and Bermudians are permanently blessed with miles of pink sand and gin-clear water, but come January they brace for brutal winds and horizontal rain, the honeymooners keep away, and tourist beaches become a playground for local dogs, bare feet and paw prints side by side in the sand.

Compared to the interior of Canada, winter in Bermuda will always feel positively tropical. And so, Sandi, who had settled in Calgary and who was working long hours, thought a frisky fourteen-month-old Cleo would love the warm weather and constant attention a visit to "Aunt" Sonja in Bermuda would bring.

Cleo had already become the consummate international jet-setter. Her impeccable manners and placid demeanor wooed even the most militant of flight attendants and caused protracted deplaning for anyone seated behind her. And it was obvious she relished all the time she could get with Sonja's male Min Pin, Odin. The two dogs bonded with the familiarity of cousins thrilled to have one another at family gatherings, prowling the backyard together, chasing lizards, mocked by the calls of kiskadees, romping in the lush Bermuda grass as palm fronds whispered overhead. Sonja loved to watch them engage, politely taking their turns dominating and submitting, smiling as they played out their mouthy bravado and then, exhausted, cherishing each other's company as they slept it off. And like an anxious mother hovering by the sandbox, daughter Sonja always felt the weight of her responsibility for her canine guest's safety. Not only did she know how much Cleo meant to her mother, she sensed that this creature supplied all the things that were missing in their own mother–daughter relationship. Sonja wasn't jealous or resentful, and this had never been discussed, but she only had to hear her mother talk about Cleo to know an emotional void had been filled by a surrogate. To some extent it was a relief knowing her mom had found a vessel for her emotional outpourings. But the pleasure of sharing Cleo for a few weeks was always offset by a degree of worry, not least because of the poor dog's eventful medical history in such a short amount of living.

It started back in Canada when Cleo was only five months old. Already a gifted canine socialite, Miss Popularity had been unable to contain herself when she and Sandi pulled into their familiar doggy day-care parking lot. As unpredictable as it is common, a classic scenario unfolded.

Sandi was sliding out of the car with Cleo cradled in her arms when another dog trotted past. For whatever reason—new kid in school, the exciting prospect of making a new best friend—this sighting proved irresistible, and Cleo transformed into a coursing greyhound intent on a hare, shifting from neutral to sixth gear in an instant, legs scrambling, accelerating, desperate to find traction. Sandi had milliseconds to choose: clamp down and risk breaking Cleo's neck, or attempt to get her to the ground as quickly as possible. The lesser of two evils resulted in a drop, a screaming human, and a whimpering dog no longer interested in the chase, holding her right rear leg off the ground.

Nausea, fear, and remorse took turns beating up on a woman who had waited so long and cared so much for this Min Pin puppy.

Yes, the leg was broken. Yes, Cleo had decided to ignore the basic principles of biophysics by selecting an unusual fracture configuration in the shaft of the long bone in her thigh. In a five-month-old dog, the growing portions of the bone known as growth plates should be the weakest points, the locations where the majority of young dog fractures occur. Contrary Cleo had decided to flout that rule. She had also chosen to break at a site where the conservative options of a splint, a cast, or cage rest were either contraindicated or ill advised. Unfortunately for Sandi, five-month-old Cleo was in need of a major surgical fracture repair using stainless-steel plates and screws.

In the days before Cleo's surgery, Sandi discovered that sleep was for people with less guilt in their lives. Yet the procedure went well, Cleo healed, and in those requisite eight weeks of quiet recuperation, Sandi and Cleo tightened their bond. Reluctant to crate Cleo and abandon all her hard-won socialization skills, Sandi purchased a backpack specifically designed for dogs. With Cleo safely constrained like a canine papoose, the two shared even more time together, doing household chores, shopping, and going for long walks on two legs. When Cleo eventually skipped free of her confinement, she did so without hesitation, as though her broken leg had never happened, an observation that moved Sandi to tears, torn as she was between joy and a guilt compounded by a dog's unconditional forgiveness.

The second fracture wasn't too far behind though, and once again, indirectly, doggy day care played a role. Cleo was having fun roughhousing with a Labrador puppy, oblivious to the weight and size disparity, when she pulled up lame on a front leg. She had broken two of the bones in her paw, an injury that was amenable to a fiberglass cast, though Cleo violated proper cast protocol by using her immobilized leg to stir the water in her water bowl. New casts came and went and with them the inevitable, unavoidable sores and cuts that come with a dog struggling to tolerate an itchy, bulky, heavy package wrapped around a sweaty foot. But once more Cleo healed just fine, and once more Sandi did not.

"I'm a lousy pet owner," she told her vet when the cast came off and Cleo finally got a decent chew on her toes. "I'm not good enough for this little dog. I don't deserve her. She needs a home with someone who can look after her safely and properly. She just gets hurt around me."

No doubt some of this reckoning contributed to Cleo's sojourn in Bermuda that January. Perhaps, with all those diabolical guilt demons dancing in her mind, she trusted Sonja more than she trusted herself to take good care of her dog. Cleo, of course, was just a puppy doing what all inquisitive puppies do—discovering her world, making mistakes but ultimately getting away with it. If Sandi had known what would happen next, she would have gladly insisted Cleo suffer a winter of discontent in Calgary.

SONJA pulled into her driveway, cut the moped's engine, and removed her helmet. Shaking out her red hair she noticed her husband, Dave, standing behind her.

No greeting. No "how was your day?" or "glad to have you home." He just stood there, one hand on his hip, the other hand scratching an imaginary eyebrow itch, watching her dismount, and instantly she was tuned in to his awkward body language.

"What is it? What's wrong?" asked Sonja, certain that something bad must have happened.

His palm was out, patting the air between them in a calming gesture, only twisting the fear even tighter in her chest.

"It's Cleo," said Dave.

When Sonja heard Cleo's name an adrenaline wave surged in and she felt it propelling her forward, into his face.

"What do you mean? Is she all right? What's happened to her? Where is she?"

"She's in the house, curled up next to Odin on their bed."

Dave's soft tone and patient delivery made Sonya realize she had been shouting and rambling. She heard his reply but she still didn't understand. She was moving past him, not listening as he called after her.

"It was an accident. I don't understand how it happened."

In the kitchen, across the terra-cotta tile, two little dogs looked up, pricking their ears as they heard Sonja's heels clicking in their direction, and for a second Sonja was confused as to what could possibly have made Dave so upset.

And then Cleo stood up and walked toward her, her nubbin of a tail offering a greeting, and Sonja saw it, saw how the little dog refused to put her right hind leg down, saw the swelling around her right thigh, the distension puckering her previous surgical scar, a slight parting of the hair revealing its ugly white line.

As she stood there, paralyzed, her brain caught up with Dave's words. Sonja didn't turn around. She could sense his presence behind her.

"When did this happen?"

She made no attempt to hide the accusatory tone in her voice, and they both knew she was really asking a series of different questions altogether. What did you do to her? What happened on your watch that went so terribly wrong? How did you let this happen?

"Shortly before you came home," said Dave.

His voice was at her back, her eyes were focused on Cleo, her mind's eye focused on her mother. She spun around wearing a facial expression trapped somewhere between incredulity and panic.

"How shortly?"

Dave shrugged, trying to convey concern and not terror.

"I don't know, half an hour."

Sonja turned around and saw him now, for the first time, all casual in jeans and a T-shirt that said "comfortable," not anxious, as she thought he ought to be.

"Christ, Dave, why didn't you call me on my cell? Why didn't you take her straight to the vet?"

Dave looked down at the floor, glanced up, looked down again, swallowed, and finally met her eye.

"Because it's probably nothing. Because she will probably be fine in a couple of hours."

Incredulity crept into Sonja's glare.

"Since when did you get a veterinary degree?" And then, "I don't believe you."

She brushed past him, Dave feeling her breeze by like a ghost as she went to a linen closet and found a clean beach towel. She picked up Cleo as though the dog were broken glass, easing her bit by bit into her cotton stretcher before gentle levitation.

"Well if you won't take her, I certainly will."

She picked up his car keys sitting in a bowl on the kitchen counter and headed for the door. Dave thought about reaching out to her but caught himself, as Sonja seemed to anticipate his move, veering her body out of his reach.

"She got caught up in her own leash," he shouted after her. "She twisted and fell down. It wasn't my fault, Sonja. Honest."

But Sonja had no time for excuses and closed the door behind her, sealing him on the wrong side of their relationship.

Dr. NICK Glynn, Odin's regular veterinarian, made short work of diagnosing Cleo's injury: sudden-onset lameness; pain on palpation of the right thigh; lower leg dangling in the breeze like a silent wind chime. A quick X-ray sealed the deal—Cleo had refractured her right femur at the junction between normal bone and the bone plate from the previous surgery.

Glynn put up the X-ray on a viewing box for Sonja and watched her response. At first Sonja wore a tight grimace, every muscle frozen, a full-facial Botox, and then a freckled hand flew up and clasped her lips tightly, muffling a scream.

Eventually she loosened her grip and said, "I don't understand. My husband swears she just got caught up in her leash. How can such a minor thing result in such a major catastrophe?"

Glynn tried to get a read on this woman reeling from shock. He didn't think she was pointing fingers. Instead, he sensed fear and a desperate need to understand and justify what had happened. If not for herself, then for someone else.

"You said this is Cleo's third fracture, right?"

Sonja managed a nod.

"And she's only fourteen months old?" asked Dr. Glynn.

She nodded again, hypnotized by the X-ray, the proof, the crack in Cleo's white bone big as a crevasse. How was she going to tell her mother?

"Sorry, what did you say?"

He repeated, "Cleo's only fourteen months old?"

"Yes, yes," said Sonja, back now.

"Fed a regular canine diet? Adult, not puppy?"

"That's right. She gets the same food as Odin. For treats she gets blueberries, grapes, cranberries, and carrots. She also gets a wild salmon oil pill every day. Do you think she could have some sort of birth defect in her bones?"

Glynn pursed his lips, took a deep breath, and turned his gaze to the X-ray, as though the answer might be there. In truth he was raiding his mental database, flicking through a Rolodex in search of diseases that predispose young dogs to fractures.

Sonja had raised an excellent point. Fractures resulting from everyday, prosaic activities beg the question, is there an underlying problem with the bone? Is the bone weak and therefore vulnerable, and if so, is that weakness a congenital problem, because the dog is so young, or is it an acquired disorder that has developed early in life?

He would need more time, as well as his textbooks and the Internet, but his memory tossed out a list of words: *calcium, phosphorus, vitamin D, sunshine, rickets,* and, to his surprise (and, one would imagine, the surprise of those who taught him pathology at vet school if they knew about it), osteogenesis imperfecta, known in people as brittle bone disease.

Of course, lacking all the details of how these factors specifically influenced Cleo's bone structure and anticipating that this was precisely what Sonja sought, he packaged his insight in the following manner.

"I think that's a very good question. It is hard to imagine that poor Cleo can have this much bad luck in such a short lifetime. We should definitely take some blood samples and a urine sample for analysis to make sure we're not missing something obvious."

In fact, unbeknownst to Sonja, Cleo's vet in Canada had previously hunted for, and failed to discover, an underlying cause after the second fracture. Still, she agreed, especially if there was a chance to find some explanation for her mother other than a failure to properly care for her dog.

"But what about this?" she asked, forcing herself to tap a finger against the image at the break, like a tongue searching for the pain of a loose tooth.

"Cleo's going to need surgery, yeah," said Glynn. "The kind of surgery we might not be comfortable doing here—you know?"

Sonja's eyes widened and for a brief moment it was if she was sucked up in a vacuum. All that was left was a whisper.

"So where will she get the surgery?"

Here Glynn smiled, offering confidence and reassurance.

"I have a friend who works at Angell in Boston. It's a huge animal hospital. One of the best in the world. I'll give him a call right now."

"You're saying it's safe for Cleo to fly? With a broken leg?"

Glynn pursed his lips, nodding his appreciation of her concern.

"You're right. It's not ideal. There's no good way to stabilize her

fracture for travel, but she's definitely small enough to fit under a
seat and with the benefit of a few pills I guarantee she'll be comfortable for the flight. It's direct as well." Then Glynn added, "Less than
two hours," and regretted it, thinking he sounded like a travel
agent.

Sonja was silent, suddenly feeling tired and demoralized.

"Don't worry, everything will be fine," said Glynn. "I'll go and make
that call."

And he left Sonja and Cleo alone in the examination room. Sonja
looked at the X-ray and looked at Cleo snuggling in her towel, trying
to get comfortable. She ran a hand across the dog's skull, flattening
the velvety ears, while Cleo's wet eyes blinked open, checking who it
was, and content with the discovery, she closed them again.

Sonja wondered if this innocent dog was somehow destined for
disaster on her watch as some sort of payback for the way she occasionally treated her mother. In the next few minutes she would have
to put her fears aside, pick up a phone, and call Sandi, and what
made it worse was knowing exactly how their conversation would
play out. This was when her mother was at her best, in a crisis, able
to separate personal feelings from what needed to be done. In times
of fear and uncertainty Sonja would let down her defenses and allow
Sandi to tend to her emotional needs, allow Sandi to play the loving
mother. This was when they were always at their closest, and the certainty of her mother's unconditional support only reminded Sonja of
how unresponsive and cold she herself could be, especially when she
felt the oppressive weight of Sandi's neediness.

The bustle of the hospital continued all around them—barking
dogs, a woman's voice asking for a prescription refill, the copycat
parrot she had noticed on the way in voicing his opinions—but inside the examination room there was silence as Sonja and Cleo came
to an understanding. It would be awful telling her mother the bad
news, but at the same time, here was an opportunity to prove herself,
to handle the situation and take care of Cleo in a way that told Sandi

she understood, respected, and approved of this special dog's role in her mother's life. Sonja would drop everything, fly all the way to Boston, and fix her up. Whatever it took, whatever it cost, she would make it happen and the world would right itself and all would be well once again.

5 THE GODDESS LUNA AND A RUSH TO JUDGMENT

NOBODY ever suggests that what I do for a living is boring. They might say "gross" or, occasionally, "wicked awesome" and I've certainly witnessed facial expressions ranging from respect to sympathy to dismay, but no one, to my knowledge, has ever labeled my career choice as boring. *Unpredictable* would be my one-word synopsis because implicit in this adjective is the certainty of surprise. No amount of training will ever fully prepare you. Education may teach you the science but you have to live this job to discover the art.

I leave home in a shirt and chinos and change into my pajamas when I get to work. I ask way too many questions, crawl around on the floor, and wear a hearing aid around my neck. Sometimes I even risk life and limb (well, mainly limb . . . okay, maybe a finger or two), but the point is there is always an element of danger. There is also mystery and intrigue, passion and intensity, fear and hope. I get to say "Sweetheart" without feeling sexist or inappropriate, and petting, kissing, and public displays of affection are encouraged in my workplace. Arguably, I have the best job in the world. I am a veterinary surgeon and I am a lucky man.

Anything could happen from the moment I pull into my

parking space and turn off the engine of my car. I practice (and few words could be more appropriate) at the Angell Animal Medical Center, located on the fringe of Boston's hospital district, yet another enormous brick building that from time to time attracts disoriented humans looking for a "real" doctor. Working with seventy other veterinarians, my days in this state-of-the-art facility are, by definition, design, and desire, unpredictable to say the least.

It may be no more than fifty yards and twenty seconds from the click of my vehicle's central locking mechanism to the swish of the automatic doors at the hospital's entrance, but there is ample opportunity to be accosted. It could be an anxious owner who has just dropped off his or her pet for surgery, armed with more pressing questions, eager to ensure that I have brought my A game, my mind sharp but not overly caffeinated. It might be my first appointment of the day, early and wandering the perimeter of the lot, a gimpy canine patient staking claim to a patch of yellow snow as his owner looks my way and juts a sharp chin in my direction as if to say, "Ready to see us or what?" But on one mean morning in January, nothing but black ice and a dusting of pet-friendly ice melt stood between me and the warmth of our vast reception area.

"Is it Friday the thirteenth?"

Sweeping in from my left, keeping pace as I headed to my office, came one of our interns, Dr. Elliot Sweet, greeting me with that question.

"Because if it's not, last night had to be a full moon."

We were walking together, as though he happened to be going my way, and it seemed obvious that he needed to confide. In fact it was a Tuesday, though I could forgive his disorientation. The telltale stubble on his cheeks told me all I needed to know. Dr. Sweet had been working the overnight shift.

"Did one of your clients appear overcome by the Roman goddess Luna?" I said.

He stopped me with an enormous hand on my shoulder and a smile that said this would be worth my while, and he set the scene.

The doors to our emergency service are open 24/7 and last night the waiting area had been packed with a variety of patients hoping to be seen. Among them were a Persian cat who had mistaken his owner's stash of pot for his own stash of catnip; a Weimaraner puppy with a cut pad, blissfully ignorant of the bloody crime scene he was creating across the hospital floor; and a Pomeranian with a chronic, greasy, malodorous skin problem that, according to his cranky owner, simply could not wait until tomorrow.

And then there was Mr. Turret and his dog, Dillon. Mr. Turret's resonant mantra had been heard long before he breached the automatic doors, his arrival all the more dramatic for the silence that ensued as he stormed into the center of the waiting room.

"Rabies," he boomed, dropping the piece of twine that loosely tethered his placid mutt, his great hands extending before him, joining his eyes in pleading to the audience, circling before the waiting room turned theatre-in-the-round.

Mr. Turret commanded attention. He was an enormous barbarian of a man with untamable black hair contiguous between head and beard through which poked a bulbous ruddy nose and quick menacing eyes. Only the horned helmet and the evidence of rape and pillage were missing.

"For the love of God, it is rabies."

He stressed every word, enunciating with Pentecostal precision.

"Rabies, the Lord's blight upon man and beast. I know it and you know it. Just look at him."

Suddenly he strode toward the strung-out guy clutching the floppy Persian cat.

"Look before you," he said, gesturing dramatically in the direction of his dog, like a magician's assistant accentuating a trick, the cat and its owner too stoned to feign interest.

"You see it, sir. I know you do. See the devil's froth and spittle, see it pouring from his innocent lips; see those kind and devoted eyes possessed by Satan's defiant stare."

Dillon sat perfectly still, unperturbed, watching his master's every move. However, to the trained eye, Dillon swallowed with increased frequency, effort, and considerable discomfort. The corners of his lips were wet and accumulating saliva, in a manner remarkably similar to those of his ranting owner.

"Rabies. Can there be any doubt?" Mr. Turret scanned his audience and, getting no reply, leapt to Dillon's side, squatting beside him.

"Can you smell it? Well, can you?" He cocked his head back, forcing a long sniff, in and out, copious nasal hair caught in the flow, and to his delight one or two in the audience cautiously joined in.

"Am I right?" Mr. Turret nodded and kept on nodding as he encouraged the tentative in an olfactory investigation that yielded little more than confirmation of the new and pervasive aroma of alcohol in the room.

"Of course I am right. It is the devil's virus. The rabies. And mark this." He stood towering above them, holding out the back of his hand for all to see.

"Satan has bit me too." He pointed to what looked like an innocuous scabby cut near his thumb. "That's right, he has possessed my dog and now he comes for me. Now, my friends, on this very night, he is coming for us all."

His final words might have stretched into a maniacal cackle if it were not for the attempts of a hospital supervisor to take Mr. Turret by the arm and steer him, and his ambivalent pet, toward a wooden bench.

Even from his sitting position, with the dog lying at his feet, the sermon continued, spittle flying, his arms gesticulating far and wide regarding the plague that Dillon would unwittingly inflict upon mankind.

Enter our bright and shiny overnight doctor, Dr. Sweet. Elliot may have been a relatively new veterinary graduate, fresh-faced though prematurely balding, yet despite his awkward, gangly, mumbling and bumbling manner, he possessed a dedication to animals and owners alike that was fueled by a heart of gold.

The supervisor collared Elliot, shoved a hastily created record into his hand, and insisted, with an enigmatic smile, that he take the madman and his dog off into an examination room. Elliot did as he was told, guiding patient and owner, though failing to halt the incessant, vociferous sermon that condemned poor Dillon to a slow and gruesome demise.

"Rabies, rabies, my dog's got rabies."

Mr. Turret would not be pacified. His belief in his diagnosis was total, unwavering, although eventually simplified to a single word that he repeated over and over again, in a whisper that softened while Elliot began to perform a physical examination on Dillon.

"Rabies, rabies, rabies." Two syllables merged into one wobbling, hypnotic sound, a rhythm percolating into the tired and sleepy gray matter of this hardworking intern, as Elliot stretched open Dillon's mouth and found exactly what he had suspected he would see in the back of the dog's throat

Mr. Turret leaned forward in his chair, the whisper reduced to repetitive lip sounds as he waited for the verdict.

Conversely, Elliot leaned back in his and took a deep, cleansing breath.

"I am one hundred percent certain that your dog does not have rabies" is what Elliot had *meant* to say. But, unfortunately, he did not. Chalk it up to brainwashing, sleep deprivation, or some inherent phonetic deficiency—Elliot left out, forgot, or slid by the single most important word in his sentence: *not.*

There followed a brief moment of silence in which neither man spoke. But just as Elliot realized the absolute horror of his mistake, divine judgment, swift and final, descended upon Mr. Turret.

Even the Persian cat, now munching his way through his second bag of Cheetos from a vending machine, sat up when he heard the relentless screaming headed back toward the waiting room.

"The devil's benediction! He is rabid, he is. Dillon is rabid, and I am rabid too. Dear God, you have forsaken us both."

Mr. Turret dropped to his knees, shoulders pitching forward in time with his sobbing; drool, mucus, and tears trapped in luxuriant whiskers as he heaved, wailed, and swiped at his face.

It was another twenty minutes before Mr. Turret finally accepted that the cause of Dillon's problems had been a chicken bone lodged in the back of the poor dog's throat. .

ANGELL boasts twenty-six examination rooms—all fully equipped, basking in fluorescence, and uniformly painted "yellow finch" with a tinge of institutional green. Room 12 is my domain when it comes to most of my interactions with the public, a room tucked away in the far reaches of the building, a room with a tiny examination table and large floor space, an arrangement that encourages me to interview my patients on their terms, at ground level.

Up until my follow-up consultation with a twelve-year-old female yellow Labrador named Rory, I had not given Dr. Sweet's speculations about the lunar cycle a second thought. Cats and dogs had come and gone; advice and medications were dispensed, elective surgeries scheduled. Their owners had been attentive, with questions smacking of meaningful Internet surfing. Nothing we discussed had been remotely wacky or verging on irrational. Little did I know that Rory, and her "mom," Mrs. Nadworny, were about to buck this trend.

As it happened, Rory was well known to me, for two very different reasons. First of all, where I come from, "Rory" is a male moniker (in fact, Celtic in origin, it means "red king"). Consequently I kept referring to *her* as *him*. Gender confusion is a huge faux pas for any veterinarian and after countless slipups and polite reprimands

Mrs. Nadworny finally pointed out that the name "Rory" was short for Aurora, from aurora borealis, the northern lights.

Secondly, and most important, for the last eighteen months poor Rory had been living with a significant lameness in her left front leg that I had failed to define, let alone cure. As I walked to the waiting room, I promised myself that the least I could do was make sure I kept Rory's gender correct.

Mrs. Nadworny, professionally dressed, seemingly on her way to or from some sort of high-powered job, humbled me with her enthusiastic handshake, bright eyes, warm smile, and easy conversation— the kind of greeting usually reserved for a success story, the kind of greeting that reminds me how lucky I am to work with pet owners who appreciate my intent to heal even when my results fall short.

Her four-legged companion was equally forgiving. Though not a fan of hospital visits and prone to bouts of trembling during examinations, Rory relinquished a coy tail wag when I tickled under her chin. She led the way back to my room, her head bobbing with each stride, a patent reminder of her unsolved ailment.

In these situations, I like to start by backtracking with the owner and refreshing my memory of the chronology of the workup. It gives me a chance to step back and take a new look at the big picture, secretly praying for a bolt of inspirational lightning. I hope it gives the owners a chance to see that I have been methodical and conscientious in my quest. I also imagine it gives them a chance to reflect on how much money they have spent on my clinical dead ends.

Mrs. Nadworny reached into her Marc Jacobs handbag, silenced her BlackBerry, and leaned forward in her chair to narrate Rory's history while the retriever at the center of it all cowered by her side shedding fur, hairy tumbleweeds gathering at their feet. I noticed how evenly Rory balanced the weight on her front legs, as though she were faking a miraculous intervention that must surely enable her to go straight home.

"If you remember, you started with her elbow," said Mrs. Nadworny, matter of fact, nothing accusatory in her tone.

"Yes I do," I said. "The X-rays confirmed a mild case of elbow arthritis, but not bad enough to account for the severity of her lameness."

Mrs. Nadworny nodded her agreement.

"So that was why you started to worry about her shoulder. You took more X-rays, you took some fluid from the shoulder joint and injected it with steroids."

I found the appropriate section of the cytology report, the cellular analysis of the joint fluid.

"Mild chronic inflammation in the shoulder joint," I read, "yet I see a note here that says the steroids failed to improve the lameness."

"Nothing earth shattering," she said. "Juicing my dog didn't make that much difference."

She smiled, as though enjoying the narrative and I wondered if this was cathartic for her.

I went back to the record and here Rory had disappeared, fallen off the radar, lost to follow-up, hovering in a state of limbo in which the veterinarian might make believe "no news is good news." I could imagine Mrs. Nadworny gave up on me, sought a third opinion from a better clinician than I. Or perhaps the problem resolved itself with a tincture of time. Based on the little of Rory I had seen so far, none of these conjectures was correct.

"What's been going on since then?"

Mrs. Nadworny looked at Rory, looked at me, and said, "Promise you won't laugh."

She hesitated for a moment and I wondered whether I was required to make a verbal promise or perhaps a pinky swear.

"I took her to a chiropractor."

If she imagined I would be amused, appalled, or offended she would have been disappointed.

"Really," I said, all morning-show smiles, business as usual. "How did it go?"

Many of my clients worry that I will be skeptical about alternative treatment options. Maybe an image of Rory lying on a table, relaxing into her neck adjustment, the vertebral crack just shy of a fracture, does give me pause but who am I to criticize? After all, it's not as though a chiropractor could do any worse than me. Or at least I hope not.

Mrs. Nadworny wrinkled her nose.

"Hard to tell. Maybe it helped a little. Anyway, we moved on to acupuncture."

Her sentences were interspersed with a tinge of nervous laughter, but once again I nodded and maintained serious eye contact. Truthfully I was far more intrigued by the notion of acupuncture. I wasn't at all sure how Rory would tolerate having the polarities of her chi restored with tiny needles, and I have read that when you get really critical of the scientific data supporting the use of acupuncture in animals there is little compelling evidence either way. But I am comfortable with the notion of stimulating the body's natural endorphins to relieve pain, and besides, it's hard to argue with five thousand years of Chinese medicine.

"And?" I said, assuming my asking was rhetorical given their visit today.

"She didn't really like it and, again, it was difficult to tell whether it was making a difference."

"Okay," I said and stood up, thinking we had caught up to the present, ready to begin my examination. "So we're back to good old Western medicine?"

Mrs. Nadworny gave me a practiced mischievous smile as she confessed, "Not exactly."

"Look," she said, as I backed down into my seat, "I am the biggest cynic ever. But my husband and I felt like we had tried everything so we thought, why not, what harm can it do?"

"What harm can what do?" I said.

"A pet psychic," she replied, wincing with each word, her shoulders rising up, neck shrinking down, as if bracing for my outrage, or perhaps the intensity of my guffaws.

I should have taken the opportunity to study her over the rims of my glasses, removing them slowly, with a heavy sigh of disappointment, a deliberate shake of the head as though she had gone too far. But I never had a chance—she was already into her next sentence, defending her position.

"I know, I know, but you have to understand that I'm the kind of person who believes in God because I'm afraid not to. I read my horoscope every day. And occasionally, on a girls' night out and after a few margaritas, I've even had my fortune read."

I thought again about Dr. Sweet's comment about the shape of last night's moon—he may have been on to something.

"Our town has this annual fair, you know, stuff for the family to do, bring along the kids, and there's this New Age store, one of those places you'd never go into with kids because it's all crystals and glass." Mrs. Nadworny gave a little shake of her head as she said, "But whatever—anyway, I saw they were advertising psychic readings for animals and I'm thinking, hey, for twenty bucks compared to what I've already spent, why not."

I nodded a "can't argue with that."

"So Rory and I go and check it out."

"Is this during the day or the night?" I asked and watched as this question caught her off guard.

"Ten o'clock in the morning."

I didn't reply because I was too busy imagining Mrs. Nadworny rapping her knuckles to the rhythm of a secret knock and whispering a Wiccan password through a sliding peephole before being engulfed in plumes of swirling incense and the music of Enya.

I came back to reality.

"Forgive me but all I'm seeing is a dark creepy room, candles, long shadows, and a swarm of carnie folk."

Mrs. Nadworny shook her head.

"No, nothing like that at all. When Rory and I entered the store we were led to a back room. There were about a dozen 'readers' sitting at tables," she said, miming quotation marks with her fingers. "A few people were seated opposite them, and everyone was speaking in hushed tones. I may have been looking for the woman in the black shawl or at the very least, a neck tattoo and numerous body piercings, but I was introduced to this well-dressed, fortysomething woman who looked like a soccer mom."

My raised eyebrows conveyed surprise. I kept the disappointment to myself.

"She seemed very nice, very comfortable around Rory."

"How much did you tell her about the lameness?" I said.

Mrs. Nadworny immediately understood where I was going.

"Yes, I decided to give her a little but not a lot. I simply told her Rory had been lame for some time in her left front leg but no one seemed to know why."

Rory had a tendency to hold her left foot off the ground when seated, in the manner of "giving paw," so essentially Mrs. Nadworny had given the psychic nothing.

"So she rubs and squeezes and Rory trembles, but other than that Rory just sits there."

I'm still imagining faraway looks, pensive nods, a one-sided dialogue broken by intense moments of apparent concentration, ear lined up with snout, waiting for the silent communication to get through.

"Then she told me two things that grabbed my attention. First she said Rory was stressed because there was something troubling going on in *my* life. Now I know this is incredibly vague and superficial but at the time my husband had just been laid off and I was coming to the end of my contract at work so, to be honest, the term *stressful* was an understatement."

"What was the second thing?"

Mrs. Nadworny paused and studied me, as if anticipating my response.

"You were always convinced that the problem was in Rory's shoulder."

She was right. Rory's shoulder was still my prime suspect.

"Well, completely without prompting, the psychic says, 'You know it's not her shoulder. It's her wrist.' "

Narrowed eyes and a sideways glance betrayed my skepticism as I asked, "And you never mentioned anything about the shoulder?"

Mrs. Nadworny shook her head.

"That's why we're here," she said. "I want you to check out Rory's wrist."

I deliberated a beat, considering her request to abandon a scientific workup in favor of a metaphysical inkling divined by a canine swami.

"Sure," I said, crossing the room and squatting down on the floor next to Rory. "Let's find out what she will tell me, aside from 'Not you again!' "

I did the elbow thing, I did the shoulder thing, and once again I struck out with nothing. Mrs. Nadworny arched her eyebrows as I hovered over Rory's wrist, as though I had been keeping her on tenterhooks. Out of a misplaced sense of courtesy I arched mine back, trying to hide the fact that I was simply going through the motions, indulging her and her fanciful pet psycho.

Confident, embracing this cynicism, I flexed and extended the joints of the wrist, thinking about how best to break the news when I felt a palpable click between the bones.

Subconsciously I must have hesitated long enough for Mrs. Nadworny to pounce.

"Did you find something?"

My fake smile became a nervous smile as I repeated the maneuver and once again my fingertips discerned the alignment of the small bones of Rory's wrist, feeling them jostle and settle with an unnatural and reproducible snap.

How could I have missed it? Suddenly this malady seemed so

obvious. Had I been bested by an animal guru with supernatural powers?

"Um . . . well . . . I'm not sure why, but there *does* appear to be something unsual about Rory's wrist."

Mrs. Nadworny studied me with a mix of surprise and downright satisfaction.

Still reeling, I tried to regain control by suggesting we get an X-ray of Rory's wrist, and half an hour later my humiliation was upgraded after objective black-and-white proof revealed that one of the small bones at the back of her wrist appeared to have been displaced.

Poise abandoned, my mouth suddenly dry, I sputtered:

"It's . . . well . . . unusual . . . this bone here . . . this bone here shouldn't be here. It's the kind of injury we occasionally see in racing greyhounds."

Mrs. Nadworny looked at me, astonished.

"I can't believe you said that. People were always telling me that Rory races around like a greyhound."

Don't get me wrong, I love Labradors and there are few breeds out there with better endurance skills or a better work ethic, but I felt like Mrs. Nadworny was comparing a Toyota Land Cruiser with a Lamborghini. I knew the comment was meant as nothing more than a dog park compliment for Rory's enthusiastic play during her heyday but somehow the improbability of the statement and the peculiarity of the injury suddenly hit me like a two-by-four. The clinician in me, temporarily waylaid and bullied by the talents of a paranormal canine communicator, finally came to his senses.

"Excuse me a moment," I said. "I'll be right back."

Sometimes, in the heat of the moment, even an experienced vet will forget that our four-legged patients are kind enough to bring along a perfectly good and normal opposite leg for comparison. Rory's front right leg had never had a problem. It was the "control" I had foolishly chosen to ignore.

I checked out her other wrist and convinced the radiologist that our ability to interpret the first X-ray would be enhanced by getting the same view of the opposite side. This was done, and armed with new discoveries I sought out the devoted and long-suffering Mrs. Nadworny.

"Your pet psychic was right, there is something strange about Rory's wrist, but I can feel the same click in her opposite wrist and look," I positioned the images of the left and right leg on a viewing box, side by side for comparison.

"They're identical. The bones may not be in perfect alignment but this is normal for Rory. She's simply a dog who can click the joints in her wrist."

Mrs. Nadworny took another look at the X-rays. I could tell she saw the truth hidden amid their shades of gray and it had burst her bubble.

She turned to me unable to hide her disappointment and I wanted her to see that I too shared this sentiment, buying into her psychic's hunch as much as she had because we were both frustrated and motivated by a desire to help this poor Labrador. If Rory entrusted her secret to a soccer mom in a New Age store that was fine by me. Cut me a slice of humble pie if it means the patient gets better! Of course it was quirky and unconventional but it was rooted in what counts—trying to advocate for a creature in pain. I might joke about the cycles of the moon and crazy clients but there is a big difference between well-intentioned and irrational, indulgent behavior.

"I'm sorry," I said. "Once again I can tell you what it is not, and not what it is."

Mrs. Nadworny patted my elbow, gave me an appreciative smile, and then cracked up laughing.

"I'm sorry," she said, "I was just remembering how I was so impressed by what she told me about Rory that I instantly slapped down another twenty bucks and demanded she give me a reading."

I really didn't want to ask and fortunately Mrs. Nadworny bailed me out.

"I should have known better because how many real psychics start out by asking 'What seems to be the problem?' I mean, isn't that what they are supposed to be telling you?"

THERE was a package of X-rays waiting for me outside my examination room door, no doubt a gift from my final patient of the day. I stole a peek and my memory conjured a conversation with a referring vet in Bermuda. Time to put a face with a fracture.

If I'm being honest, the miniature pinscher is not in my all-time top-ten favorite canines when it comes to veterinary bonhomie. Please believe me when I say I have nothing against the breed (ranked twenty-second in popularity by the American Kennel Club in 2008). This is purely professional negativity based on the fact that, for some reason, most of my experiences with Min Pins have involved them becoming genuinely bipolar around people in white coats, transformed from angelic lapdog to homicidal junkyard dog with the first touch of toenail on metallic examination room table. When I think of Min Pins I imagine the kind of dog that might force Cesar Millan to reach for his rabies pole or tranquilizer-laden dart gun, the kind of dog that comes with an owner warning "Yeah, sometimes she doesn't like vets," which we all recognize as international code for "Dial 911 now, so the ambulance arrives before you bleed out!"

Sonja Rasmussen may have stood alone in the waiting room but the small pet carrier seated on the bench beside her was the give-away. It bore a sticker with the airport letters for Bermuda—BDA. She was tall, in a long winter coat buttoned up tight, with her hair tied back in a loose ponytail, long red hair in contrast to pale winter skin, shy freckles in hibernation. Taking tiny steps back and forth, arms folded across her chest, she was keeping vigil, features at the mercy of one all-consuming, all-powerful force—anxiety.

"Ms. Rasmussen?"

Preoccupied with her worries, she was taken by surprise, and gave me a nervous smile as I reached out to shake her icy hand.

"Dr. Trout?"

I nodded and she looked relieved.

"Thanks for seeing us at such short notice."

I shook off her unnecessary gratitude.

"Please, you're the ones with a two-hour flight to get here."

And with this I dipped down and risked a peek at the savage behind the bars.

"And this must be Cleo."

My body braced for a playful "great white" lunge, a flash of ivory, and a throaty growl. Instead a docile, polite detainee in a black-and-tan jumpsuit stepped forward, pressed her nose up to the bars, and began sniffing my fingertips. She didn't make a sound, not a cry or a whimper. She simply wanted to say hello. I berated myself for my foolish rush to judgment.

We small-talked our way back to my exam room, Ms. Rasmussen clearly impressed with the hospital although she confessed she had already done plenty of homework on both Angell and me.

Once inside, I placed the carrier in the center of the room and opened the little plastic door. Cleo stretched, dipping on extended front legs, a perfect downward-facing dog yoga position, before hopping out, talented and nimble on three legs. The right hind leg hung at an unnatural angle, toes lightly scuffing the floor as she picked up the many layers of scent from previous patients.

Sonja unbuttoned her coat and squatted down, calling her name as Cleo hopscotched over. Wag would be too strong a word for the movement in that little nubbin of a tail. Frenetic twitching might be more appropriate. Regardless of what it was, the rate definitely picked up in response to Sonja's call and I remember wondering, does a dog's tail beat to the rhythm of her own heartbeat, or to the rhythm of ours?

"Please, take a seat, Ms. Rasmussen. Cleo seems quite happy to explore while we chat about her history."

"I'll do my best," she said, "but Cleo's not my dog. She belongs to my mother. I'm just looking after her for . . ."

Sonja's sentence stopped short, as though she had been stung by her own words, her being here the ultimate indictment of her failure.

"Why don't you start with what brought you to your vet, to Dr. Glynn, in Bermuda," I said, easing my interjection into this awkward pause between us, though, even to me, it seemed clumsy and affected.

She leaned forward in her seat, knees together, hands together, working something small and invisible between her fingertips, like imaginary worry beads.

"Cleo was on a leash in our backyard. We have a Min Pin of our own, Odin. The two of them love to play tag, chase each other around. My husband said that somehow the leash got tangled up, twisting around her back leg, and she fell down awkwardly."

To me, it seemed like Sonja spoke carefully, economically, as if she were delivering a prepared statement. Though it was obviously painful for her, the brevity and simplicity of the description left me curious about what she might be holding back and why.

Delicately I poked and prodded, came at the story from different angles, hunting for something more serious, more reasonable, but Sonja had little more to add. This left me with a relatively minor incident resulting in a major trauma, an unsettling notion in such a young and apparently healthy dog.

"Do you think there's something else wrong with her?" she said. "I mean this is the third time she's broken a bone and she's only fourteen months old. Did *we* do something wrong?"

If this was a human hospital and my patient were a seven-year-old girl with a vague history of trauma and serial fractures, even an indifferent fan of *ER* would suggest contacting social services. And yes, sadly, the unthinkable can occur. Occasionally dogs and cats arrive at Angell and other hospitals with nonaccidental physical injuries and even Munchausen syndrome by proxy in which the pets are victims. But to be honest, this despicable possibility didn't even cross my mind. Anyone who had been with me looking into the eyes of Sonja Rasmussen on that January afternoon would have seen clearly, unequivocally, how much this dog meant to her and her family. Frustration permeated her every word, and she visibly ached for me to make all their pain go away. She was so tightly coiled, almost petrified, as if she were still on the plane, someone afraid to fly, agonizing over every second she spent trapped inside a metal cylinder a mile above the earth. Despite her best efforts it had taken a few days to coordinate a flight, necessary travel paperwork for Cleo, and time off work. She knew this wasn't a life-threatening disease, but even with medication to alleviate the pain, Cleo had to be sore. Far worse than the occasional squeak when she lay down or got to her three feet was the expression on her face—confused but entirely void of accusation. It was more than forgiveness, it was unbreakable trust and likely it crushed Sonja every time. It made her desperate to get to Boston and let the healing process begin, and now, finally, with the end in sight, the strain had became magnified, betrayed by the panic and guilt in her voice, as her resolve began to crack.

I crabwalked closer in my swivel chair, mindful of Cleo, who had taken an interest in me, methodically sniffing the hem of my pants as if her nose were a TSA wand frisking for metallic objects.

"Of course not," I said. "Fractures in toy breeds of dogs are quite common, especially when they're young. They're always jumping out of owners' arms or getting underfoot. I can't tell you how many times I've walked through the wards on a Monday morning and seen a Yorkie or a Chihuahua or a Pomeranian with a bulky fluorescent bandage on their leg and known exactly why they were here and what happened. I've even heard some surgeons joke about shoring up the opposite leg before it breaks."

Sonja smiled but I could tell I had hardly dented the surface.

"But three times, and twice in the same leg? This dog means everything, and I mean everything, to my mom. You will never meet a more devoted or attentive pet owner and yet here we are."

"Believe me, this has nothing to do with you or your mother or your husband." My assertive tone took her by surprise, but I felt like she needed some strong reassurance. "The break occurred at the point where the stainless steel plate from the first fracture repair ends and normal bone begins. This junction can be vulnerable to normal stresses and strains. It was an accident, plain and simple. My job is to make sure we're not missing something other than bad luck. Now I've reviewed all of the notes from Dr. Glynn and Cleo's vet in Canada, the blood work, the diet, and the bone quality on the X-rays and there is absolutely nothing jumping out at me. You've done pretty much everything possible to discover an underlying problem and come up empty-handed." And then, with an attempt at levity, I added, "Or should I say, almost everything."

In response to her confusion, I smiled, silently saying "relax, everything will be fine," and got to my feet.

"Come here, sweetheart," I said and Cleo skipped right over to me. I opened my hand to pick her up and as I did this she edged her flank into my fingers, as though she were positioning me to scratch her where *she* wanted, as though I wouldn't be smart enough to understand what she was up to.

"You're funny," I told her, lifting her under her belly and carrying her over to my table, confident no dangerous metamorphosis into Cujo would ever take place with this dog. Sonja came over to join us, and I began my examination.

Cleo's head was small, her features delicate and distinctly feminine. Each stroke of my cupped hand caught her little pricked ears. She appeared relaxed and comfortable, with the eyes of a wiser, older dog that had been through this routine a thousand times. The closest she would come to a snarl was when I lifted her lip to inspect a healthy pink gum line and the Hollywood-white teeth of a young dog.

Pulling on the stethoscope draped across my shoulders, I listened to the normal rhythm of her plum-sized heart, feeling Cleo's skin twitch briefly when she flinched as my left hand came around the inside of her thigh, locating the femoral artery, the beat inside my head synchronized with the pulsing blood under my fingers. I waited. The rhythm, the synchrony remained. My stethoscope moved around her chest, up, back, across, jumping between quadrants, listening for crackles and pops. All I heard was the faintest summer breeze, air moving freely and deeply into healthy lung tissue.

I scratched under Cleo's chin, or so she thought, and watched her melt, all bashful, enjoying the pressure as I hunted for swollen lymph nodes at the angles of her jaw. Submandibular clean. I slid back and in front of her shoulders. Prescapular clean. Left hand only, left side only, I squeezed in the meaty muscle behind her left knee. Popliteal clean.

I reached under her body, nails against skin, the belly scratch causing her to relax her rectus abdominus muscles so I could feel the loops of bowel, the edge of her liver, the position of her spleen, and a bladder full of pee. I was hunting for anything abnormal or painful, but apart from a need to use the ladies' room, Cleo was giving nothing away.

Obviously the elephant in the room was the dangling right hind leg and I had no intention of manipulating the limb anywhere near the fracture. Gently I laid my hand over the swollen thigh, fur hiding the black and blue that lay beneath. Cleo turned to watch me, her expression curious, not defensive or bracing or impatient. It would have been perfectly reasonable for her to snap, to ward me off, but I didn't sense a warning. For a few seconds we stared at each other.

"I'm trusting you not to bite me," I tried to convey. "And I hope you can trust me not to hurt you."

Whatever language passed between us, it worked. Cleo let me check out her knee and ankle and toes, and I kept the fracture perfectly still throughout. She never squeaked or moved in protest.

I thanked her with a pat and returned her to the floor and her ongoing olfactory investigation, then invited Sonja to have a seat.

"What an absolute sweetheart," I said. "I have to confess that a lot of the Min Pins I deal with can be a little . . . how shall I put it?"

"Testy?" Ms. Rasmussen suggested, and I could tell she got it.

"Thank you," I said, appreciating her understanding. "Of course she has every right to give me a hard time, letting me check her over with a broken leg."

"But can you fix it?"

She could stand it no more, the need to know written all over her face, and it had been wrong of me to keep her waiting.

"Of course," I said. "I can fix Cleo's broken leg."

I could almost feel the air leaving her lungs with the "thank God" sigh of relief.

"I'm going to have to raid the war chest and get a little creative, but as far as I can tell there's no good reason why we can't put her back together again."

For a moment she seemed lost, overwhelmed, and because I still had an important point to make I leaned forward and unleashed a three-letter word guaranteed to bring her back.

"But," I said.

It worked.

"There is one more thing I think I should do at the time of surgery. I want to take a small piece of Cleo's bone and submit it to the pathologists, have them take a look at it under a microscope and make sure there's nothing wrong."

Sonja nodded but I sensed she wasn't really listening. I briefly went over anesthesia and epidurals and narcotics, insisting that Cleo would be extremely comfortable and pain free, and I paused, as I occasionally do, waiting for a nervous owner to interject some variation of "Do you think I could have some of what she's getting!"

But Sonja said nothing, and as I spoke and watched her watching me, I realized something about her had changed. It was as though she had made up her mind. She had decided to trust me, unreservedly, and now Cleo's and every member of her family's future was in my hands. I believed she wanted to hear what I had to say, but it didn't really matter now that she had committed to my care.

"Would you like me to speak to your mother?"

For a few seconds she seemed to give my offer serious consideration before shaking it off.

"Thank you, but that won't be necessary. I'll call her later."

And once more Sonja Rasmussen drifted off, visibly uneasy at this prospect.

"So let me put the paperwork together, the various requests for anesthesia and radiology, an estimate, and then I can take Cleo back to the wards. And please, don't worry about her feeling lonely. I guarantee this little dog will be so popular with the technicians I'll have to organize visiting hours."

As I ticked boxes and scribbled details, Sonja picked up Cleo in her arms, whispered in her ear, and gave her a kiss. At the examination room door, our exchange took place and I watched the blood squeezed from Sonja's lips as they clamped down, pinching her guilt into a pale scar that she would wear until this was all over, until, hopefully, Cleo's broken leg was reduced to a vague memory, something to "remember when." My heart seized at her attempt to mask it, to twist her pain into something approaching a passable smile, while all it revealed was how much effort it took. Despite my attempts to absolve her of blame, she still wore the burden of responsibility for what had happened to Cleo like a heavy, unwieldy cloak. I wondered if it would disappear after this was all over. I wondered if I could help to make this woman really smile again.

As Cleo lay in my arms, the two of us watched Sonja head out to the front desk looking like a mother leaving her child in day care for the first time. In a daze, she checked out, negotiating the unsightly financial paperwork, signing without reading, unable to process how she got here and why.

"Don't look so worried," I said to Cleo. "I'm sure she'll be fine."

6 THE HEART OF THE MATTER

FOR some, the idea of brushing a dog's teeth is no less ridiculous than teaching him or her to use a flushable toilet. They sneer or roll their eyes in disbelief at the increasing demand for root canals, crowns, and braces, arguing that dogs have been doing just fine for centuries, gnawing on bone or rawhide. Since when does a dog owner need to purchase a toothbrush and edible chicken-flavored toothpaste?

This question occurred to Eileen as she and Helen sat patiently in the Angell waiting room before their appointment with the cardiologist, Dr. Molotov. Arguably, with twice-weekly brushing, Helen's dental crisis would never have evolved to the point where close proximity to her breath required a "severe" terror alert. Then again, given her sorry state when she entered their lives, the niceties of oral hygiene must have been low down on a list of bare necessities for survival. Eileen imagined Helen living, for the most part, like generations of dogs before her, wandering and scavenging, devoid of meaningful contact with humans. Now that she had become a modern canine and moved into the heart of a family, killer halitosis could seriously curb quality social time. And aside from the smell issues, a decade of neglect also meant unremitting mouth pain. The poor dog's teeth needed professional attention, even if that demanded a detour to a cardiologist to get things done properly.

So why did Eileen feel nervous about this appointment? In part, she realized, it was due to Helen's age, the fear of putting a geriatric animal through any elective procedure, especially when the dog's entire medical history was a mystery. There was also her inkling that Dr. J. had either heard something she shouldn't, or couldn't hear something she should, during her examination of Helen's chest. But most of all it was how this urchin dog, in her life for such a brief time, had so completely, so effortlessly, crawled into Eileen's heart, padded down, and come to rest. Helen had this way about her when she looked at you in response to every small kindness, like a Make-A-Wish kid living every day at Disneyland, unable to believe her luck.

"Helen?"

Eileen looked up to see an older woman in a long white coat standing over her. The woman wore no makeup and Eileen supposed pigment had never flirted with the long gray hair secured by a nest of bobby pins to form a tight precise bun. Thick glasses made her eyes look even smaller, giving her a chaste, mousy look—like an austere parochial school educator. But when Eileen said, "This is Helen," the woman glowed, as if this meeting were a fortuitous pleasure and privilege.

"Hello," she said, "I'm Dr. Molotov, one of the cardiologists on staff. If we may, I'll have a listen to Helen's chest, then we'll take a closer look at her heart with ultrasound. Would you please follow me?"

Eileen and Helen trotted along behind her, moving deeper into the heart of the hospital, guided toward a room with an entranceway labeled "Echocardiography." Here Dr. Molotov began her examination, starting with Helen's history.

"I wish there was more I could tell you," said Eileen. "Helen was a stray. She's been with us a couple of months now. I had her vaccinated and tested for heartworm. She was heartworm negative. Hopefully you have a fax from my vet for the rest of her blood work."

Dr. Molotov smiled and nodded, turning over a number of stapled sheets of paper in her hand. She ran a finger all the way down the page.

"You're doing a wonderful thing for this dog," she said. Despite the compassion visible behind the thick lenses, this candid remark took Eileen by surprise. She managed a self-conscious, whispered "thank you" as Helen was picked up and placed on a table for examination.

Quite where this reject cocker spaniel acquired her dog-show manners Eileen did not know, but for the gentle hands of Dr. Molotov, Helen stood square and still, appreciative of the tactile affection, even if her old spaniel ears filtered out all the compliments.

"Okay then, let's see if Helen will let us take a look at her heart."

With the assistance of a female technician in plum-colored scrubs, two neat symmetrical patches of fur were shaved, one on each side of Helen's chest, and she was laid down on a transparent plastic table with a small square window cut into its center. The overhead lights were dimmed so as to optimize image contrast on the screen. The ultrasound machine was a bulky, high-tech, hospital-white unit, touting buttons and dials and sliders and mouse pads beneath a large screen bearing Helen's details in its top lefthand corner. The main body of the image was shaped like a generous slice of cake. Dr. Molotov selected a probe, applied a liberal coating of blue gel to its head, snaked it under and through the hole in the table, and made direct contact with the bald skin of Helen's chest. Instantly, within the sweeping radar triangle on the screen, beating muscle, chambers, and valves came into remarkably sharp focus.

Methodically, images were produced and measurements made.

Eileen watched as probes came and went, twisting this way and that, slicing the beating heart into transverse and longitudinal sections, the flow of colors adding splashes of blue and red paint dancing to the whoosh and slosh of venous and arterial blood. Eileen felt lost, her eyes moving between the digital chaos on the monitor and the calm smile of the dog she loved on the table.

"Please God," she thought. "Give this poor dog a chance at a real life."

"Very good," said Dr. Molotov.

For a second Eileen thought it was over, that "very good" meant Helen must have a clean bill of health for her heart.

"Let's see if she will be just as helpful for the other side."

Eileen kept the groan to herself while Helen, more than happy to oblige, flipped over and was wriggled into position above the aperture by the technician. Same beat, same dance moves on this opposite side, the side Dr. J. had hesitated over months before. The eternity dragged on, the desire to know if everything was okay building to an unbearable crescendo. And then, as if she were delivering a throwaway line she might have slipped into the conversation at any time, Dr. Molotov said, "Well, I don't see anything wrong with her heart. Her measurements check out fine for an older spaniel. Her valves appear to be in perfect working order."

Eileen inhaled deeply, overcome by the mixture of relief and pride welling up inside.

"So that just leaves us with a couple of chest X-rays," said Dr. Molotov, wiping the *Ghostbusters* slime off Helen's chest. "We should be able to do them right away, and based on how good Helen was for the ultrasound, I doubt she'll need any sedation. Let me take you over to the radiology waiting area."

Eileen and Helen were led down a corridor to a small waiting room occupied by an elderly gentleman with a golden retriever lying at his feet.

Man and dog existed in an invisible shroud of nicotine. He, the man, was long limbed, angled forward, elbows on thighs, his body speaking the language of someone unable to relax. His gaunt features relinquished a brief forced smile as Eileen and Helen took a seat.

The dog shared this lean, skeletal appearance—another example of master looking like dog, or maybe it was the other way round. This was a particularly blond golden, the bony features of his skull prominent, unnaturally unmasked by wasted muscle. He lay with his chin resting on the cool floor, his eyes looking tired and unfocused.

For a while the four of them maintained their silence, like strangers on an elevator watching the numbers over the sliding metal doors count down.

A technician in Oxford blue scrubs appeared.

"I'm here for Helen, for her chest X-rays," he said.

"Do you need me to come with her?" asked Eileen, handing over her leash.

"No, that won't be necessary," he said. "The X-ray machines are just around the corner. If she lies still we'll be back in a few minutes."

Eileen watched them go and then turned back to the old man and his dog, suddenly aware that Helen had been taken out of sequence.

"I'm sorry," she said, "I feel like I'm jumping the line."

The old man waved away the apology with a large, weathered hand. It smacked of a lifetime's manual labor but Eileen focused on the indelible dirty yellow V between his cigarette fingers.

"No biggie," he said, tar and gravel clinging to every word. "Sam's supposed to be seeing the cancer doctor before he gets his X-rays. We've got nowhere to go."

Eileen leaned forward and down to run a hand along Sam's head, neck, and back, feeling every bone along the poor dog's spine, the damning reality of an emaciated dog. It was remarkable how much a dog's fur could hide. Perhaps, thought Eileen, it was more telling that Sam made no response to a stranger's touch. No look back. No swish of the tail. The old dog continued to stare straight ahead.

"I get the feeling this is going to be his last set of X-rays," said the man, the words sounding detached, as if he were trying them on for size, seeing if they fit, if he could say them to a stranger and keep the pain and fear inside him from spilling out. He dropped his head slightly, focusing on a spot on the floor next to where Sam lay, and seemed to take stock of how he had done, how it had felt. He seemed unsure of his performance, a tough old man trying to save face in public, to deny how much he was being hurt by his best friend's unrelenting demise.

Suddenly, for Eileen, this fragility on both sides of their relationship filled the room, as if she could share his unimaginable burden of losing his dog. She stared at him, reading the battle playing out in the wrinkles around his eyes, unable to find the right words. Any words. Eileen had had pets her whole life but she had never been in a situation where an animal had endured a relentless illness and lost.

"Eileen."

It was Dr. Molotov, standing before her, large manila folder in hand, Helen at her feet on the end of the leash, appearing pleased all this overrated medical attention was over.

"We're all done so why don't you come with me."

Eileen took Helen's leash from Dr. Molotov and followed her, the silent farewell from the old man as she left no more than a subtle nod, dry lips pursed, a message that said, "Don't look so worried, *your* dog's going to be just fine."

Directly off the radiology waiting area was a private room with viewing boxes where owners could be shown their pet's X-rays. The room was dark until Dr. Molotov turned on a viewing box, removed an X-ray from the folder, and hung it in place, the fluorescence transmitted through the shades of black and white creating an eerie glow. She stepped toward the door and closed it behind them, the action too deliberate to go unnoticed by Eileen. Eileen turned to face her, hoping to speak first, the preemptive strike, but the shadows couldn't mask the sadness written on the doctor's face and that moment of speechless shock was all it took for Dr. Molotov to get there first and say, "I'm so terribly sorry."

THE rest of what followed was a blur.

There were the words of the messenger, Dr. Molotov, a woman unable to conceal her surprise and disappointment as she delicately marinated every phrase in genuine kindness and empathy.

There were the X-rays themselves, the cold hard facts regarding this dog's past and future. They were bold and blatant, leaping from the film, inducing a dumb nod of understanding even to the untrained eye.

What Eileen walked away with was a new, foreign, and paralyzing vocabulary, ugly phrases absorbed like blows in a beating, frightening medical terms that rained down on her until she could take no more. Pulling herself together, placing one foot in front of the other, she walked out of the room with Helen in tow. Perhaps what struck her the most as she passed through the radiology waiting area was the absence of the old man and his fragile retriever, as if neither of them had ever been there in the first place.

Back home, with Ben, she went over these verbal wounds one by one, the ones that stuck, the ones she had to say out loud: *massive tumor . . . potentially inoperable . . . probably malignant . . . terminal cancer . . .*

All the while the tears kept coming and the little black dog at her feet wondered what all the fuss was about.

Ben held Eileen in his arms, pained by his inability to protect her from this grief. The shock came in waves, the brief lulls while tissues caught the tears an opportunity for carefully chosen words.

"So the tumor is in Helen's lungs?"

He felt the nod in his chest.

"But she has no problem breathing. She runs. She plays. And I've never heard her cough."

Eileen pulled back, wiping her nostrils.

"I know," she said. "But something wasn't right when Dr. J. checked her over the very first time. She said she had a problem hearing her heartbeat."

And then Ben lost her, could see and feel her slipping away, those few seconds of composure melting into an expression of dread, words distorted by her heaving sobs.

"I sh-should have had . . . her ch-chest X-rayed . . . sooner. This is all m-my fault . . ."

These would be the first of many second guesses, Ben knew, but he beat them into submission, sent them into exile, and tried to give pragmatism a chance.

"Who knows how long it's been there?" he said. "What if Helen's had this thing for months, even years? Surely that makes it less likely to be malignant and more likely to be benign?"

The shuddering inside his arms continued, as if she had not heard him. Ben bided his time.

"Here's what you do," he said during the next respite. "You go and meet with an oncologist. Find out what they have to say. Let's not jump to any conclusions before we have all the facts."

Eileen chose to hear this, her nod and audible swallow suggesting that his message had gotten through. She pulled back and glanced down to lock eyes with the dog at her feet. Innocence stared back, she was certain of that, and though Eileen hunted for more, she could be confident that one emotion was missing—fear. In all her years shared with animals, she had never sensed a dog or a cat was afraid to die. What do they know that we do not? Why are we the only ones burdened by the fear of death? In those big brown shiny eyes Eileen saw it, so obvious and uncomplicated. For all her fussing and struggling to interpret the minutiae of Helen's expression, it was all there, written in the unspoken language of contentment and security, one dog's blatant declaration of trust.

7   ORDINARY DAY

T HE uninitiated may be forgiven for thinking the "soaping" of hospitalized animals alludes to a daily ritual of sudsy patient cleanliness. In fact SOAP is a convenient acronym for a brief yet thorough early-morning evaluation of clinical well-being, followed by a summation and a statement regarding the day's purpose.

"*S*" stands for *subjective* and calls for me to make a spontaneous, gut-feeling appraisal of how my patient reacts to my presence.

"Hi, sweetheart, how are you this morning?"

I opened the cage door, squatted down, and squeezed into Cleo's overnight accommodation.

"Did you sleep well? You look like you did. I hope your neighbors kept the noise down."

Cleo rushed forward to greet me, jubilantly waltzing on three legs (and two left feet) before crawling into my lap and poking her face into mine.

"Look at you, all fresh and frisky," I said, scratching her under the chin, impossible not to. When I let up, Cleo's ears pricked, head canting to the right. I mirrored the maneuver, the puzzled expression. She paused and then tried to see if I made more sense with her head listing to the left.

"What is it? What are you after, little one?"

There was a giggle behind me and I turned to see a technician cleaning bowls in a sink stealing a glance over her shoulder, amused by my coquettish remarks. The snout rooting in the breast pocket of my shirt brought me back to the task at hand.

"Hey, stop that, you little rascal."

Now I understood her confusion. Cleo was looking for food. She had assumed I was about to deliver her breakfast and, finding me empty-handed, planted her face in my shirt pocket like she was strapping on a feed bag.

"I'm sorry," I said. "I'll get you something to eat as soon as you wake up from anesthesia. But first of all we've got to fix that leg of yours, okay?"

Cleo appeared to listen, but it was obvious that Uncle Nick had lost most of his credibility with this indecent disruption of her gastronomic routine. I decided I would write Cleo up as B.A.R.—bright, alert, and responsive (accurate, if unimaginative)—and moved on to the *O* part of the proceedings.

Objective refers to all the hands-on stuff and the numbers it generates. Cleo's heart rate said she was calm and, more importantly, not in pain, as did her breathing. Her belly felt fine and she stood quietly, if a little self-consciously, for her rectal temperature, which was in the normal range.

"Good girl, Cleo," I said, producing an enormous orange marking pen resembling a giant Popsicle, designed for tagging livestock. At first, I could tell all was forgiven. An ice lollipop might not have been the breakfast of champions but Cleo obviously thought it was better than nothing. One lick, an unpleasant aftertaste, and her confused expression told me I was right back in the doghouse.

Which of Cleo's legs was broken was patently obvious, but in veterinary medicine, every patient has three right legs. This is why operating on limbs fills almost every surgeon with a degree of trepidation. Forget about falling off a cliff or running down a crowded street in nothing but your underwear, my worst nightmare is the omnipresent possibility of taking a patient to surgery and operating on the wrong leg. My patient cannot sanction my decision or offer me any last-minute verbal reminders ("Remember, it's this one, Doc").

For surgery involving the right leg, I need to clarify between *right* front, *right* hind, and *right* meaning "correct." In an attempt to avoid any mistakes we have a strict policy requiring the clinician responsible for the patient to label the leg with a swath of waxy orange paint or some other mark that categorically defines which limb will be going under the knife.

For Cleo, my orange daub was redundant but I still identified the broken leg. If I didn't do it now, the anesthesia technicians would be all over me to do it sooner or later. Cleo watched me swipe the orange crayon in a safe zone, below her right knee, her gaze turning from my hand to my eyes, her expression suggesting I would have to do better than this to redeem myself.

A stands for *assessment*, and though I might have touched upon Cleo's charisma and stoicism, I kept my wording practical, pertinent, and informative for the other doctors or technicians who might interact with Cleo but not know the details of her case. She was a healthy young dog with a right femur fracture that was three days old. The fracture was at the site of a previous surgical repair. Her blood work and urinalysis were normal. Any concerns I had about some sort of a predisposition to fractures, an underlying pathology, did not fit here. They had no basis in fact. There was no section in the patient record for niggling doubts or the tingle of my "spider sense."

P stands for *plan* and this was easy. Take Cleo to surgery this afternoon for right femur fracture repair. I might have said more—leg heals, Cleo does great, daughter overcomes sense of guilt, and everyone lives happily ever after—but I still had to call Sonja and then I had a special case to see.

———

For a twentysomething, twenty-first-century woman, Sonja Rasmussen was guilty of an unimaginable communications faux pas. Lost, broken, or forgotten, whatever the reason, she was without a cell phone. In this throwback to the Dark Ages, the only available means of contact was the telephone number to her hotel room in downtown Boston.

She picked up the phone before the second ring, and I imagined her perched on the edge of the bed, ready to lunge, picked-over room-service food on a nearby silver platter, ordered because she had been afraid to go down to breakfast and miss my call.

"Hi, Ms. Rasmussen, this is Dr. Trout."

"Please, call me Sonja, how's Cleo?"

"She's great. She's funny."

"What do you mean?"

I caught the stiffness in her reply, the silent tension between us, as though I had meant "funny peculiar" and had news for her.

"I mean she's entertaining, quite the character, though she was less than pleased to be denied her breakfast this morning."

"Oh, I see," she said, her tone more measured. "When is she going to have her surgery?"

"Well, I have an urgent appointment coming in shortly and from what I'm told it might need to go first. So Cleo will be second in line."

Silence gave away her disappointment.

"It will probably be first thing this afternoon," I said.

"And how long do you think it will take?"

"I'm not sure," I said. "Couple of hours, then I'll need to take some X-rays to make sure everything looks good. I can't imagine I'd be calling you later than five."

An audible sigh crawled into my ear.

"I'll go out of my mind waiting here all day for your call. Maybe what I'll do is go shopping this afternoon and then swing by the hospital around five o'clock. Would that be okay? That way I can speak to you in person."

"That sounds great," I said. "I can show you the postoperative X-rays when you arrive." And then I added, "How's your mother doing?"

It was really none of my business but I imagined they had spoken after Cleo's consultation.

"She's good," said Sonja, clearly caught off guard by my question. "It should be the other way around, but she's the one looking after *me*, helping *me* keep it together."

There was a pause and for a moment I thought she was going to say more, but she didn't. I wouldn't want you to think I handle all my conversations with pet owners like a homicide detective interrogating a prime suspect, but once again I sensed an element of mystery shrouding what she said or rather what she didn't say, omissions speaking louder than words.

"She sounds like a remarkable woman," I said.

Another pause, as though my remark had taken her by surprise.

"Yes," she said, "I guess you're right."

I CALLED the cat's name, Henry, and a man wearing a black turtleneck sweater and suede jacket stood up. He made a deliberate adjustment to the parting of his neat black hair like a slow military salute, picked up his copy of the *Boston Globe* in one hand, and strutted toward me swinging a cardboard cat carrier in the other. The guy looked like a character from central casting, the wannabe author type. I was wondering where he had hidden the Starbucks Venti Chai and the laptop containing his unpublished novel.

"Sorry to keep you waiting, Mr. Sharpe."

I gestured toward the open door of a nearby exam room.

"I'm not Mr. Sharpe," said Dan Brown Jr., brushing past me,

rudely depositing Henry's mode of transportation on the table between us. "Henry is my fiancée's cat, not mine. I'm just the delivery boy."

I checked the owner's name on the patient record and read
"Susan Sharpe."

"I'm sorry about that," I said, "but maybe you can still answer a
few questions about . . ."

Without invitation, Henry's chauffeur had taken a seat, unfolded
his newspaper, and disappeared behind the pages of the business
section.

". . . about Henry's problem."

My words trailed away to a whisper and he appeared not to notice,
turning a page, snapping the paper taut. He eased back in his seat,
happy to let me get on with whatever it was I did when I admitted a
patient, and I realized here was a man who would rather be stuck at
home organizing his sock drawer on Super Bowl Sunday than talking to me about his fiancée's cat.

I resolved to battle on.

"So, Susan would be the person who brought in Henry through
the emergency service last night?"

His head remained level, eyes rolling up above the page to meet
mine, transmitting a "you still here?" look before giving in to a reluctant nod.

"And I see from his record that Henry has a long history of urinary tract problems. Has there been blood in the urine, frequent
visits to the litter box? Why did he need to be seen last night?"

Of course I already knew the answers to these questions. The
intern who saw the case in our ER had briefed me on Henry's
predicament, his record having grown to encyclopedic proportions
after years of difficulty going to the bathroom. Like many tomcats,
regardless of whether or not they are neutered, Henry had a talent
for growing microscopic crystals in his urine. Sometimes these crystals can form discrete stones, but oftentimes they produce a sandy,

gritty sludge that builds up in the narrowest part of his manly plumbing, which happens to be the penis. The result is a painful and potentially life-threatening blockage because of Henry's habitual inability to pee.

"Look," he said with the raised brows of a man losing his patience, "she brought him in, she discussed the surgery with the doctor, she was told to drop him off this morning, but she had to work so here I am. The only thing I know for sure is he's costing me a fortune and he wakes me up growling in the night every time he takes a whiz."

He tried a smile, like an off-the-rack suit, apparently didn't like the way it felt, and put it right back as the hypnotic pull of the Dow Jones got the better of him. I let him drift, preferring to head over to the carrier and open the box.

Henry was an arresting orange tom with a tail that shot up like an antenna, a twitching feeler in search of attention. I lifted his twelve pounds onto the table and he was on me, head butting, pressing his flaming flanks into my chest, sidling to and fro as I reached for my stethoscope, deafened by the steady grinding purr of a flirtatious cat.

His head was broad, the head of a cat neutered later in life, and his ears and face bore the scars of a former street fighter. When you went to stroke him he pushed into your hand, hard, as though he objected to a delicate touch, his tough old skin longing to be roughed up.

"Hang on there little man, hang on," I said, swinging him around so that his head was away from me. Only now did I notice the extra toes on his front feet, the polydactyl paws of so many New England cats.

"I just want to have a feel of your tummy."

Henry stopped purring as soon as I moved my right hand under his abdomen, guarding with a defensive muscular crunch. I gave him a noogie and he relaxed enough for me to feel a bladder that had distended to the size of an orange.

"I know, Henry," I said, picking up his tail and hunting for his penis, "this is not very dignified but it has to be done."

Henry began dancing back and forth on his back legs and this time the purr had ripened into a grumble. He let me catch a glimpse, no more, but it was enough to confirm redness, swelling, and considerable soreness. Poor thing, his barbed feline tongue had rasped the tip of his penis raw trying to relieve the gritty impaction trapped inside.

"I'm sorry, little man," I said, rubbing down his neck. All forgiven, Henry twisted his big head off to the side to make sure I worked a few good scratches into the base of his ear.

I put him down on the floor so he could explore the room and washed my hands in the sink.

"So," I said, turning my swivel chair back to front, straddling it, and sidling up to the back of a newspaper, "according to his records, this is Henry's third episode of getting blocked. And you know what they say: 'Three strikes and you're out!' "

I didn't expect the baseball metaphor to get his attention but he angled the paper forward and down so I could meet his steely eyes.

"What are you saying?"

"I'm saying, I think you're making the right decision. It's about time Henry was plumbed a little differently, down below, if you know what I mean."

My turn of phrase had the desired effect.

"No, I don't know what you mean."

"Really," I said, feigning surprise. "Susan didn't tell you all the details of the surgery?"

"No. Like I've been saying all along she just asked me to drop him off. What are you going to do to him?"

I wasn't sure whether he was suddenly Henry's advocate or begrudged being left out of any decision that might affect his checkbook.

"It's a procedure called a perineal urethrostomy. Essentially I'm going to amputate Henry's penis and give him a new, wide opening that will make it much easier for him to urinate."

The paper fell to the floor as Deadbeat Dad came to his feet, incredulous.

"You're going to do what? Lop off his penis and give him a sex change? Is that what you're telling me?"

His hands reached for his hairline, fingers stretching back the skin at his temples to produce an instant frantic facelift.

"Susan would have told me about this. She couldn't have understood what was involved. She said the doctor was young. She probably didn't get all the gory details."

I knew for a fact that the intern who saw Henry last night had done an excellent job of describing the surgery, the postoperative care, and the potential complications. She told me the owner had been putting off the inevitable for some time. Susan had done everything she could; modifying Henry's diet, monitoring his urine for crystals and bacteria, periodically bringing him to the hospital to be catheterized and flushed out when the signs of obstruction started to return. She simply couldn't stand to see Henry suffer anymore.

"She's the one you need to be talking to. Not me. She should have been here. I can't believe this. I shouldn't be making these kinds of decisions. It's not even my cat."

"I can give her a call," I said, "if it will make you feel better."

He raised an index finger and rummaged in a jacket pocket and pulled out a Post-it note on which various telephone numbers were written.

"Yes. Here," he said, handing it over. "I was supposed to give this to you anyway."

I studied the note.

"Any suggestion where to start?" I said, picking up the examination room phone and getting an outside line.

He consulted his watch.

"Try work, she might be in by now."

The call was picked up and an insipid recorded voice listed my options and had me hold for three minutes before an actual human being transferred me to the appropriate office, only to get an answering machine.

I shook my head.

"Try her cell," he said.

I dialed the number and a woman picked up on the third ring.

"Hello."

"Hi, Ms. Sharpe, this is Dr. Trout from Angell."

In the background I could hear the click of heels on salted concrete, the sound of passing cars, and the customary refrain of horns. I imagined a woman caught in the daily tide of silent iPod-wearing androids scurrying to work.

"I have Henry here. What a great cat. But your fiancée asked me to call to make sure you were clear about the exact nature of this morning's surgery."

Static crackled, and the odd syllable filtered through but I was losing the signal.

"Ms. Sharpe. Hello."

I was talking into the hiss of white noise. I pressed redial and a recorded message informed me the cellular subscriber had moved out of the service area. Perhaps she was belowground riding the T.

"No luck," I said, "but not to worry. I'm sure Ms. Sharpe understood exactly what was going to happen to Henry. However, I will need you to sign his consent form."

From nowhere, Henry leapt into his prospective stepfather's lap, an orange ball staring the man in the face, quizzically, adding to the burden of his responsibility.

For a few seconds I let him stew as he grappled with his responsibility to sanction an unexpectedly radical procedure without a definitive verbal approval from his fiancée. This man's relationship with Henry's true guardian was absolutely none of my business, but it was hard for me to ignore his attitude toward her cat. He had made it perfectly clear he was performing a chore, an act of appeasement akin to dropping off a car at the shop for an oil change. His moment of vacillation over the surgery felt like it was borne out of misplaced, virile anthropomorphism rather than genuine concern. Henry's medical record was a testament to Susan's dedication, while her unaccompanied visit to the emergency room and her failure to discuss the nature of his surgery seemed to be a testament to their dissociation when it came to this feline member of their love triangle. Henry coerced him into a couple of mechanical pats to his head and I wondered if this man had it in him to change his attitude. Part of me hoped he would have to if he truly wanted to win Susan's heart.

"Tell you what," I said. "I'll give Susan a call back in the next fifteen minutes. That way there won't be any surprises."

He picked up his paper and I traded Henry for a written estimate and a consent form for him to sign at the front desk.

"Don't worry," I said, "I'll take good care of him." The fact that I seemed to interpret his consternation as concern for Henry only seemed to amplify his unease.

We shook hands, his grip firm, the exchange feeling more like an endorsement of a major deal. He was probably just grateful for me bailing him out. But the romantic in me liked to imagine he was finally seeing me as a doctor and not simply a mechanic, seeing himself as a concerned party and not simply a chauffeur.

PERINEAL urethrostomy for the surgical treatment of feline urethral obstruction has been around for nearly forty years and I can honestly say that I have never thought about it as a gender-bending exercise. Henry's surgery was everything it should be, a textbook modification in his anatomy designed to provide as patent an outflow as possible. Surgery would not prevent him from producing grit and sand in his urine. It would, however, minimize the potential for this sludge to create a blockage. Susan's fiancé would not be out of pocket for hormone therapy. Henry was not about to become a feline fashionista or develop an affected, effeminate meow. He would be the same little man he always had been—fiery, demonstrative, and macho—though he would be required to wear a satellite disk for the next few weeks to stop him from licking at his stitches.

With Henry recovering nicely and Susan thrilled that everything went according to her plan, I crossed paths with Dr. Beth Maganiello in the surgical prep area.

"What's with this Min Pin of yours, little Miss Cleo?" said Beth.

Dr. Maganiello is a critical care specialist, but given her interest in anesthesia and pain management, she is intimately involved in protocols and monitoring for many of our more challenging or brittle surgical patients.

"Quite the character, isn't she?"

"I'm sure she's lovely," said Beth, scrolling through the pages of her record, "but I've yet to meet her. I was actually referring to her history. You think she's healthy apart from fracture number three?"

Beth wore gray scrubs and a red headband that seemed redundant given the shortness of her hair. Her trademark pair of retro tortoiseshell glasses had been discarded for contacts, clearly a recent transition given the frequency of her blinks.

"As far as I can tell. Two different vets have looked for an underlying cause of bone weakness and come up empty-handed."

She frowned, visibly underwhelmed by the blood work.

"Maybe she's just unlucky."

"Maybe," I said, and then, moving ahead to the crux of what this was about, "When you anesthetize her, will you be serving a well-balanced but robust narcotic for starters, followed by a smooth, clean induction agent, finishing with aromatic and intoxicating gases mingled with the delights of your legendary epidural cocktail?"

She regarded me with a weary expression, the sharp intake of breath, the one that says "are you finished?" overplayed enough to reveal her amusement.

"Don't worry," she said, "we'll make sure she's nice and comfortable despite what you have planned for her leg."

I smiled, knowing Cleo was in truly excellent hands, and half an hour later I was paged to the surgical prep area in time to see her fall asleep, relaxing into her anesthesia.

A tube was inserted into Cleo's trachea and she was hooked up to a machine that would deliver anesthetic gas and oxygen. A heart monitor designed specifically for veterinary use was turned on, firing up with its electronic rendition of "If I Could Talk to the Animals" from the Rex Harrison version of *Doctor Dolittle*. Colored leads were fastened to her skin and a white probe gently attached to her little pink tongue, measuring the oxygen saturation of her blood. A small square of fur was shaved on the underside of her front foot, positioning a Doppler ultrasound probe to assist in recording the highs and lows of her blood pressure. All was well as Cleo sailed into oblivion.

"Where would you like me to shave her leg?" said a technician armed with an electrical clipper. She followed my finger as I delineated the margins of what was about to become Cleo's surgical bald patch. The technician nodded her understanding and then appeared to disregard my design, defining a tidy small square over the base of Cleo's spine where Dr. Maganiello herself would deliver Cleo's epidural.

At this stage in the proceedings I usually have about fifteen more minutes before my patient will be ready for surgery, and I took this opportunity to leave Cleo in the surgical prep area and pass by the scrub sinks, through the swinging door, and into the OR to go shopping for orthopedic implants and all the necessary instrumentation. I was going to need power tools, tissue retractors, bone-holding forceps, bone-reduction forceps, suction, electrocautery—the usual, indispensable stuff of all orthopedic surgery.

Armed with the X-ray of Cleo's broken leg I scoured the aisles for a plate with the appropriate length, width, number of screw holes, and thickness. We have it all in stock, from tiny plates you can break with your fingers to plates so thick you need huge table-based bending pliers to produce the smallest kink in their stainless steel. After all, veterinary surgeons routinely repair fractures on dogs as small as a Chihuahua and as big as a Great Dane or bullmastiff. Is it any wonder our stock of orthopedic implants needs to be so versatile?

One of the other surgeons on staff pushed through the swinging operating room door, dripping hands out front, and muttered behind his mask, "I think you might want to check on your patient."

Then he was past me, headed for his sterile gown and latex gloves, his suggestion delivered on the fly, but it was still easy for me to catch its gravity, even if I could not comprehend its reason.

My first thought was of Henry the cat, recovering from his surgery, and the possibility of a little postoperative hemorrhage given the vascular geography of his procedure. Hiccup, yes. Major complication, unlikely. A mixture of faith and confidence in my work had me heading out of the OR and back toward the prep and recovery areas, yielding to concern but keeping panic at bay.

Nothing about the scene before me felt credible or reasonable, but from a range of thirty feet, the image punched into two separate parts of my brain—passive, visual pathways recognizing that the problem lay with Cleo, followed by the emotional recognition, as I screamed her name over and over inside my head.

Cleo appeared in glimpses, in the gaps between swarming scrubs, the critical buzz of their body language easy to read. As I drove forward, wanting in, there was a split second in which I closed my eyes, really little more than a blink, but enough to visualize all the details smoothing out, becoming clear and discernable. The crisis had been averted, everyone wearing smiles of relief, riding the high of an adrenaline rush with a happy ending. There had to have been a leak in the endotracheal tube sitting in Cleo's windpipe. The tube had been pushed in too far. The tube had become kinked. A monitor lead had become dislodged. Cleo had been swimming in the safe waters of her tranquil anesthetic void but she went down too deep. Now she was back on the surface, breathing fresh air, no harm done. They say that anesthesia is 99 percent boredom and 1 percent sheer terror, and on this occasion relief had triumphed over regret.

But the blink had come to an end by the time I reached her, and it was as if someone had handed me my glasses, a soft impression swiftly replaced by a sharply focused image.

Cleo's vibrant pink tongue had turned a listless crimson. The orderly blips and spikes of a normal heart rhythm were replaced by static interference of seismic proportions. with the anesthetic gas turned off, a dissociated hand squeezed a one-liter bag, driving pure oxygen into lungs that no longer wanted to breathe for themselves.

Beth Maganiello's voice penetrated my head, her calm piercing the turmoil, hooking me with her certainty and control. I could feel the groundswell of commitment all around me. Beth had become the conductor, the technicians her orchestra, and it was clear everyone had practiced long and hard for this performance. Every instruction came across as clear, incisive, and calculated, as though she had been waiting for this moment her whole life, knowing precisely which resuscitative drug to use, at which dose, and when.

Anesthetic emergencies require one leader and I believed Cleo would be better off with Beth. Besides, I needed to be physically involved, connected, drawn to the organ that mattered most—Cleo's heart.

"How long?" I asked, my question vague, but Dr. Maganiello instantly knew where I was going.

"Couple of minutes in full cardiac arrest," she said, reading the EKG monitor, making an interpretation of the changing situation, deciding to switch up to a different drug, dialing up the dose, overseeing the delivery, and watching for the response. It was like a game of chess, your opponent a macabre genius armed with merciless combinations. You must anticipate, react, and outsmart. A body trapped in an anesthetic crisis will fight to survive, will whisper clues and signs to outmaneuver, outplay, and defeat its deadly adversary, but as I glimpsed the pile of discarded syringes littering the table, I sensed the game was already swinging in the wrong direction.

My hand reached inside Cleo's thigh, feeling for her femoral artery. The pulse was weak at best and the technician performing cardiac massage winced through the painful cramps in her hand.

"May I?" I said, eager to take over.

Leaving my left hand in search of a pulse, I placed my right hand under Cleo's chest, thumb on one side, four fingers on the other to offer resistance, and began squeezing, fast and hard, two beats per second, 120 beats per minute, a little rib and muscle all that separated my hand from her heart. And now I could feel it, the force of my compression pumping blood, producing a pulse under my fingers as it rushed through the artery.

"Do we need to defibrillate?" I asked, finding it difficult to interpret the pattern of her EKG.

Beth said, "No. She's not in ventricular fibrillation. I wish she was."

I felt like there was something veiled in her response. I thought the technicians around me sensed it too. I took a second look at the empty syringes on the table. Each one was labeled for a specific drug. I couldn't see them all, but of those I could read there was atropine, a drug used to speed up a slow heart rate; naloxone, an antidote to reverse the effect of any narcotic used in the anesthetic protocol; and epinephrine, synthetic adrenaline, used to increase the heart rate and force of contraction. There were many more I couldn't read, but I began to suspect that Beth's cryptic message meant she was running out of options.

Time is the enemy during a resuscitative effort and it vanishes as easily as time spent watching a great movie or reading a good book. In just four or five minutes of cardiac arrest an animal will succumb to serious irreversible brain injury. Keeping positive, staying in the moment, I came to believe that if I could feel a pulse in Cleo's back leg then oxygenated blood had to be reaching her brain. Acidic cramps were beginning to ripple through the meaty muscle of my thumb and palm, gathering intensity with every squeeze, and as I watched Beth pulling out all the stops but failing to jump-start her heart, I began to welcome the respite of a more physical pain.

"Hold off a second," said Beth and I knew she meant just that, enough time for her to study the cardiac monitor without the interference of my manual compressions.

"Okay," she said, and I started again.

"What are you thinking?"

Beth never skipped a beat, her delivery cold, clinical, and direct.

"I'm pretty sure she has torsades de pointes. It's a bizarre heart arrhythmia seen in people. Just stop for another second."

She pointed to the screen.

"There. It's a really fast rhythm, and see how the shape of the complexes is constantly changing. Carry on."

"So what can we do about it?"

"There's nothing to do. I've tried beta blockers but they're supposed to be preventative, not therapeutic. It's one of the leading causes of sudden death in young, otherwise healthy people. There is no treatment."

She had a pen light out, shone it in Cleo's left eye, watched for a response, and swept it across to the right eye, like the beam from a lighthouse. I saw it all and she knew I saw it and neither of us needed to say it out loud. Cleo's pupils were fixed, dilated, and unresponsive. Even if, by some miracle, we were able to get her heart pumping again, the absence of reaction to bright light shone directly into her eye suggested some degree of brain trauma had already occurred.

"Do you want to open her chest?" said Beth.

I felt the magnitude of this question, but my mind was elsewhere. Thus far I had been a clinician, waging physical and pharmacological war, concentrating on saving the life of an animal that happened to be my patient. And now, with this question, the patient transformed back into a dog named Cleo, a remarkable Min Pin, the beloved pet of a mother I had never met and a daughter haunted by guilt. These hands crawling all over her body, trying so hard to keep the life inside from slipping between our fingers, these hands weren't enough hands to save poor Cleo.

Some people refer to a cardiac or respiratory arrest as a crash, which sounds dramatic, chaotic, and violent. In truth, our response is prompt but measured, based on anticipation and an understanding of pathophysiology when systems begin to fail. It is the antithesis of chaos, a determined, coordinated, cohesive effort to resuscitate an animal in a crisis. There was no feeling left in my hand but it never lost a beat. If anything, this was when the real "crash" hit, my own emotional crash, when the certainty of losing her, all the evidence, the reality, rushed up to meet me, decelerating to a complete stop and in that instant I thought, "She is dead, and you are responsible."

"What?" I snapped back to the scene.

"I said do you want to open her chest?"

I was still with Cleo, attached and not letting go, but I began to feel the waves of doubt and disbelief. Up until this point there had been no pointing fingers, no recriminations. This was the situation and we had to deal with it. What went wrong and how we got here began as a hiss, a caustic whisper as I thought again of Sonja and her poor mother and what I was about to put them through.

"What do you think?" I asked, though I already knew the answer and Beth's hesitation was more than enough to tell me I was right.

When external massage of the heart is failing, it is widely accepted that direct physical contact, internal massage, has a better chance of success. I don't doubt that this is statistically true, but over the last twenty-five years I, personally, have never witnessed a single case in which a dog or cat in full cardiac arrest benefited from such a violent intervention. The chest overlying the heart is hurriedly shaved, and after a splash of antiseptic solution a scalpel blade slashes down and through skin and muscle, creating a rent between the ribs wide enough to squeeze in a gloved hand. It makes perfect sense that the quality of cardiac compressions will be superior, but internal massage can be physically challenging for small dogs and cats, the actual space available restrictive. Yes, you can inject drugs directly into the failing walls of the heart, apply direct electrical stimulation, but every arrest is unique and in this particular situation, based on the EKG, the sequence and nature of the drugs used, neither Dr. Maganiello nor I believed there was anything to be gained.

"No. I don't think so." I stopped short of adding the word *either* because although I believed she agreed with me, this judgment call was mine and all mine.

"Do you want to call the owner?" said Beth.

I nodded and had someone replace me, to keep pumping her heart just in case. I found the hotel phone number and made my futile call, hearing it ring, praying Sonja would pick up and praying she wouldn't.

I came back.

"I can't reach the owner," I said, hearing the flat defeat in my voice.

Beth didn't respond but met my eyes and said everything that needed to be said.

8 BEFORE AND AFTER

ONE minute I was in the OR, dressed in blue surgical scrubs, paper mask, and bouffant cap, rummaging the shelves and sterile packages like some eccentric bargain hunter, and the next I was standing alone beside Cleo, surrounded by the medical detritus of life saving and the oppressive silence of failure. Before, everyone had gravitated to the scene, desperate to help and play their part. Now, bodies drifted away, awkward yet reverential, eyes averted or cast down, full of pain and incomprehension. How fast a wonderfully untroubled and ordinary day can change.

I realized I had been stroking Cleo's head and this didn't feel strange in the slightest. I wasn't thinking straight, but at that point one regret had managed to push its way to the front of a long line— if only I had been able to contact Sonja Rasmussen during the resuscitative effort. Part of me believed it might have helped mitigate some of the initial shock she would be subjected to when I saw her later. Though it is inconceivable how anyone can be capable of processing such information via a phone call, there could have been comfort in knowing what was happening to Cleo in *real time*, being involved in the decision of how far she wanted us to go, getting to the hospital as soon as possible. It wouldn't have made the slightest

difference in the outcome but perhaps she could have felt a part of
process, connected, however remotely, to the passing of this special
dog. As I ran my hand over Cleo's body one last time, I began to realize the magnitude of the task before me—my obligation to inform
this patient's next of kin.

WITHOUT it, none of this would have happened. Without it, Cleo
would never have been admitted to the hospital, let alone undergone
anesthesia. I'm talking about a consent form. It's a rather simple
sheet of paper on which is written a paragraph or two of dusty dis-
claimers in the hieroglyphics of legalese, but at the bottom of the
page there is space reserved for written approval, room to sign away
our own lives or the lives of those we love.

Regardless of whether the patient has two legs, four legs, or no
legs, informed consent creates a contract of trust, a statement of understanding that says "I know you will do your best, but I know there
are no guarantees in life and I know that every medical intervention
comes with risk." But how many of us hesitate and realize the message might actually be aimed our way? How many of us seriously re-
consider whether to go ahead? For most, the perfunctory language
washes over our anxious, desensitized minds, hardly more relevant
than a statement pointing out that people can be killed by lightning.

And if I told you the statistics would it make your decision any
easier? Roughly speaking, you have a one in fifty thousand risk of
anesthetic death as a healthy human patient in the United States. In
other words you are ten times more likely to die in an automobile accident than during a medical procedure that requires general anesthesia. But when it comes to our pets the stats become far more
menacing. During the 1990s, peer-reviewed scientific studies looking at private veterinary practices in North America and South Africa
reported the risk of anesthetic-related death in dogs to be approxi-
mately one in one thousand procedures. So why, in the twenty-first

century, does it appear to be far more dangerous to go under the knife for a dog than a human being?

Believe me, the last thing I want is to be a fearmonger among a group of understandably anxious pet owners contemplating anesthesia for their pets. Anesthetic risk is a complicated, multifaceted issue, and isolated statistics based on a limited number of studies hardly constitute a blanket statement. Some specialists in veterinary anesthesia have suggested our preoperative screening of animals is less thorough than that of our human counterparts, vets being constrained by the number of tests they can perform based on direct cost to the client. Perhaps some veterinarians offer less monitoring equipment for animals under anesthesia, less highly trained, specifically dedicated staff to oversee these patients in their unconscious state. In some cases, the surgeons themselves may be partly to blame. Veterinary anesthetists rarely get to meet the animal with the owner, possibly missing out on pertinent nuances of medical history. Rumor has it those of us wielding the scalpel are always in a hurry, resenting any bottleneck that encumbers the flow of cases into the bright lights of the operating rooms. It might be time for surgeons to take a breath and allow the "gas passers" their chance to review the patient's entire record more thoroughly before doling out their magic potions. Whatever the reasons for this disparity between anesthetic risk in people and animals, owners should recognize that veterinarians are striving to close the gap while providing their pets with the safest, smoothest, and most painless temporary siesta possible.

After all, what's our alternative? Unless we want to revert to some sort of Civil War reenactment, knocking back a shot of whiskey and biting down on a bullet, modern surgery and all that it offers is only possible with our acceptance of the dark and mysterious art of general anesthesia. Huge gaps exist in our understanding of how chemicals produce a desirable state of unconsciousness, but we accept the ambiguities that surround this artificial sleep because the alternative is unthinkable. And for so much of what we do to cats and dogs, simpler, safer, less invasive options of sedation or local or regional anesthetics, let alone hypnosis, do not exist.

Aside from the dangers of general anesthesia, the surgeon must also weigh the merits of surgery versus the potential for harm. We look at the primary disease, what it is going to take to fix it, the patient's overall health, and the chance of complications. Realistically, for Cleo, her surgical risk was minimal. She was young and, aside from her broken leg, in great shape. Her preoperative workup had gone well above and beyond what might constitute a minimal database for a similar patient of this age with a similar problem. And yet here I was, faced with the worst-case scenario—the anesthetic death of a seemingly normal animal.

Risk might be more acceptable, more forgivable, if pet owners and clinicians could anticipate the danger. But we know that the more serious the situation, the more involved the procedure, the more fragile this balance between risk and reward. If we decide to play golf in a thunderstorm we should be prepared to accept a higher risk of being struck by lightning.

Beyond the consent form and passing references in conversation, I only ever focus on anesthetic risk with normal healthy animals for one of two reasons. Either I detect a peculiarity in the physical examination, on an X-ray, or hidden in the numbers of the blood work, or the owner pushes me for a money-back, lifetime warranty and a guarantee that all will be well, a 100 percent return to full function. Neither caveat had come up with Cleo, and though Sonja Rasmussen had appeared nervous and upset that her mother's dog needed to undergo another major orthopedic surgery, I believed she had confidence and faith in my ability, and the ability of those who worked with me, to fix her dog and set Cleo on the road to recovery.

In human hospitals it has been shown that relatives prefer to be present during a crisis, to witness the resuscitation. In this way there is no mystery, no wondering what happened, what more could have been done, and as they watch everything unfold, they sense the determination of those committed to the fight. Their fears and questions must be addressed by dedicated support staff, prepared to answer questions and educate, but in practice such disruptions do not occur. The comfort comes from proximity to those you love.

For Sonja Rasmussen, any chance to prepare and brace for the bad news had passed. At five o'clock she was going to walk into this hospital, expecting me to smile, pat her on the shoulder, and let her know everything went fine. I gave her no reason to expect anything else. Sonja never had a chance to say anything other than a cursory good-bye to Cleo, and now she was about to live every parent's worst nightmare, left with memories of a mundane, forgettable parting rather than something meaningful, something she would have cherished, if only she had known this would be their final farewell. Cleo was not the daughter who goes off to war. Cleo was the child who leaves for school and never comes home.

Over the past twenty years, I can recall no more than a handful of unexpected anesthetic deaths (but still an uncomfortable number to think about). Every one requires the clinician to make a full report on the circumstances leading up to the crisis and the efforts taken to correct it, and to speculate on the reasons for the outcome. Debriefing of the entire team is essential. If we could not help Cleo, we owe it to her and her family to learn from her loss so that the next time, and sadly there will be a next time, a more fortunate animal may benefit from our understanding and experience.

Beth Maganiello had personally chosen all the anesthetic drugs, calculated their dosages, and performed the epidural injection herself. She had been circling around Cleo, trapped in a holding pattern of no more than ten feet throughout the entire brief period Cleo was under anesthesia. All the usual suspects—allergic reaction, drug overdose, excessive anesthetic depth, decreased ventilation of the lungs—and many, many more had been given serious consideration, but we lacked the hard evidence to point the finger of blame.

Yes, we had all seen the bizarre heart arrhythmia on the monitor, tagged with its improbable French label, making it sound deceptively sexy or romantic as opposed to just plain deadly. But what caused it to occur? Was it genetically programmed as an electrical cardiac defect, invisible, impossible to predict, impossible to prevent? Was it triggered by a specific anesthetic drug? Chances were we would never know for sure. Torsades de pointes literally means "twisting of the points" and is supposed to describe the visual characteristics of the abnormal electrical activity on an EKG. For me this translation captured the sinister essence of what transpired, as though something cold and steely sharp had been at work. No matter what terminology I used, Sonja Rasmussen and her mother deserved to know why their dog had died and, for right now, I had no answer to give them.

I STILL had two hours before my pager announced the arrival of Sonja Rasmussen. Two hours to think about nothing else. I could imagine her sitting in the waiting area, as before, alone, anxious, coiled, desperate to be sprung by my surgical success, reading the fear in me from the moment she saw my face. I cannot let this happen, I thought. I will not let her suffer this pain in public. Could I smile, act as though all had gone well, waving away her barrage of questions until I had her alone, behind closed doors, then drop the pretense and my bombshell? Could I try to catch her before she entered the hospital, on the sidewalk or in the parking lot? There appeared to be only one reasonable option. I called the front desk and informed them that Ms. Rasmussen would be arriving at five o'clock to meet with me. She should be escorted to an examination room and I should be paged. I purposely avoided detail. The last thing I wanted was a premature consolation, an ambiguous remark from a well-meaning stranger. All the same, I knew I was taking a chance and I remained concerned that the perceptive Ms. Rasmussen might sense some kind of a glitch—that this prearranged setting was a preface that could only mean bad news.

Alone in my office, I sat behind my desk, getting a feel for this new weight on my shoulders and the relentless tug at my heart. My patient was dead and I was responsible. I owned her passing. The fact that I never so much as raised a scalpel blade to Cleo's skin made no difference. Perhaps it would have been easier if I had made an obvious blunder—a heart problem my ears failed to hear, a liver enzyme off the charts and somehow overlooked—something more tangible than my weak misgivings over a hat trick of broken bones. The agony of death would be shared by those of us left behind but I must take the blame. I would brace for the anger, absorb the accusations, and offer honesty and humility.

As a veterinarian I should always be competent, caring, and communicative, but our innate talents and, more importantly, our ability to learn, are best tested in a crisis. Be it the operating room or the examination room, how we deal with a crisis situation can set us apart. In the OR, I have witnessed the surgical ego manifested in temper tantrums that lay blame on the technical failings of equipment or on the challenge of striving for perfection. Not that swearing or tossing instruments fools anyone. Everybody sees the fear and reads the insecurity. None of us are immune, but for the most part I try to acknowledge my fallibility because the surgeon who doesn't get scared from time to time is like the surgeon who claims he never has complications. And I confess, as I waited for my encounter with Sonja Rasmussen, I felt fear—fear of her overwhelming sadness.

Police officers, military personnel, and health-care professionals will tell you there is an art to delivering bad news. I know for a fact there are many veterinarians out there far more gifted in this department than I, but I do know some of the basic moves. When I met Ms. Rasmussen, my opening line would not be the dangerously vague "I'm sorry but we lost Cleo." It would not be the geographically indeterminate "Cleo has gone to a better place" either. I knew

I had to get right to it. No pussyfooting, no preamble, no excuses. Deliver the blow and deal with the consequences.

At some point during the two-hour wait, self-reproach paid a visit, the "what ifs" and "if onlys" attacking like mosquitoes at dusk. I knew it wouldn't change anything but I accepted the bites as part of my burden. I didn't see any point in swatting them away. I just hoped they might be something I could get used to over time.

Let's not forget that Cleo had been a second-opinion case, so I needed to telephone her veterinarians in both Bermuda and Canada. The conversations were remarkably similar—a description of the anesthetic protocol, a summary of the resuscitative efforts, an inability to offer a specific explanation, and a sincere apology for having failed the dog, the owner, and their trust in me and the hospital. In both instances I was overwhelmed by their understanding, their compassion, and their appreciation for everything we had done. I had tried to be descriptive and dispassionate but no doubt sadness laced my every word. Perhaps they were relieved that it had not been them, that they had not attempted the repair themselves. More likely their empathy lay with the fact that they knew exactly what I was experiencing because they had been through similar situations themselves.

There was one topic I knew I must broach with Ms. Rasmussen, though I wasn't sure I had the stomach for it. Truly unpleasant as it was, perhaps unthinkable with the shock of loss so fresh and superficial, I must make a difficult but necessary request for a post-mortem examination of Cleo's body. In veterinary medicine we might use the term *necropsy* rather than *autopsy*, but the premise remains the same, a scientific exploration of a dead body in order to discover what went wrong.

Cleo's body was being held in a large walk-in refrigerator, pending a decision Sonja could never have imagined having to make. Desensitized by TV shows like *CSI* and *Bones* that lure the audience into vivid autopsy scenes with the phrase "viewer discretion advised," we all have access to a relatively unsanitized view of what a postmortem examination entails. So why would I suggest submitting Cleo's dead body to such an investigation when reaching inside her chest to work on her heart had seemed too invasive when she was alive?

For me, the answer lies in the distinction between life and death and the transition between the two. Beyond the certainty of knowing there was nothing I could do to heal Cleo's failing heart, part of me recognized a need to keep her body intact. If she was going to die, at least let her die with dignity, not slashed open and hastily stitched back together. Sonja Rasmussen might want to see Cleo's body. Keeping her whole simply felt like the right thing to do as she passed from our world into the next. In death, however, the situation had changed because the essence of what I had known as Cleo had moved on. What remained of her was something she no longer needed, something she had left behind, and in this instance, I believed she was offering us all a chance to learn the truth.

THE liquid crystal display on my pager announced her arrival—"Sonja Rasmussen here to see you"—the words feeling awkward, like a hostess whispering in my ear at a noisy party rather than a somber declaration before a wake.

When I scrolled down, the pager display told me she was in Room 25. Most of our examination rooms have two doors, one providing an entrance to the public, the other providing an entrance to the staff from a central work area. The staff door has a peephole, a tiny fisheye lens to prevent people from barging in on an examination in progress. I remembered that I had this chance to pause, to take a final look into Ms. Rasmussen's world of "before," but I decided against it. Accepting the invisible violence in my chest, I took a deep breath, opened the door, and stepped inside.

There was Sonja smiling, relaxed, as though she could taste the relief, glancing up at me under her red eyelashes. Once again she was wearing that long gray winter coat, numerous bulky shopping bags at her feet, as though she had been enjoying herself splurging on Newbury Street as a distraction.

I had my hand on the handle, closing the door behind me, when I noticed the door at the other end of the room had been left wide open, affording me the sights and sounds of a bustling waiting room. My anger at this failure to achieve my goal of privacy rushed up to meet me, all consuming. I could feel my facial muscles betraying anxiety and I willed them to regain concern and solemnity.

Who left that door open? Don't they understand what is about to happen?

No time for "Why would they? How could they?" No time to blame myself for this glitch.

After only the briefest eye contact, the open door forced me to look away. I moved past Sonja, knowing she was searching my eyes the whole time, feeling like the action of closing the second door was loaded, inappropriately intimate, and a signal of hesitation.

I felt the silence tighten all around us and Ms. Rasmussen tuned in to it, up now, on her feet as I began to speak. Adrenaline had worked its predictable sorcery in my mouth, the sudden absence of saliva making the consonants crackle, underlining the tremble dancing on my tongue. I cannot remember the exact language I used, but I remember it happened fast, terror building in her eyes as I watched my words worming their way inside her, helpless as her pain took shape, suddenly bright and hot and razor sharp.

The scream came first, a piercing, agonizing wail filling the room, and then the weight of the disaster took hold, pulling her down, and she collapsed in increments, agony giving way in layers, from top to bottom, like a tower crumbling to the ground leaving nothing but rubble.

Hand clasped across her mouth, she warned me she couldn't breathe, that she might be physically sick. Clearly my message had found its mark, but then she asked me to repeat myself as though I must have made a mistake, as though the last twenty seconds had never taken place.

I was kneeling on the floor beside her for the repeat performance. She began to swear, not in anger but in anguish, curses bent by pain into another frightening scream. If it was possible, she lost even more color, blanched enough to accentuate her freckles once more. Her body began to shake, and like a nervous fool I was talking through her tears and mucus and her fight for air, describing the details, how we tried and did everything we possibly could and how it came from nowhere and how we got nowhere. Feeling helpless I watched her reel and swear and cry, pummeled by my description, trapped on the ride, beginning the transition from shock to grief. The pain had taken all the light from her eyes and I watched as they faded toward waxy and dull.

Every examination room is stocked with a box of tissues in case of an emotional outburst. Precisely where they were hidden in Room 25, I had no idea. It would have been tactless to walk in, box in hand, telegraphing my bad news as if I were wearing a black armband. So I was forced to reach for the only alternative at hand—brawny, coarse paper napkins—the kind used to mop up urinary accidents. Ridiculous the way a small thing could make a difference, leaving me convinced I had compounded her sorrow as she worked rough wads into bleeding black mascara.

Not that Sonja appeared to care. After her initial shock, the pain began to change its shape, becoming tidal, hitting her in waves that would crash and ebb away. She got it together. She fell apart. She smoothed her breathing. She began to gasp in jagged little breaths. After a time, her questions began in earnest and so I told my story over again, slowly, in detail, retracing every step, and she listened intently, interrupted occasionally, but I could tell she heard only 50 percent of what was said if I was lucky. In the end, at this stage, I felt as though there were only a few facts that really mattered. I needed her to know that healthy young dogs are not meant to die

under anesthesia. I needed her to know I didn't have an explanation
at this time. I needed her to know that we all fought long and hard
to save Cleo's life. Most of all I made her see the assurance in my
eyes that Cleo's passing occurred without fear or pain, that we may
have been relative strangers, but she left this world surrounded by
people who cared.

"I told my mom how nice this hospital was and how Cleo was getting the best possible care and all about how great you were and we
all did our research on you and we know everything about you right
down to your pant size and we thought we were doing everything
right."

The words came out too fast, without a single blink, and when the
outburst trailed off, it was replaced by tears and I watched her head
dip, shoulders finding their weeping rhythm. There have been few
moments in my professional career when I have felt more crushed
or more of a failure than that day sitting with Sonja on the cold exam
room floor.

"How do I tell my mom? She knows I am meeting with you. This
is her baby. I can't call her. I can't tell her all is well."

I offered to be the one to call her mother and break the news but
she was unsure. I asked if she could discuss what to do with her husband, or a sibling, to get some advice as to how to proceed. Again she
hesitated, but for the first time, behind bloodshot eyes, I glimpsed
the cogs of accountability beginning to turn. She began to pull herself together, but not before delivering her coup de grace.

"I'm so sorry," she said. "I can't imagine how hard this has been
for you. Do you have to be somewhere else? Is there something else
you need to be doing?"

This, by far, was the low point. After all I had done to this family,
Ms. Rasmussen was apologizing to me.

Time was all I had left, all I had to offer, and it was a relief to give
it away. This was Sonja's moment of grief and I would share it for
as long as it took, knowing she needed to maintain the dialogue,

knowing that as soon as she stopped and left this room, she and grief would be spending a lot more time together alone.

At some point I asked about a postmortem examination and Sonja handled the question with calm and understanding. She said she would have to think about it and talk to her mother and I insisted they take all the time they needed.

I wondered what she would remember of this meeting, what little details would be forever imprinted—the smell of antiseptic, the sight of a Neiman Marcus logo like the one gracing the bag at her feet, the sound of animal footsteps parading just outside the door. I didn't know but I knew this moment would linger for her in a visceral way, as it would for me.

When we stood face-to-face, about to say our good-bye, somehow the formality of a handshake seemed ridiculous. She had every right to be angry at me, to hate me, to blame me. Instead she leaned forward and opened her arms wide and we hugged. As we parted I made a point of locking eyes, wanting her to see that although I did not share her tears, she was not alone in her grief.

She picked up her bags, covered with now inconsequential names and logos of boutique stores from another world and another time, and I walked her into the lobby. Icy January air baited us as we stood too close to the blast from the automatic entrance doors. I offered to call for a cab but she declined, as though she had made up her mind to walk even before I asked, and I could tell it was the right decision. I promised to call first thing in the morning, and Ms. Rasmussen stepped out into the darkness.

9   BEING STRUCK OFF!

H E decided to join me on the drive home from work, determined to carpool, that niggling, contrary little voice I get inside my head whenever I'm emotionally vulnerable. You know the one, the diabolical confidant that despises the distractions of talk radio or NPR or books on CD, insisting we proceed in silence, ready to strike with a viperous jab or a whispered innuendo. Oh, he was in fine form that night, savoring the crush and crawl of Boston commuter traffic to offer his highlights from the day's audio and video, and long before I pulled into my driveway, simple melancholy and remorse had been superseded by his implication that there would be far more alarming ramifications following Cleo's death.

Not to be left out, paranoia also hitched a ride and insisted on staying over for dinner with the family. On the outside I was poor company, distracted and monosyllabic, with no appetite. On the inside I was feasting on an "all you can eat" buffet of panic-inducing words and phrases—*lawsuit, negligence, punitive damages.*

Shortly after the plates were cleared, I excused myself to the office for a little online search and reassurance mission, beginning with a trusted favorite, the Web site for the Royal College of Veterinary Surgeons.

Mouse scurrying, I sent the curser arrow flying across the screen like a medieval warrior, ready to fight these demons with pragmatism. As I mentioned, this was not the first time (and sadly, it was unlikely to be the last) that I had been responsible for an anesthetic death. However, on this occasion, I had yet to speak to Cleo's real owner. What if Sonja's mom was far less understanding, but rather litigious and hungry for retribution?

"Get a grip, Nick," I told myself. "Remember, there is a big difference between 'things went wrong' and 'you did something wrong.' "

Then I clicked on a drop-down menu that said "disciplinary hearings" and heard a chuckle, courtesy of my copilot from the ride home.

Sure, Nick, live in that dream world if it helps you sleep tonight, but what if Cleo's postmortem examination tells a different story?

I churned inside, knowing there was some truth to this notion, as I opened a series of press releases regarding British veterinarians who had landed in trouble with one of our profession's governing bodies.

The concept of "when good vets go bad" is wholly unpalatable, unacceptable, the stuff of tabloid fodder and shock journalism. It is one thing to be outraged that your pet's doctor has no veterinary education and has been found guilty of impersonating a vet, but quite another when the person you entrusted with the care of your pet has an addiction to controlled substances, or neglects the fundamental tenets of his veterinary oath. Vets are just as human as MDs, dentists, pharmacists, and chiropractors, just as flawed and susceptible to the same weaknesses and vices as all of us. So why do we feel so pained, so violated by unprofessional veterinary conduct?

Perhaps the answer lies with the victims, placed in harm's way by us, the pet owners. Pets attain a heightened sense of innocence since their place in the health-care system is passive, at the mercy of their most trusted advocates, their owners. If we failed to spot a problem, were blind, conned, or worst of all, failed to look, the burden of responsibility will come back to haunt us.

To be fair, veterinary misconduct is extraordinarily uncommon, and I was thrilled to note that the disciplinary body of the Royal College of Veterinary Surgeons deals with only a handful of cases every year. On the whole, most of these transgressions are unpleasant but predictable: driving drunk, abuse of available narcotics, forging health certificates, threatening or aggressive behavior toward clients and staff. Back when I was in veterinary school in England, glaring lecturers would warn that the consequence of any professional misconduct would be that most heinous and damning conviction, the most definitive punishment of all —being struck off! More evocative than "losing your license to practice" or "being disbarred," I believe this phrase was meant to strike fear in the hearts of cavalier veterinary students: I always envisaged a crusty, gowned gentleman in a powdered gray wig working his way down a ledger, fingering my name written in bold curlycued copperplate, and savoring his chance to take quill to ink before scratching it out as though it had never existed. The years of study, the credentials, the credibility—swept away in a single stroke. Indoctrinated by this image, no wonder I was flustered and questioning my professional liability.

I moved on to Google, and felt myself succumbing to all the endemic negativity of the Internet.

"When a pet or other animal is injured or killed by a person or another animal, the owner is often entitled to damages even if the animal was not harmed on purpose."

"Malpractice lawsuits against veterinarians have seen nearly a seventeen percent increase in the last decade."

It became apparent that the legal standing of our pets is a complicated and emotional issue. Many laws are outdated, and they vary considerably from state to state. Assigning the family dog the same status as inanimate property like a lawn mower or a hair dryer just doesn't cut it in this new millennium. Pets are animate, they have feelings, they have the capacity to demonstrate pain and suffering. Pet death has the potential for significant emotional repercussions for those left behind, regardless of how it came about. The problem lies in defining this loss of companionship and proving the degree of emotional distress that ensues.

Semantics have only complicated the picture. There are arguments for a label of pet guardian versus pet owner, for defining pets as sentient property (any warm-blooded, domesticated nonhuman animal dependent on one or more humans for food, shelter, veterinary care, or compassion, and typically kept in or near the household of its owner, guardian, or keeper), for pecuniary (replacement value) versus punitive (assigning emotional value and punishing the wrongdoer) damages. I came away with the feeling that pets continue to be a legal work in progress, though progress seems to be inadequate, fickle, and highly dependent on jurisdiction.

Our twenty-first-century love affair with the animals in our lives appears to have placed veterinary medicine and the legal system at a crossroads. Today, almost half the law schools in the country offer courses on animal law, moving beyond the prosecution of animal cruelty cases to the kind of work that usually applies to human offspring, such as setting up trusts to bequeath money to a pet after an owner's death and dealing with pets in divorce custody disputes. The arguments against punitive damages have so far held up and still pack a powerful punch. Will punitive damages encourage a flood of lawsuits, significantly increasing veterinary malpractice premiums? Will veterinarians seek the security of practicing defensive medicine, thereby reducing the overall quality of health care for our pets? Will vets be forced to raise their prices and make responsible pet ownership a luxury? These questions will need to be resolved because now that our dogs have discovered the family bed, they won't be returning to the kennel anytime soon!

I logged off, haunted by one tidbit of information that stuck.

"The plaintiff has to prove emotional distress, to support the allegation."

All I could see was the image of Sonja Rasmussen, collapsing to the floor when I told her about Cleo's death, and I thought, "If that wasn't emotional distress, I don't know what is."

THAT night, hypnotized by the glow of red numbers from a bedside digital alarm clock, my mind refused to shut down for sleep, preferring to continue obsessing about thorny veterinary situations.

I thought about a colleague named Neil, as flamboyant and passionate a vet as you will ever meet. Thirty years of general practice had done nothing to quash his excitement for the job, his desire to connect with animal and owner alike. You would think he had discovered how to split the atom when he dragged an owner from his examination room and forced her to look down his microscope and gape at the magnified ear mites swimming on his oily slides, her cat's head-shaking disorder unearthed. Determined to befriend a nervous rottweiler, convinced he had learned all the necessary pointers from an episode of *Dog Whisperer*, he would risk a reassuring pat even if it meant his hand was gnarled to the consistency of a spent rawhide chew. And faced with a surly dog in need of a nail trim, Neil would choose charisma over chemical intervention every time, growling as he took the patient's scruff between his teeth, inciting memories of the dog's mother and life as a submissive puppy before setting to work with his nail clippers.

His style was sufficiently unique that he either attracted clients to his fan base or repelled them to his partner in their practice. However, one client, the inimitable Ms. Adelaide, owner of a Persian cat, Arthur, began to seriously question her allegiance to Neil and his unconventional approach to his patients.

Ms. Adelaide was a former Broadway actress whose commanding stature, raptorial features, fulsome gray locks, and dramatic affectations dwindled to insignificance the moment she set foot inside

Neil's clinic. It hit her in the manner of a third martini, creeping up on her, catching her off guard with its dangerous blend of antiseptic haze, confined spaces, blood, and needles. She lost all pretension, as though her part were being played by a timid understudy.

It didn't help that Arthur insisted on making up for his mother's infirmity in hospitals by morphing from a state of placid domesticity into feral savagery, swiping and hissing as soon as he was extracted from his carrier. Arthur's indignation would build to a crescendo, his cry winding up from a low growl to a high-pitched scream like a high-revving motorbike.

I'm reluctant to use a weathered cliché, but a perfect storm had been brewing for some time, not least because Arthur's illness made him a frequent visitor to the hospital. Arthur was infected with feline immunodeficiency virus, FIV, a close cousin of the notorious human retrovirus HIV. FIV only infects cats, but in many ways it behaves in a similar manner, hiding out for months or even years, biding its time, teasing the body with unpleasantries such as gingivitis, sores in the mouth, and fevers. A weakened immune system leaves its victims vulnerable to infections. They lose interest in food, they lose weight, and ultimately, they lose the battle.

Still, with supportive care and prompt attention to secondary infections, FIV-positive cats can do great, and that was why Arthur found himself on an examination table, poised to strike, eyes wild, trash talking, taunting Neil with a feline version of "You talkin' to me?"

"I need to give him a shot," said Neil, pulling out needle and syringe as Ms. Adelaide backed up, body pressed flat against the wall as though by centrifugal force.

"You need to get an assistant. Someone who can keep a hold of him," she said, her words squeaky and terrified.

Neil considered the woman, who appeared to be bracing for a firing squad.

"For Arthur?" he said. "Don't be so silly. This will be quick. I just need you to put a hand on his back end to stop him from rearing like a bronco."

She asked again, more plea than demand, and once more Neil swatted her uncertainty aside.

Reluctantly Ms. Adelaide stepped forward, Neil flirting with Arthur's swiping paw, taunting him with a dainty finger wave as his other hand swooped in with a secure grasp of his scruff. The maneuver, swift and forceful, did little to assuage Ms. Adelaide's fears.

"Don't worry, Arthur's simply remembering the good old days when his mother used to pick him up in her mouth. Now, put your hand here. That's right."

The rest happened so fast: the needle piercing tough feline skin, the plunger depressed, the injection delivered, Ms. Adelaide letting go, Arthur's legs snapping out from under him like a Cossack dancer, Neil's hand jerking upward, and the shiny steel of the needle flying straight into a new and unexpected target—the back of Ms. Adelaide's hand.

If we freeze the action right here, before Ms. Adelaide has had a chance to scream or declare she is about to faint, with Neil mystified and still armed with his dangerous implement, we can ponder the many thoughts that *should* have been running through his mind:

- Make sure the client is okay by seeking or at the very least offering to get her medical assistance. Call a doctor or drive Ms. Adelaide to the nearest hospital.
- Apologize profusely and pray she forgives you.
- Document the entire event in the medical record, including all communications during the aftermath.
- Contact your malpractice insurance company, describe the event, and seek their advice.
- Tell Ms. Adelaide not to worry, you will send her the bill later.
- Don't be so ridiculous as to charge Ms. Adelaide for stabbing her in the hand.

• Don't be so ridiculous as to *not* charge her, since this is tantamount to an admission of wrongdoing.

Later, one or more of these thoughts might have stood a chance, but in the heat of the moment Neil instinctively did the one thing he believed would best demonstrate how perfectly harmless this accident had been.

"No harm done," he said, plunging the same needle into his forearm, trying to keep the demonic out of his smile.

"Oh my God," screamed Ms Adelaide, "you've given me cat AIDS!"

And it wasn't this impossibility that suddenly lunged at Neil, it was the realization that he had foolishly but voluntarily shared needles with a virtual stranger.

Personally I have never thought to use self-mutilation as a "get out of jail free card," but here's the thing: as unorthodox and unprofessional as Neil's spontaneous approach to this accident may have been, as easy and justifiable as it would have been to seek alternative veterinary care, Ms. Adelaide remained loyal to Neil. Despite the drama, the eccentricities, and the sharing of bodily fluids, Ms. Adelaide could overlook her personal incompatibility with Neil because his determination to help Arthur, at considerable risk to himself, remained transparent and unwavering. When a pet owner has the vision to see genuine intention, even huge blunders can be overlooked.

And besides, no one else in the practice wanted to handle her cat.

THE second horror story that kept me awake that night concerned a surgical colleague whom I'll call Mike and a nine-month-old male basset hound called Pickle. Basset hounds are intended to have short bowed legs, but Pickle's right front leg was not growing properly. It was so twisted that his paw turned out at ninety degrees to his body, the poor dog's walking gait looking more like a flapper dancing the Charleston.

Pickle was owned by an assertive woman in her early twenties, vocal about the cost of her pedigree "lemon."

"For as much as the dog cost, I reckoned on breeding him," she said. "But what with his gimpy leg an' all I might as well get his balls taken off. I mean, who's gonna want to pay for some of them genes?"

Mike was confident that the deformity was traumatic in origin and not hereditary, and he went on to discuss corrective surgical options. The owner thanked him but did not want to schedule the procedure. Mike forgot about the case until Pickle showed up unexpectedly some six weeks later ready for his surgery.

For a couple of hours, saws hummed and drills buzzed until symmetry was restored, Mike shrewdly shaving and prepping both front legs to include them in his sterile surgical field so he would have a normal basset leg for comparison. Pleased with the result, he was ripping off his gloves and mask when an astute technician noticed an additional request on both the anesthetic and the surgical paperwork.

"It says here that Pickle is getting neutered as well."

Mike had only a vague recollection of the original consultation, but the financial paperwork confirmed that the fee for Pickle's sterilization had been signed for by his owner. Pickle was repositioned and a routine castration performed.

Everything looked great on the postoperative X-rays. Mike tried to call Pickle's owner with the good news but was forced to leave a message on her answering machine. The next day, as expected, Pickle was reluctant to use his bandaged leg, but he was hungry, happy, and eager to go home. Mike called again, once more routed to the machine, where he left precise details regarding Pickle's home instructions and invited his owner to get back to him.

She did the following morning. When Mike arrived at work he

was bombarded by all manner of messages to contact Pickle's irate owner as a matter of extreme urgency. Second-guessing and a hefty dose of pessimism had Mike imagining Pickle thrilled to be home, leaping from the car, his surgically corrected leg falling apart at the moment of impact. Worse still, absurd paranoia had Mike achieving symmetry on Pickle's front legs by doing the unthinkable and operating on the wrong leg!

He prayed for something simple—the communication breakdown in his failure to speak to her directly, Pickle licking out a skin staple, or getting his bandage wet. But when they finally spoke and this young woman unleashed her disgust and fury, Mike discovered the problem had nothing to do with the leg at all. It was only when Pickle's owner had paid her bill and turned to leave the hospital, thrilled to see her dog trotting out in front of her, happy to be going home, that she noticed something more than just his front leg had changed. Between his back legs lay a flaccid empty sac, no longer containing the balls it was entrusted to protect.

At first she wasn't sure, but when she inspected the place where that essential component of his reproductive manhood used to reside, it was obvious no one was home.

She claimed that she had not requested the castration, adamant that Pickle was a breeding dog, from a long line of champion stud dogs, purchased specifically to breed, with a potential to make her tens of thousands of dollars. Breeders across the country were lining up demanding his services, all ready to pay, and now that they couldn't, somebody else was going to.

It turned out that Pickle's future sexual prowess was curtailed by a clerical error, a mistake in the preparation of Pickle's paperwork on admission. However, a signature and consent for castration had been given, witnessed and countersigned, the claim of "too nervous to read the details" considerably weakening his mother's assertion.

Lying in bed, thinking about Cleo and thinking about this case, I realized how fortunate Mike had been. Okay, so Pickle never had a chance to prove himself as a canine Don Juan, but he healed, his leg's function restored to normal. There was some unpleasantness, the necessary letters and phone calls and lawyers, but in the end what mattered most was surgical success and a healthy dog with an excellent future. Ah, what I wouldn't have given for making a surgical mistake like Mike's, something disastrous but not fatal—catastrophic hemorrhage and multiple blood transfusions or even an infection necessitating an amputation. I would welcome these calamities if they meant I had a dog that was still alive.

And then my mind traveled to its most depressing, most telling destination and I thought about what would have happened to Cleo if I had done absolutely nothing at all, if Cleo had been managed conservatively, with nothing but medications to alleviate pain and six weeks of strict cage rest. No anesthesia. No attempt at a surgical repair. Nothing. The painful truth caused my breathing to shift, deep and swift, with the certainty that Cleo would be deformed, she would always walk with a limp, but this special little dog would still be very much alive.

As I lay there, hoping sleep would soon rescue me, a possibility began to take shape. Somehow I needed to make this right, to get a second chance. I desperately wanted a shot at restitution for Cleo's passing. I simply had no idea how I might get it.

<table>
<tr><td>10</td><td>**CAREFUL WHAT YOU WISH FOR**</td></tr>
</table>

I **CALLED** Ms. Rasmussen at her hotel shortly after eight o' clock the following morning, and as soon as she recognized my voice, I could almost feel her falter as she was transported straight back to ground zero, and our last encounter.

I gently forced my way past pleasantries that sounded so trite and redundant after what we had shared.

"Did you have a chance to speak to your mother?"

"Yes, yes I did. In fact she's already on her way to Boston. She's flying in from Calgary today. She would like to meet you in person if that's okay."

"Of course," I said, trying to hide my surprise and reflex trepidation. I suppose I had imagined a long-distance phone call, uncomfortable, no doubt painful, but ultimately remote. If Sonja's mother was prepared to drop everything and, at considerable expense, take the very next available flight across a continent so she could look me in the eyes when I told her what went wrong with Cleo, this could only mean trouble.

"When will she be here?"

"Later this afternoon," said Sonja. "Will that work for you?"

"Sure," I said, hearing the nervous levity in my voice. "Should I bring my lawyer, a Kevlar vest, an armed bodyguard?" I wanted to ask, but went with "If you don't mind me asking, how did your mother handle the news?"

Sonja Rasmussen paused, as if she wanted to find the right words. "She was brave, for me," she said. "She was everything I expected."

A rather oblique response, I thought, now even more curious about the relationship between Sonja Rasmussen and her mother and the integral role of a little dog named Cleo.

"Please, there's no hurry, but I wondered if you came to a decision about Cleo's body."

"Yes, of course," she said, as though grateful to be reminded. "My mother wanted me to tell you to go ahead with the . . . the examination of Cleo's body."

And there it was, the request for a formal investigation into the cause of death. Ideally, a postmortem allows the doctor to achieve full disclosure while providing the owner with an opportunity to lay unanswered questions to rest. A postmortem was the right thing to do and I had been the one to encourage it, but now, given this impromptu but official appointment with Sonja's mother, I began to feel as though it was a quest for proof of liability rather than a search for answers from which we all might learn.

"Will it still be possible to have Cleo privately cremated and her ashes returned to us?"

"Yes," I said, seeing a problem and a solution at one and the same time. "I visit a practice in Bermuda several times a year to help them out with surgery. I'll be there in the next week or two. It's the least I can do to personally deliver her remains by hand."

As she thanked me, I realized that I had no idea how one goes about air travel with the remains of a deceased animal, but I could not allow Cleo to be delivered to her final destination in this world chauffeured by a stranger in UPS brown.

"I'm really sorry about the way this all turned out," I said.

Another pause and I wondered if Sonja caught a tear, or maybe she had nothing left to cry.

"I hate to rush you," she said, "but I have a flight to catch back to Bermuda."

I'm sure she was telling the truth, I know she was emotionally distracted and rightly so, but all I heard was a failure to acknowledge my apology.

"My mom's going to take a cab straight from Logan Airport. When she arrives at Angell should she have you paged?"

"Absolutely," I said.

And suddenly we were both lost for words, our second awkward good-bye, severing a bond neither of us had wanted to form. I imagined Sonja checking in at the airport, life so much simpler than when she had departed Bermuda. No holdups at the check-in desk riffling health certificates and veterinary paperwork. All that empty space at her feet. No worries about Cleo whimpering at thirty-five thousand feet. I had robbed her of this chore, this burden, and in doing so I felt like a thief.

"Have a safe flight," I said to be saying something.

"Thanks," said Sonja Rasmussen. And then, as if it was important for me to know, she added, "My mom's name is Sandi. I think you will like her."

THIS time I was taking no chances over the location for our meeting, and I had a specific room in mind, a room situated at the end of a corridor, purposely set away from the hustle and flow of the hospital. It is as inviting as such a room can be—subtle, with warm lighting, a noticeable contrast to dispassionate fluorescent strips. There is a large couch, comfortable chairs, easy-on-the-eye, tasteful art on the walls, plenty of boxes of tissues, and pamphlets, reading material on euthanasia, coping with loss, the stages of grief. In the past, this room has offered a sanctuary, a quiet refuge for owners to say good-bye to their pets. But on this day, for the first time, I would meet a stranger and tell her how I failed her and her dog, how that good-bye came too soon, and how, thanks to me, she never got to be a part of it.

I knocked before entering, stepped inside, and closed the door behind me, sealing my own fate.

Sandi Rasmussen remained seated on the couch as I walked over, introducing myself, a somber timbre to my voice, as though I were about to tell her the bad news she already knew. I offered her my hand, wondering if she might refuse to shake it, but she took it, and I felt as though her grip was more than a formality, intended to hold me, to provide her with a moment to look up and into my eyes. I imagined I would be doing the same thing in her position, searching the depths, hoping to discover all the hidden characteristics that make me tick.

"Will you be honest with me? Are you genuinely sorry for what happened? Was I right to trust you with the care of my precious Cleo?" She might have been asking any one of these questions as her big russet eyes stared inside mine and I had no choice but to let her in.

Without a word she gestured for me to take a seat, this woman in a pink turtleneck sweater, woolen scarf, and glasses. There must have been a winter coat hanging up nearby but I didn't see it. I backed up and into a chair opposite, sitting forward. There was nothing comfortable or relaxed about what I had to do and I wanted my posture to let her know I took this responsibility seriously.

"I'm so sorry to meet you under these circumstances," I said, and Sandi nodded, exuded serenity, and forced a smile. "If I may, I'd like to go through everything that happened with Cleo, from the beginning to the end and if, at any time, something I say doesn't make sense, please, feel free to stop me, and I'll try my best to answer your question or try to make things clear. Does that sound okay?"

The words written here might sound slick and rehearsed, but I assure you, sitting in that room, with the tremble in my voice, a thick layer of dread and helplessness coated everything I said and did. Though I wanted to give her a synopsis and eulogy at the same time, I tried to focus on my simple, premeditated plan—do whatever it takes to make things bearable for this woman.

Her nod filled the room, cued up my nervous throat-clearing cough as a prelude to my speech.

"Firstly, I think we need to bear in mind that for all Cleo's various blood tests, everything came back as normal. We did look for an underlying problem, but never found one."

As soon as the words got away from me I realized how defensive, how arrogant this sounded. Cleo's backstory *was* important, the source of our niggling doubt that her tendency to break was something more than bad luck. But this opening smacked of "don't blame me, it's not my fault." Sandi's subtle recoil felt like a slap, an unspoken demand for me to start over.

"I mean . . . what I'm trying to say is . . . Cleo *appeared* to be a healthy young dog. I examined her the morning of surgery and her lungs were clear, her heart sounded fine, and she was a happy . . ."

"I wonder if I could hear about the anesthesia," said Sandi, her voice startlingly soft, her interjection catching me off guard, though her sentiment felt almost apologetic. Of course she wanted to get to the details. She already knew the punch line.

"Sure," I said, "yes . . . of course . . ." Any mental image I had of the salient points I needed to cover in my synopsis dissolved. I had lost my place, my rhythm was gone, and I could tell Sandi sensed it too. Involuntarily my open palms were sliding back and forth on one another, slick with guilty sweat like those of a criminal about to confess. I tried again.

"Cleo's record was carefully reviewed by another specialist, Dr. Maganiello, and based on her findings an anesthetic protocol was . . ."

"No," she said, talking over me, once again her soft cadence more effective than if she had screamed. "I just . . ." She paused, collected herself on a breath she held before letting go, leaving me hanging in the tension between us. "Please," she said, her gaze dropping away from mine, momentarily breaking the connection, before coming back to me, letting me catch a heightened, desperate level of intensity in her eyes. "I just need to know what happened."

Sandi Rasmussen delivered a plea that begged me to bag the cold medical explanations and jargon and simply tell her the truth. Even to my own ears I had sounded uncertain and worst of all, unconvincing. If I wasn't careful this conversation would turn into what I had feared all along—an inquisition.

Then, for the first time, I noticed Sandi was wearing a bracelet on her wrist, and as I looked closer I could see it held a gold heart pendant engraved with a single word, *Cleo*. Not that I didn't already appreciate the importance of this dog in this woman's life. Not that I wasn't already trying my best to make this tragic encounter meaningful. But seeing her name, written in gold, was like a cue card, a keyword that brought me back—focused, lucid, and in the moment.

The story started to unfold with the anesthetic protocol in simple, understandable terms—why we chose it and what it was intended to do—and a delicate account of exactly what transpired, how we reacted, what went right, what went wrong, the emergence of the fatal heart rhythm, Cleo's failure to respond to all our measures.

Sandi listened intently, crying freely, making no attempt to wipe away a single tear, a detail I noticed and I wondered if I was meant to notice.

I paused for a second, giving my words a chance to sink in, giving Sandi a reprieve before I spoke about what I considered to be a particularly important point.

"I'd like you to understand that I had to make a decision about when to stop trying to save Cleo."

Sandi regarded me and I sensed she was pleased that I was bringing up this point without being asked to do so.

"I had to make a judgment call. I could have tried to perform direct massage on Cleo's heart. It would have meant cutting her open to do it. Normally I would have left the decision with you, the owner, or in this case, Sonja. But as you know, Sonja wasn't available. There wasn't time to deliberate. I had to rely on knowledge and experience and what I would do if Cleo were my dog. The option to keep going seemed futile, maybe even gratuitous. I truly believe now, as I did then, it would not have made the slightest bit of difference to the eventual outcome."

Sandi stood up, took a few paces away from me, as if gathering herself. I didn't know whether I should just shut up and let her have the floor, but I felt like there was still one critically important detail that needed to be discussed.

"One other thing," I said and Sandi turned to face me. "There's this question that keeps bugging me and won't go away. If I had a chance to do it all over, from the first moment I met Cleo, knowing what I know now, would I have done anything differently?"

Sandi nodded and her eyes summoned my answer.

I shook my head.

"I've thought about this a good deal over the last twenty-four hours. And a big part of me wishes there was somewhere to point, even if it means pointing at myself. I don't know what I missed. I don't know whether there would have been anything to find even if I knew where to look. Perhaps the postmortem examination will provide some answers. But for right now, I don't think I would change a thing, apart from how everything turned out."

Sandi bowed her head, fingers working Cleo's bracelet. She moved forward and stood over me as she spoke.

"I came a long way to meet you today and not because I am angry at you."

Her self-possession was disarming, the calm and assurance in her voice unnerving in someone who had probably not slept and hardly eaten anything during the past twenty-four hours. I swallowed down the lump in my throat.

"I came here, needing to meet you, face-to-face, so that you would understand."

I nodded but on the inside a part of me flinched.

"And, I need you to do something for Cleo."

As soon as she spoke her dog's name, I could hear the love in her voice, but confusion had taken a hold of my brow. I tried hard to twist it into concern and nodded again.

"Let me tell you a little something about my Cleo. You've met her, so you already know that for a Min Pin she was an absolute sweetheart."

I smiled, and so did she, and something gave a little between us.

"Cleo loved people. She was my transparent dog. What you saw was what you got, as though you could see into her soul. And she loved to socialize. In the first four months she was with me, I made sure two hundred strangers picked her up and held her. We went to schools, retirement homes, malls, anywhere with people and noise and distractions. I had her meet men in hats, men in sunglasses, men with mustaches, men with beards. I got her used to skateboards, strollers, bikes, and motorbikes."

This was not what I had expected. Where was the agony? Where were the accusations? I had failed this woman and her dog and here she was, on a mission to compress the essence of a dog's life into a short story. She was considerate with her words, weighed their impact before letting them fly. I could have pretended to listen, my smiles, my nods, my laughs motivated by politeness and relief. I had anticipated confrontation, even hysteria, and here was reminiscence and, without a doubt, joy. Her narrative was simple, perhaps ordinary, but it was her passion that had me entranced.

"Cleo loved to swim in the ocean. I know, weird for a Min Pin. She was always polite, never bit another dog, and she cared about other people's feelings. Dogs' too."

A memory pushed forward and Sandi smiled.

"She used to go to a doggy day care and they looked after this. sheltie who always sat alone, off to the side, trembling and frightened to play with the other dogs. And I would drop Cleo off and watch how she would carefully sidle up to her, inching her way closer and closer until she and the sheltie made contact. I'd pick her up and the girls would tell me that all Cleo did all day was sit next to this nervous little sheltie. And this went on for days, Cleo passing up her chance to play with her buddies so that she could sit next to this stranger and somehow make her feel better. And slowly, like kindergarten kids in a playground, Cleo won her confidence, convincing the sheltie no one was going to get hurt and it was okay to have some fun."

I didn't say anything, but the clinician in me was starting to feel sentimental and exposed. You take the kids to see a Disney movie and you're the one pretending you've got something in your eye while they're the ones indifferent to the plot and spilling popcorn on the floor.

Sandi was laughing.

"What?" I said.

"Well, the only dog getting hurt at day care was Cleo herself."

I sighed into a smile. I liked her attitude. This woman should have been sleepwalking, stumbling through a fog of sorrow, but she had it together, her composure unnerving. To her credit, her words did not have the polish of a prepared speech. Instead they glowed with the warmth that comes of speaking from the heart.

"Cleo loved children, she absolutely loved them. Anytime we were out in public, if she saw or even heard children, she insisted we go and see them. She would whine, tug on her leash, whatever it took to reach them. She would stand on her back legs, paw at the air, and insist they come down to her level so she could climb onto their lap and sit there, hoping to be petted. We don't have any small children in our family, yet for some reason she had this attraction to kids.

"Of all the places we would visit, airports were her favorite. She was my constant companion and she always came with me on business trips, so while we waited for flights, Cleo would look for children. Find a group of kids and yours truly would be right in the middle of the mix, entertaining her new fans. She loved to do tricks and by five months of age she knew how to sit, stay, lie down, get off, give me five, roll over, leave it, kiss, shake paw, and spin. I don't know whether she was more popular with the kids or their parents grateful for the distraction.

"There was this one time when we were in the Ottawa airport and Cleo was pulling her usual stunt, making a group of kids ooh and aah, when all of a sudden she left them and trotted over to this little girl who was sitting off to one side with her mother. Standing on her back legs she pawed at the girl's chair, got her attention, and very gently licked her hand. The little girl checked with her mother before patting Cleo's head and slowly, over about ten minutes, just like with the sheltie, Cleo made contact, climbing onto the girl's lap and gently lying down. This was not Cleo around kids. Normally she would be out of her mind with excitement, yet with this little girl, Cleo was being careful and gentle. I looked over at the mother to make sure everything was okay and I noticed she was wiping away tears. When their flight was called she came over to me to thank me for bringing a smile to her little girl's face. The girl's name was Megan and they were on their way to the SickKids Hospital in Toronto, where Megan was being treated for bone cancer. It was so strange, this mother thanking me for what Cleo had done, for what this little dog had instinctively known was the right thing to do."

And this was where I lost it. As a veterinarian I have always been able to keep my emotions in check in these difficult situations with clients, staying strong as part of my responsibility to the animal, especially during the gentle good-bye of euthanasia. But this time was different. The animal that had brought us together had already moved on, painlessly and peacefully. Maybe it was relief, the wait over, the encounter heartbreaking and sad but not bitter, not angry. Or maybe it was the woman running the narrative, the ease with which she conveyed her dog's essence, so simple and understated yet brimming with pride and the privilege of having had any chance of sharing Cleo's presence. Or maybe it was the subject matter, a dog with a gift for making a sick child smile, lost forever. For whatever reason Sandi Rasmussen split me open.

It started in the muscles around my top lip, taking me back to my childhood, and by the time I recognized the telltale tremble it was too late, the first fugitive tears getting away from me, her words reaching into my chest, making me gasp, hearing that initial catch in the breath before the real crying began.

I stood up, wiping my palms down my wet cheeks, trying to suck it up, to get a grip, but Sandi sealed my fate. Without hesitation, she stepped forward, opened her arms, and gave me a hug.

It didn't last long. Several deep breaths and my diaphragm decided to behave, responding to instruction, overriding emotion. We parted, but her hands maintained their grip on my upper arms. I shook my head,

"I'm so sorry. I can't believe it. I'm the one who's supposed to be consoling you, not the other way round."

She smiled, and now, in her eyes, I could see all that she had lost and the proportions of the enormous void in her heart. Only by her being here, face-to-face, telling me these small stories, letting me in, could I even begin to appreciate the size of this emptiness, of all that this dog meant, and how much of this special animal would remain with her.

"I need you to make me a promise," she said. "Cleo would never blame you for what happened to her, and neither will I."

She caught herself, and suddenly laughed.

"I was going to say she didn't have a bad bone in her body, but you and I know that's not true."

I joined her, thankful for the release only laughter can bring at such moments.

"But I would like something positive to come of this."

I wasn't sure where this was going but I knew enough to keep quiet.

"I want you to promise me to take Cleo's spirit on a journey, to realize all the wonderful qualities she embodied and to pour all the skill, effort, and talent you had intended for Cleo into the lives and health of other unfortunate animals."

At this point I wasn't saying anything simply because I was stunned into silence. Without doubt, this had been a powerfully affecting experience and I had been awed by Sandi's grace, her otherworldly wisdom, and her magnanimous approach to this tragedy. No one can tell you how to grieve. There is no correct way to grieve. Suffering is not proportional to the volume of our tears. Sandi's grief was striking, unusual, and in its own way, special. This appeal, however, had thrown me, and though I was never going to refuse, I had no idea what this would entail, let alone how it could possibly be fulfilled.

Naturally I nodded my assent, gave my assurance, as though nothing would please me more or be simpler to achieve. But looking back, this should have been my cue to ask for guidance. Okay, so I had inadvertently shown her my soft side, but this was hardly an admission of spiritual beliefs—an appreciation of the soul, of heaven, of a greater understanding of life's purpose. Then again, this might have been part of Sandi's plan, forcing me to make my own interpretation, to define a purpose that I alone saw fit.

We hugged one more time and then, in silence, I led the way toward the main hospital entrance.

Before we said good-bye, Sandi turned to me and said, "Be generous, and if you get a chance, please let me know what happens."

She smiled and once more I felt myself having to fight against the grief and kindness in her eyes. How could someone in so much pain appreciate that loss was simply a part of life and not an end of life?

I watched her go, disappearing into a waiting room full of animals, watching her as she was forced to witness the reunion of humans and sick animals with a future together.

11   INCIDENTAL FINDING

S the daughter of a registered nurse, Eileen possessed a judicious balance of medical smarts and emotional sensitivity. And like so many other pet owners in her position, she dove into the Internet, attempting to discover the truth, to sift some nuggets of hope from the unfiltered mounds of negativity. She kept an open mind and focused on being informed, regardless of the injustice of what she discovered and how much it hurt.

The first surprise came packaged with an assurance that her spaniel Helen was not alone. Far from it. In fact, Eileen discovered, 45 percent of dogs that live to ten years of age or older ultimately die from cancer. That's four million dogs in the United States developing cancer every year.

The second surprise came as a statement she needed to see in writing. She had heard it before on TV interviews, a well-intentioned platitude, easy to appreciate, even easier to brush off, reserved for the less fortunate few. This time, however, the phrase hit home and she grabbed it, grateful, vowing to keep it with her. It was nothing more than a simple sentence, but it would be her new philosophy.

"Cancer is not the same as death."

A few days later when she and Helen returned to Angell, Eileen felt prepared, rational, and open-minded about what the oncologist might say.

Dr. Able was not the cancer specialist of her dreams. That is to say she had imagined a much older man with less hair on his head and more wisdom lining his face. This man seemed altogether too young for all those letters after his name, his double-boarded specialist status and all those years of training in both medical oncology and radiation oncology belying the gold-rimmed John Lennon glasses and a neatly gelled Tintin haircut. To her surprise and satisfaction though, Dr. Able seemed like a man used to the introductory reaction playing on Eileen's face. Though secretly he might enjoy it, he was quick to prove he had earned his credentials.

He began with a detailed history, provided by Eileen as observer, running through her statement one more time and feeling frustrated by everything she didn't know about Helen's former life. They moved on to the physical examination, Helen at ease, tail wagging off the chart, apparently forgiving Dr. Able his joke about someone being in desperate need of a Tic Tac as he examined her mouth. He saved the stethoscope for last, taking his time, in no hurry now that her secret was out.

"There are two kinds of approaches we oncologists use," he said, inviting Eileen and Helen to take a seat as he rolled closer in his swivel chair. "One could be described as a guardian, the other a teacher. Based on a given diagnosis a guardian will tell the owner how best to treat the problem without much input from the owner, whereas a teacher will educate the owner, give them all the data regarding treatment options, but not offer any help in the decision-making process. There are clearly flaws with both approaches."

His smile did little to reduce Eileen's confusion, so he pressed on.

"Some owners like to be guided, to have their vet make the tough calls for them. But if things turn out badly, then who foots the blame?"

Dr. Able drove a thumb into his chest.

"Some owners like to be involved in the decision-making process but sometimes this can feel frustrating, even overwhelming."

"So what kind of an oncologist are you?" said Eileen.

"I'm like most oncologists," said Dr. Able, "a bit of both. Mixing it up, focused on keeping our goals realistic and never losing sight of patient quality of life."

Eileen saw that he meant what he said. She liked what he was saying and could feel her earlier apprehension about this young man beginning to subside.

"I've looked over all Helen's blood work, her cardiac ultrasound, and her chest X-rays. Normally I would insist on a definitive diagnosis before recommending a specific treatment option but in Helen's case I believe we can argue for an exception."

"Because almost all canine lung cancers are malignant," said Eileen.

If she was expecting to score points with an appreciative arching of a single eyebrow, Dr. Able did not deliver. Then again, she thought, almost by definition, if you have taken the time to seek out a veterinary oncologist, you are highly likely to go to your meeting armed with a wealth of pertinent cyberspace factoids. Perhaps Dr. Able would have been more surprised if she had kept quiet.

He rose to his feet and switched on the X-ray viewing box. Eileen instantly recognized the picture on the screen, the enormous white mass in Helen's chest, an ominous moonlit cloud scudding across a night sky. Seeing it again was like recognizing your attacker in a lineup.

"Here's the mass." His index finger traced the outline. "It's quite large for a dog of Helen's size."

He paused to look over at Helen snoozing on the floor, an apologetic expression on his face, as though he didn't want to be talking about her behind her back.

"It's also solitary, meaning it is more likely to originate in lung tissue rather than having spread to the lungs from somewhere else."

A thought suddenly occurred to Eileen and she was surprised that it had not struck her sooner.

"Is it possible Helen spent her life among people who smoked?"

She was remembering Sam, the sad old golden retriever she had patted while waiting for Helen's chest X-rays. The smell of nicotine and cigarettes had permeated the room. Had his frightened owner inadvertently contributed to his best friend's demise?

Dr. Able frowned, a moment of deliberation playing over his features.

"The jury is still out on secondhand smoke increasing the risk of lung cancer in dogs, though it does appear to cause an increase in the frequency of certain cancers in cats. To be honest, I'm not sure it matters *how* it got there. What matters is how we deal with it from here on out. Most dogs with this disease would show up at their vets having been coughing for weeks or even months. An owner might report their dog had slowed down, been reluctant or unable to exercise. When it comes to Helen, I think you should consider yourself lucky to have found a problem you never even knew existed, before it could produce a single clinical sign. It's called an incidental finding and we don't get to find them too often."

Eileen latched on to this word *incidental*. It sounded like something unplanned, casual, even minor, and for some reason she imagined a fender bender on the far side of a busy highway, something that makes you slow down and check it out but ultimately something you can choose to drive right by.

"Could it have been there for some time?"

Dr. Able answered without looking at the image, as though he no longer needed its help, as though he instinctively knew where Eileen was going.

"Maybe," he said. "But probably not."

He paused for a beat and added, "It can be a whole lot easier when disease comes packaged with a problem you can see or hear or smell. Owners often consider incidental findings to be a mixed blessing:

for some they offer a welcome opportunity to act sooner, for others
they create an unsolicited burden of having to act at all."

He tapped the X-ray cloud twice with his finger.

"We can't pretend this never happened. I think we have to accept
it as the ultimate 'heads up.'"

Eileen followed his finger and did not avert her eyes.

"So where do we go from here?"

Arguably, more than any other speciality, veterinary oncologists
have chosen to deal with pet owners who are desperate for hope. A
few of these owners will be on a reconnaissance mission, meeting
with the oncologist in order to satisfy their curiosity and their con-
science that at least they looked into the future and didn't like what it
held. And of course, there is absolutely nothing wrong with this motivation. Then there is the other end of the pet-owning spectrum,
this meeting proof of their intent to keep their animal alive at all
costs.

Dr. Able already appreciated that the old black spaniel sleeping on
the floor in front of him was special. She had to be. She might be
"the best dog in the world" or "the best dog Eileen has ever known."
Not that the malignant tendrils brooding inside this dog's chest
could give a damn. Courtesy and respect for this disease can only go
so far. It will fight dirty and Dr. Able knew that sometimes you have
to be prepared to give back as good as you get.

In formulating a plan of attack it pays to keep a grip on reality.
Sugarcoated speculation is for the purveyors of snake oil. Dr. Able
had a responsibility to scientific fact, evidence-based medicine, and
the data of the journals he devours. It was time to balance empathy
with honesty, to temper encouragement with the truth.

"It would be nice to have a biopsy but sticking a needle into a lung
mass is not without risk, even with ultrasound guidance. In theory,
taking it out gets rid of it *and* gives us our diagnosis."

Eileen was all over the caveat.

"What do you mean 'in theory'?"

Dr. Able pursed his lips and sucked back on his teeth.

"A couple of things about this mass bother me. First," he extended his thumb, "its location. Ideally a tumor should be located on the edge of a lung lobe where it can be cut out more easily. Helen's lump is deep, at the base of the lung, which makes it far more difficult to get."

Eileen took a noisy, deep inhalation and let it out, thinking "Most people give out the good news first."

"Second," out came the index finger, "primary lung tumors have the best prognosis when you catch them early. A no-brainer really, the smaller the tumor, the less likely it is to have spread to the regional lymph nodes. X-rays are notoriously difficult for detecting enlarged lymph nodes but we do know that solitary masses less than five centimeters in diameter carry the best prognosis."

"And how big is Helen's mass?"

It was Dr. Able's turn to take a deep breath.

"Please, I don't want to overstate the significance of a single parameter."

But he saw she was still waiting.

"Six and a half centimeters. Normally, after complete surgical excision, with clean nodes and a small well-differentiated tumor, I would be telling you that about half the dogs will live for one year."

Eileen began working the math.

"You mean if the surgeon gets it all and it hasn't spread there's a 50 percent chance Helen could be alive this time next year."

"That's correct, but I'm telling you this thing is big and awkward. Helen's cancer may not be quite so well behaved."

"So what are we looking at?"

Dr. Able stewed, weighing the numbers like a used car dealer about to risk a lowball offer.

"I know it's not a fair question," said Eileen, softening, realizing too late that her question had sounded like a demand for a definitive answer. "I won't hold you to it, but if you could give me your best guess."

Dr. Able came right back.

"Less than eight months, maybe as little as four. But like you say it's just a guess."

Four months.

Eileen looked down at the star of the show, the shadow glued to her ankle. If she were to pat Helen's head right then she knew with absolute certainty the dog would wake up, turn her way, and smile— content to stay, content to go. Worst of all, she knew that Helen was oblivious to both the malevolence looming inside her chest and the violent campaign to defeat it soon to be waged by those she trusted.

"It might be easier to make a decision if we get a CAT scan of Helen's chest, that way we can see whether the mass is operable and have a better idea about the size of the lymph nodes."

Four months would put us into the summer.

Dr. Able waited a beat and then said, "You know choosing not to do anything is also a reasonable option. You've already gone way above and beyond for a dog you've only known for a couple of months. This is asking a lot of you. Besides all the nursing care and the follow-up visits there's the actual cost of all this treatment. You're going to end up spending several thousand dollars before we even think about the possibility of using chemotherapy."

Eileen was still lost to him, coming to terms with his worst-case offer—*four months*—but Dr. Able saw that familiar flinch when the word *chemotherapy* snaps a person out of their trance.

"I know what you're thinking," he said. "You're worried all her hair would fall out and she'd throw up and have blowout diarrhea the whole time. Truth is 75 percent of dogs on chemotherapy have no side effects whatsoever and the remaining 25 percent have the kind of minor stuff you can easily cope with at home. I'm not even sure chemotherapy is indicated but part of me thinks that if we're going to get this thing, then let's go at it with everything we've got."

Eileen nodded, to be doing something. What she had discovered on the Internet had skirted around this subject. She shouldn't have been surprised, but somehow the anonymous accrual of uncertain information had been tolerable. Here and now, whittled down to something precise and personal, the truth was worse than she had anticipated. She thought it would be bad but not this bad.

She had come armed to ask him what he would do if this were his dog, but even though this seemed like the right moment to ask, the words failed her, as though she were being unfair, assuming too much of a doctor she hardly knew.

"Can I talk it over with my husband?"

"Of course. Definitely."

This time Eileen gently touched Helen's head and, as predicted, Sleepy verified the source of the touch, approved, and bounced to her feet.

Dr. Able stepped forward.

"Here's my card. And please, if you have any more questions for me, don't hesitate to give me a call."

They shook hands and then Dr. Able dipped down to pat Helen one last time. In doing so, he said something to her under his breath that Eileen couldn't quite catch. She could have sworn he told Helen she was a lucky dog. But how could a dog with terminal cancer be so lucky?

12 | BUCKING THE TREND

RAGEDY can demolish like an explosion—swift and indiscriminate and crushing and painful. But sometimes, for some people, what remains after the rubble of confusion has had a chance to settle is an amazing clarity. Suddenly, all the obstructions and debris and pointless minutiae of our life are wiped away, and for those who can open their minds, there are new, important vistas to take in, and a different way to look at the world.

To say that tragedy is unfair assumes that life can be led according to a set of rules, that by charting a certain course and staying between the lines, all will be well. Yet tragedy is pervasive, versatile, and ingrained as a universal component of life. It's not sexist or ageist, it has no regard for socioeconomic standing, race, creed, or ethnicity. You can't pay it off. It is the blackmailer who keeps coming back for more. It is a chameleon, a con artist, able to worm its way into any life at any time. It is ubiquitous and we need to be prepared to deal with it. Nothing can be more annoying to someone embroiled in tragedy than to overhear the whispered inanity "God only deals it out to those who can handle it." Do they really think *they* couldn't handle it, would be crushed by it, or worse still, are somehow above it? As I see it, tragedy will take its turn with all of us. Perhaps they should rephrase their platitude to "God only deals it out to see *how* we handle it."

Lost and dazed in the aftermath of Cleo Rasmussen's untimely death, I knew that throwing myself into work was a good thing. I could still feel a tightening in my guts whenever I thought about her, still hear Sandi Rasmussen's ethereal request rattling around inside my head like the ball in an eternal game of Pong, but the job offered a welcome distraction and something akin to relief. It had only been a few days since our encounter and I had yet to come to terms with the promise she had made me swear. What was she *really* asking me to do?

Promise me to take Cleo's spirit on a journey, to realize all the wonderful qualities she embodied and to pour all the skill, effort, and talent you had intended for Cleo into the lives and health of other unfortunate animals.

This request was big, broad, and, from an objective, scientific point of view, flawed. Even so, I could see the conviction in Sandi's eyes, assuring me this was possible. I had no idea how to make this happen, I simply knew I had to try. This could be the path to restitution I so craved, the chance to make things, if not right, better. At the same time, I didn't want to feel rushed simply to scratch a check in a box so I could put this event behind me, move on, and forget. At the very least this mission deserved a little preparation and a good deal of thought. Besides, my meeting with Sandi had exposed a serious chink in my emotional armor. I needed to explore this wound, acknowledge its existence, and defend against future susceptibility.

The first unofficial report regarding Cleo's postmortem examination reached me by e-mail. I should have been petrified, about to be unmasked as a sloppy, even dangerous clinician. But for some reason I wasn't. I'm sure my encounter with Sandi made some of the difference, but there was conviction in my assertion that I would not have done anything different with my workup for Cleo. Fallibility and negligence are not the same thing.

Pathologists talk about "gross" findings, meaning blatant and obvious rather than disgusting and nausea inducing. Though there were still samples of tissue from vital organs awaiting microscopic examination, there was news to report. Based on visual inspection alone, Cleo's heart appeared to be completely normal. There was nothing remarkable, brittle, or delicate about any of her bones. There was, however, something unusual about her kidneys, a finding both infrequent and incontrovertible. Cleo had been born with only one kidney, her left. Her right kidney was missing.

For me this anomaly triggered speculation about a possible link between some sort of renal insufficiency and a weakened skeleton, of anesthetic drug sensitivity due to impaired drug excretion from only having one kidney. But in the light of her perfectly normal urinary function and blood work and previous unremarkable encounters with anesthetics, any possible relationship quickly fizzled out. Anyway, plenty of humans and animals can thrive on just one kidney. Why should Cleo have been any different?

A FEW weeks later, another difficult case had Cleo's death and Sandi's unprecedented request right back in the forefront of my mind.

The patient in question was a four-year-old male rabbit called Atlas, cursed by a large firm swelling attached to his lower jaw. Earlier I defined the term gross as used by pathologists. One exception to my forgiveness of their jargon relates to their affinity for culinary metaphors. By definition, pathologists are drawn to the nuances of disease, dedicated to sharing their enthusiasm through vivid oral and written descriptions, and apparently food analogies offer superior sensory impact, evoking fragrance, texture, and even flavor. The lump on Atlas's jaw demanded surgical excision and I had no doubt an epicurean pathologist was standing by, waiting for his slice, eager to describe the contents of this abscess as having "the consistency of fluffy white cheese."

Atlas had received a visit from the dentist and had exhausted more conservative options, and now it was my turn to play mission impossible, trying to best a resilient foe. Unlike a split-pea-soup cat bite abscess (my apologies, but you get the idea), so common among outdoor fighting cats, the rabbit variety does not lend itself to simple drainage. Treating it like a tumor, completely cutting it out, is the preferred approach. There is, however, a fundamental flaw in this plan—it necessitates general anesthesia.

Rabbits and gases that induce unconsciousness are about as dangerous a mix as naked flames and gasoline fumes. For starters, rabbits flout the basic anesthetic principle of airway control by refusing to open their mouths wide enough to allow easy tube placement in their windpipe. Think about it, when was the last time you saw a rabbit yawn, or exhibit a look of jaw-dropping surprise? Crowded molars and tight lips make it virtually impossible to snag more than a glimpse at the back of their throat, let alone visualize the airway. Blindly tubing a rabbit becomes all touchy-feely as the anesthetist carefully pushes the transparent endotracheal tube into the mouth, listening for the softest breeze, its to and fro matching the rhythm of a swirling mist of condensation inside the tube. If the noise of breathing is replaced by a gurgling noise, you know you've gone down the wrong way.

With the tube in place, the fun has only just begun. Rabbit heart rates can run in the three hundreds per minute, and their respiratory rate can be only marginally slower. Thank goodness for their big ears. At least they offer a decent-sized vein in which to place a catheter.

By comparison, as the surgeon, I was doing the easy stuff, and while Atlas behaved himself—no doubt dreaming of daring raids in Mr. McGregor's garden, plundering abundant carrot booty—I cut and dissected and teased the offensive item off of his jaw. Part of my plan involved implanting a handful of tiny green antibiotic-impregnated beads. These magical "petits pois" would slowly release their medicine in high concentrations precisely where it was needed rather than risking the broader side effects of a systemic assault.

Cognizant of the clock and the anesthetic risk, I moved quickly within the confines of my surgical field, oblivious to the mayhem all around. For anesthetists, where possible, access to the head is paramount and with my smothering Atlas in sterile towels and drapes, they were struggling to gauge anesthetic depth. Simple, meaningful observation of eye position and the color of his gums and lips had been reduced to blind ferreting in the manner of a nineteenth-century portrait photographer rustling under his shroud before he exclaims, "say cheese." And it didn't help that I kept on knocking off every probe and monitoring device they had on him.

"I don't think he's breathing."

Obviously the technician who made the comment put it out there in search of assistance, to raise the alarm, but for a few seconds its effect was paralyzing, making us all stop and scrutinize the drapes for the slightest flutter of Atlas's chest. I looked into my incision, trying to glean some meaning from the shade of red in the small amount of lost blood. Was it bright enough, sufficiently oxygenated for our patient to be breathing and therefore still alive?

"Can I get by," said Dr. Bain, a critical care specialist, muscling in like a serial bridesmaid after a tossed bouquet. I was so focused on my work I had failed to notice her circling the OR, as though she had sensed a looming crisis.

I backed off, gloved hands clasped in front of me as the drapes were peeled away, my surgical site contaminated by naked hands pawing for proof of life. Suddenly my efforts, my being there, became inconsequential; far greater concerns were at play. It was as though my services were no longer required. Reduced to voyeur, I watched the resuscitation unfold and naturally I couldn't help but think about Cleo. So this time I got a little bit further in the surgery, but once again I was watching an anesthetized animal beginning to die.

I am not by nature a superstitious person, though I might avoid walking under ladders, I am cautious when hanging mirrors, and I choose not to open umbrellas indoors. Like I said, most medical professionals, including surgeons, live by objectivity. Even so, there are times when superstition can still undermine a semblance of reason.

Young doctors, interns, and residents are perhaps the most prone to this. Maybe they seek the solace of knowing a higher power had a hand in their bad luck. Maybe they want to feel assured that an outcome was predestined, fated beyond their control. For example, if they are on call for nighttime emergencies there will be this tacit understanding that no one on the team should verbalize how quiet it has been for the past few nights lest they unleash the wrath of the ominous word *jinx*. That said, they may look upon a certain permutation of technician, intern, and resident and resign themselves to pulling an all-nighter because, for some inexplicable reason, that particular combination always has bad luck. Best of all, they will tell you that everything, no matter how obscure or how disastrous, always comes in runs of threes. And this was why I stared at Atlas, a creature trapped in some kind of purgatory between this world and the next, because all I could think of was Cleo. If everything comes in runs of three, which wretched case would be next?

Forty minutes passed. Technically Atlas was alive but only just. He refused to breathe for himself and the technician had been artificially breathing for him this whole time. His heart was still beating but the rate was down in the forties, a ridiculously low number for a rabbit. It waned in increments and was resistant to all chemical stimulants. Worst of all, just as with Cleo, the pupils of Atlas's eyes were fixed, dilated, and unresponsive.

"Essentially he's dead," said Dr. Bain, looking at the heart monitor. "He's been off anesthesia but he still won't breathe for himself and his heart rate just keeps falling and falling. It's like he's slowly shutting down. Based on his pupils I think he's probably already brain dead."

It was as though Atlas had opted for hibernation and was slipping away gracefully. Instead of ending his life with a screeching halt Atlas preferred to brake slowly and smoothly before coming to a complete stop.

Once again, here I was, undone by another unexpected and disastrous turn of events, but there was nothing more for me to do so I removed my gloves, called out the OR, and asked the anesthesia technicians to get going on my next case. I forced myself not to add "with all caution."

"Hey, Nick." It was Dr. Vega, Atlas's primary doctor and a specialist in exotic medicine, poking her head into the surgical suites.

"I just spoke to the owner and she's coming right down. She wants to say good-bye to Atlas while he's under anesthesia. Do you think we can make him look *presentable* before she arrives?"

"Of course," I said, thinking that he wasn't really under anesthesia but more than able to understand her request. One of the basic truths in all of surgery is that no matter what you do on the inside, the quality of a surgeon's skill and compassion is often judged by his or her handiwork on the outside. Make Atlas look pretty. Tidy up all the hastily shaved fur. Pull the catheters, the monitors that fasten and pinch and probe. Do a nice neat job of stitching the skin. If Atlas cannot reap the rewards of the hard work no one ever gets to see, at least he can leave this world looking his best.

And so I donned a new pair of gloves, picked up a few basic pieces of surgical equipment, and set to work.

About three stitches in something strange happened. This inert, unresponsive, velveteen rabbit twitched his skin. At the time, I considered the tic noteworthy but inconsequential, no more than an involuntary reflex, a final discharge from a dying nerve. Seconds later when the previously flaccid Atlas jerked his head and blinked, the entire resuscitation team succumbed to a dumbstruck moment of disbelief.

The choice phrases that ensued do not bear repeating here, but who could deny any clinician a joyful four-letter expletive or two with the impossible realization that Atlas, bless his slowly beating heart, was back from the dead. The little rascal had been faking it all along. Oh, the thrill and relief of scrambling to close the wound before Atlas literally hopped off the table.

None of us had a clue as to what happened with Atlas. It really was more like hibernation than anesthesia, as if a particularly cold winter had nearly taken him and just when everyone had given up, spring had brought him back to life. I had willed it with Cleo, imagined it unfolding as we had worked on her, to no avail. Still, as far as I was concerned, Atlas had thumped lucky rabbit paws all over any superstitious twaddle that says bad things come in runs of threes.

Nevertheless, as Atlas went off to the critical care unit to recover, I privately remained concerned. Alive was not the same as being functional. One by one his body's various systems had been saying goodnight, and a vegetative state is no quality of life for a rabbit or any animal. And if, by some act of God, he came all the way back to us, what had our surgery achieved? I had managed to leave behind a smattering of those antibiotic impregnated beads but the wound had been mauled by ungloved technicians and doctors like clumsy detectives at a crime scene. My closure had been a desperate race, the result not quite Frankenstein, but far from Joan Rivers.

By the time Atlas's owner, Leah, arrived, this remarkable rabbit had undergone a complete transformation. Leah was a young woman in her early twenties, and she had hurried to the hospital prepared to say good-bye, eyes filled with the preemptive tears of shock and pain. Instead she was rewarded with shock and joy. The creature in the critical care unit, hopping around his cage, utterly unfazed and gnawing on pieces of carrot, insisted on saying hello and "When are we going home?" In short, Atlas was acting like a normal, healthy rabbit. And as it turned out, the surgeon in me need not have worried. The wound healed beautifully and some fifteen months later, his abscess has never returned.

Not long after my encounter with the amazing Atlas another sick animal had me wondering about that elusive promise to Sandi.

"Nick, how about a gallbladder this afternoon?"

The question, delivered like an invitation to try an hors d'oeuvre at a cocktail party, came from Dr. Carroll, a specialist in internal medicine. Her trademark clinical style lay somewhere between Energizer Bunny and Tasmanian devil. She always spoke in fast clipped bursts, words unleashed like bullets from an Uzi. Her candor and dedication garnered a loyal clientele despite the fast-talking, fast-walking urgency of someone who always managed to look like she had somewhere else to be.

"Kyoza's a Siamese, eleven years old, and her liver's toast. She's not eating, her enzymes are off the charts, and her skin color lies somewhere between the yolk of a free-range egg and pureed carrot."

Dr. Carroll was talking about jaundice, the cat's failure to rid herself of the waste product called bile. Bile is normally excreted into our gut. If it can't get out, sometimes due to a blockage in the gallbladder, it will find its way into the circulation, quickly turning the skin and mucous membranes a disgusting shade of yellow or even orange.

"I don't know if she'll make it through surgery but the owners want to give it a try."

I heard the caveat loud and clear. It was the need to try, the reassurance of knowing there was nothing more that could be done. For so many owners, no matter how long the odds, there can be solace in knowing they have given their pet every chance.

"Sure," I said. "I'll see what I can do."

Dr. Carroll was already on the move, heading down the corridor.

"Hey," I shouted after her. "What's this cat like?"

She slammed on the brakes, turned, and looked at me.

"Why? Does it make a difference?"

I shrugged, shook my head. Of course it didn't matter one iota, but from a management standpoint, a difficult and testy cat requiring extensive aftercare may be more of a challenge than a granny-loving lap cat, purring amid knitting needles and cups of tea.

"I'll let you be the judge," she said and was gone.

YELLOW cat belly is weird. It's eerie, like the faces of those three men in Blue Man Group. And in Kyoza's case, the discoloration went beyond skin deep. What little fat this poor cat had left was yellow, her intestines were yellow, her stomach was yellow, and even her kidneys were yellow. Normally the gallbladder lies between the lobes of the liver like a tired old party balloon, barely distended. Kyoza's gallbladder was inflated to the point of bursting, its surface tight and thin, all ready to pop.

I set to work on this diseased plumbing, teasing and coaxing the gallbladder out of its glandular alcove lest it rupture and spill its green poison. I followed up with a little Roto-Rooter action, suctioning and flushing the duct system, making sure that all the unwanted bile could flow downstream, into the intestines and out of the body. All that remained was that old chestnut, much loved by those internal medicine types.

"Oh, while you are at it, I don't suppose you could just get me a biopsy or two."

This was a request to sample a surgical tasting menu, if you will, of tiny pieces of tissue such as the liver, jejunum, and pancreas. Eager to please I acquired my requisite specimens, cultures, and aspirates and closed little Kyoza up.

Many hours later I checked in on her in CCU. She was hooked up to fluids and monitors, lying on her side, weak and unable to raise her head. Now I could appreciate how sick this cat really was and how our anesthesia team had done an incredible job of just getting her out of surgery. They had achieved their goal, the relay baton had been successfully passed on to critical care, and now it was their turn to keep Kyoza in the fight.

I lay my hand across her xylophone chest, nothing but fur and ribs. Her eyes were closed but to my surprise, as soon as I touched her, she began to purr. Not a subtle purr either, a grinding, booming variant, like a Geiger counter homing in on a radioactive cache. Cats don't just purr when they are happy. Sometimes they purr when they are in pain or frightened. It has even been suggested that these vibrational sound frequencies possess healing properties. For me, this purring was not initiated by distress but was Kyoza's way of letting us know she was still in there, hanging on, grateful to be alive. It took me back to my question for Dr. Carroll.

"What's this cat like?"

Well, I had my answer. Kyoza was clearly a fighter.

IT IS quite common for hospitalized pets, particularly those destined for an extensive stay in critical care, to be accompanied by a favorite blanket or stuffed toy, family photos, and even "get well soon" cards. Kyoza's heartening cage accessory, however, did not seem to fit this bill. Set off to one side, inside a transparent plastic frame, was a very different type of card. I picked it up and on the front was a photograph of a gentleman called Harold Klemp. Mr. Klemp was probably in his sixties, with a receding hairline just shy of bald, functional glasses, a blazer, striped tie, and a warm smile that felt more like an introduction from a doctor than a used car salesman.

It turned out that Mr. Klemp was neither. He is the spiritual leader of a religion I had never heard of called Eckankar. Apparently I was holding what is referred to as a "Hu card," the flip side of which said,

HU is woven into the language of life. It is the Sound of all sounds.
It is the wind in the leaves, falling rain, thunder of jets, singing of

birds, the awful rumble of a tornado . . . Its sound is heard in
laughter, weeping, the din of city traffic, ocean waves, and the quiet
rippling of a mountain stream. And yet, the word HU is not God.
It is a word people anywhere can use to address the Originator
of Life.

"You have to say the word *Hu* whenever you are around Kyoza,"
said a passing technician who saw me eyeing the card. "It's supposed to give off good vibes or something like that."

I thanked her and placed the card back in the cage like a child
ordered by a shopkeeper not to touch the goods. Now I was curious about Kyoza's owners but, if I am being perfectly honest, I
also recognized a tinge of relief that these clients still belonged to
Dr. Carroll.

Kyoza struggled through the next few days, needing a feeding tube
to deliver liquid kitty gruel because she showed no interest in food
on her own. For the most part, skin and bones just lay there, staring
out at the world, what remained of her body being turned by attentive nurses every four hours because Kyoza was simply too weak to
move herself. When her biopsy results came back they provided the
explanation for her faltering recovery. Kyoza had one of the worst
cases of liver infection the pathologists had ever seen. Wily gut bacteria had taken advantage of all the sludge clogging her bile ducts,
swimming upstream to colonize her entire liver. Based on the lab results it was hard to imagine any cat surviving their malicious attack.
Perhaps all we had done was to prolong the inevitable.

A couple of days later I bumped into Dr. Carroll and braced for the
worst.

"How's Kyoza?" I asked.

She stared at me as if I had ripped up a winning lottery ticket and
tossed it in the trash.

"Didn't you see her this morning? I swear that cat should be dead but she's eating and drinking and keeping it down. I'm sending her home."

As usual Dr. Carroll had vanished before I could ask what happened, instantly teleported to some other critical case in the hospital.

I was left hanging, incredulous as to how Kyoza could have possibly pulled through. Here, like Atlas the rabbit, was another example of an animal who had defied the odds. Was Kyoza simply the product of modern medical care or were other, more subtle forces at work? Inadvertently, and maybe even fortuitously, had I been carrying thoughts of Cleo around with me like a lucky talisman? Cleo was still on my mind, but I never consciously conjured her up around Kyoza, never chanted her name, never willed her memory into my mind as I worked on the cat's diseased gallbladder. Surely the notion that somehow Cleo had helped was ridiculous. She could never have been more than a fleeting thought, a moment of reflection, if that. Perhaps a naive part of me believed that when the right case found me, I would know it for sure. At best, I managed to convince myself that I *might* have been thinking about Sandi and my promise to her. Kyoza deserved and received my best efforts in surgery, and clearly, based on the outcome, the best efforts of Dr. Carroll and the team in critical care. Undoubtedly this was a remarkable cat, but was this the kind of magic Sandi had been hoping for? This was a great story and one I imagined Sandi would greatly appreciate, but had I really fulfilled my promise to her? Had Cleo been along for the ride? I wasn't convinced even though I wanted to be. Many months later I called up Kyoza's mom, Ms. Dunne, to discover the secret to this cat's miraculous recovery and the importance of the Hu card.

"In the days leading up to the surgery," she said, "Kyoza was incredibly sick. We never knew whether she would live long enough to have the procedure, let alone pull through it. We talked to her all the time about what we should do."

Virtually all pet owners talk to their pets but how many of them expect guidance in return? In an attempt to stave off what might have been an uncomfortable weirdness to our conversation, I came clean about my interest in the Hu card in Kyoza's cage.

Ms. Dunne laughed and was happy to talk about her spiritual beliefs in a refreshing, easygoing, non-proselytizing manner. Nothing she said sounded preachy or rote.

"It was simple, silent communication. Soul to soul. Trying to discover whether she wanted to fight or bow out gracefully. My partner and I would sit vigil at home and focus our minds on giving Kyoza our love.

"Our religion, Eckankar, believes our dreams offer many insights into our lives, that they hold the promise of divine guidance. When we sleep all our mental facilities, our emotional turmoil, can come to rest and if we choose, we can surrender to divine insight.

"That night, before the surgery, my wife had a dream. She described a farmer driving a tractor trailer carrying three discrete, conspicuous objects on the tractor's flatbed. She was riding a bike, close by, and as the trailer went past her it was swept into the air, slammed down to the ground, and these three objects flew off. She watched in horror only to see the driver step out of the cab, dust himself off, smile at her, and walk away as though he was off to get a coffee, no big deal."

The skeptic in me started to get restless.

"What were the objects?"

"She wasn't sure. The only three things that came to mind were the three major clinical problems affecting Kyoza—anorexia, lethargy, and jaundice. I know what you're thinking, the analogy of the trailer with a cat shaking off her symptoms seems like a stretch but this was her dream."

I thought about it and had to agree. If I were going to force a dream that would convince me whether or not to proceed with a risky surgery, I think I could have done better than this. At least I could have been specific about the three objects.

"It always comes back to 'everything happens for a reason.' So we decided to go ahead with the surgery. Dr. Carroll made sure we understood that Kyoza might die on the table, but this was okay with us because it would be her *choice* to go and we would honor her choice."

"But that was only the beginning of her troubles," I said. "Kyoza was in critical care forever."

"All the doctors and staff were wonderful. They were incredibly respectful of the Hu card."

Time for a tactful approach.

"So what exactly does the card do?"

In the pause I could almost feel her smile.

"It is a word we say to convey peace, warmth, and comfort. We wanted Kyoza to be surrounded by the spirit in Hu and I am told that many of the technicians would speak the word whenever they worked with her. In fact, people started to refer to Kyoza as the Hu Kitty."

I waited a beat, taking in what many people might perceive to be a bizarre approach to healing. But why shouldn't we indulge people's beliefs if their intent integrates with our medical approach to the problem? What harm can it possibly do? I imagine a few of the technicians might have viewed the Hu card with the kind of skepticism normally reserved for fortune cookies, the photo of Mr. Klemp as possessing all the curative power of a picture of Miley Cyrus. But according to my own informal investigation, the CCU staff shared a universal appreciation that the card was motivated by the same fundamental desire they all shared—the goal of making Kyoza well.

"By the way, what does *Kyoza* mean?" I said, attempting to bring the conversation back to more worldly matters.

"It's Japanese, from *Gyoza*. It means 'little dumpling.' When we got her as a stray she only weighed a pound and a half and could fit in the palm of your hand like a little dumpling."

Cute, I thought.

"And how is she doing now?"

"Fabulous," said Ms. Dunne. "She has gained forty percent of her body weight. She's better than before any of this even started. She loves going for walks in her harness. When I come home and can't find her all I have to do is jiggle my keys and out she pops ready to go for a walk."

When I hung up, I summoned the images of her skinny yellow cat in CCU and an almost deceased rabbit named Atlas chowing down on a carrot, like Bugs Bunny about to ask "What's up, Doc?" and all I could think was that for such a scientific, objective, fact-based endeavor, some pretty miraculous things can happen in veterinary medicine. For the most part, when the impossible happens we have no credible explanation. Though we might hunt for the answers, for an explanation, in the end does it really matter? Kyoza and Atlas had said it all—be grateful, bear witness, and enjoy.

13 | A DOG'S CHANCE

SEATED at their kitchen table, Eileen told Ben about her meeting with Dr. Able, pushing through the cold stats, holding it together until her husband knew as much about Helen's cancer as she did. In the loud, contemplative silence that remained they stared into each other's eyes, wondering who should go first, and in the end it was the little dog leaning into Eileen who, indirectly, instigated the dialogue. It was something about the way Helen pressed the left side of her rib cage into Eileen's ankle, Eileen staring down and then sensing the tumor right there, creeping into the space between them like an unsolicited guest, lurid and obnoxious, laughing at their obvious discomfort.

"You know what sucks," said Eileen, letting the floodgates open on the day's sad news. "What really sucks is that every single morning this incredible little dog wakes up next to our bed and looks around and barks her head off because she cannot believe that compared to what she has been used to, she is still living in paradise."

Ben leaned across the table, taking his wife's hands in his.

"You remember what she was like when we found her." Some of Eileen's words were getting lost, stabbed into choppy gasps. "She's never had a chance. She's never had a family who loved her and took care of her. And when she finally gets her first opportunity to live a decent life, a real dog's life, this goddamn awful disease comes along, determined to sweep it out from under her feet."

Helen remained deaf to the anguish playing out over her head but Didi was on it, barreling into Eileen with a massive head butt and a bucket of warm drool. The slapstick comedy of flying gobs of saliva spinning end over end as the big girl shook her floppy jowls in Eileen's lap turned out to be a timely and a much-needed antidote.

Ben studied his wife, reading her compassion, her unwavering desire to do something positive for a smelly, foul-mouthed, chubby little dog, who despite these outward characteristics won their hearts with her cheerful appreciation of companionship.

"What are you thinking?" he asked, seeing her frown.

"I'm trying to imagine what Helen would want us to do. Who in their right mind wants their chest ripped open and all that that entails for an extra four months of living? And what kind of living are we looking at? We have no idea how well or had badly she might do. It's even possible she might live that long if we do nothing at all."

Ben cupped a hand around his chin signaling his turn to think.

"How would you feel if four months was all she got?"

This time Eileen leaned forward.

"You know what, and I hope this doesn't sound selfish, but when the oncologist said four months, all I kept thinking about was the possibility of giving her one summer with us, one vacation where she and Didi could run around on the beach at Prince Edward Island. I know she's never seen the ocean, I just know it. She's never chased a ball across the sand or tried to catch a crab in a tide pool. She'd love it. Wouldn't she? And Didi would love having her there too. I want to see Helen that happy. Just once. No matter what comes after that, at least she can have it once."

Right then, more than anything else, Ben was struck by the purity of her intent. It was such a simple plan. Eileen wasn't doing this for herself or because she couldn't bear to let go. She simply wanted Helen to enjoy a little canine nirvana in her lifetime. No need for some anthropomorphic, Hallmark Hall of Fame moment with Helen standing in the breaking surf, tail wagging, sun dropping off the end of the earth as she turns to Eileen and the cutesy voice-over says, "Thanks, Mom, for bringing me here." This was all about the dog. Eileen wanted Helen to live for Helen.

Hearing this, few men could have sucked down a deep breath, winced, and shaken their heads as a prelude to "I don't think so." Then again, it wasn't as though Ben could afford the surgery and the chemo and all the aftercare. The price tag on Helen's dental workup alone had been bad enough and thus far the dog breath continued to thrive unchecked, overshadowed and entirely forgotten. By any standards Ben was an accomplished and successful painter but this kind of disposable income lay far beyond what he could make with his canvas and oils. Could he really justify the cost without the promise of reward? After all, Helen was a geriatric dog with a diagnosis of terminal cancer. If she had been younger, if the disease had even a fair prognosis, it would have made the decision so much easier.

Yet Ben never wavered. He had no idea how he would do it but he would do it, because at that moment, what was passing between them was precisely what his marriage to Eileen was all about. You could forget about the romantic getaways for two, the candlelit dinner at a fine-dining restaurant, or the contents of a small, velvety jewelry box. This intimate, unadorned moment, this connection, this was what mattered. This was the substance of their relationship, the inexpressible spark that lasts and reminds you how lucky you are to be sharing it.

Ben smiled. How could he not?

"You don't have a selfish bone in your body," he said. "I have no idea how much all of this is going to cost and it's probably best that I don't know. What I do know is that throughout our marriage you've never asked for anything from me. And here you are, asking for the first time, and it's not even about you. Any husband would have to be a complete idiot to say no. If you believe this needs to be done, then let's do it."

WITH the decision to go ahead with Helen's surgery came a sudden craving to have it done yesterday.

"I don't want to do the CAT scan," said Eileen into the phone. "I just want her to get the surgery as soon as possible."

Too bad Eileen couldn't appreciate the smile playing out on the other end of the line.

"Yeah," said Dr. Able, "I get that a lot. Let me see if I can line up a surgeon. Sometimes, when they get busy it might take a while to schedule. I'll do my best and give you a call back."

Eileen hung up, stewed, lasted about a minute, and picked up the phone again, this time placing a call to Dr. Judy.

"I think it's great what you're doing," said Dr. J. "Not many people would make that kind of an investment in an animal they hardly know."

Eileen knew what Dr. J. meant, but the word *investment* sounded wrong, like Eileen was looking for a return on her money. Then again, in a sense, maybe she was.

"I can't stand this waiting for the surgery," said Eileen. "They're telling me the larger it gets the worse the prognosis, so wouldn't they want to take it out as soon as possible?"

"Who's Dr. Able trying to get to be Helen's surgeon?"

"No idea," said Eileen. "To be honest I'll take whoever's available first."

Dr. J. waited a beat and then said, "What about asking Dr. Trout?"

For Eileen, the name breezed in from the past.

"That was the doctor who operated on Didi's knee. I thought he only did orthopedics?"

"Don't know. A lot of surgeons do both orthopedics and soft tissue surgery. He knows you, you know him, and I'll bet he remembers Didi. Worth a try?"

Eileen hung up and placed a second call to Dr. Able, giving serious consideration to putting his number into her speed dial. An operator bounced the call into a paging system and after few minutes he picked up.

"I'm not really stalking you, I promise," said Eileen.

"That's okay," said Dr. Able, but without humor. "What's up?"

Eileen hesitated. The poor guy must get this all day long, pushy clients acting like big insistent moths, hovering, swooping, determined to cross his path. Uneasily, she pressed on.

"I wanted to tell you *why* I decided to go ahead with Helen's surgery. I know that probably doesn't make much sense, but I think it might help you convince a certain surgeon to take her on."

Any reticence she might have detected in Dr. Able's tone was now replaced with sly curiosity.

"You sound like you have someone in mind," he said.

Eileen smiled.

"I do."

14 THE OTHER SIDE

PASTED to the door of the radiology reading room is a photograph of a suburban street sign warning "Unnecessary Noise Prohibited," and like a combative librarian enforcing silence it sets the tone for all who enter. It may be black-and-white pictures and not words, but the reading of X-ray images is best achieved with privacy, mood lighting, and silence.

I sat alone in the physical and emotional gloom created by the three films hanging on the viewing box in front of me. In my hand I held an index card embossed with a patient sticker, a gift from Dr. Able, delivered with more of a romantic story than a clinical synopsis. Baiting a surgeon with a procedure guaranteed to crank up the adrenaline is a perfectly acceptable recruitment ploy, but in this particular case, instantly hooked by his compelling narrative, I felt the allure of something far more important than a surgical challenge. Even before I tracked down the chest X-rays, I had the sense that there was something special about this case, this dog named Helen.

No one wants to hear a surgeon say he or she is daunted by the size of a tumor or the challenge that befalls the clinician willing to take it on, but my sharp and involuntary intake of breath seemed appropriate. I checked the written radiology report on the X-rays and found an unnerving verification. The report ended:

Diagnostic Impression: Solitary mass left caudal lung lobe.
Primary lung tumor suspected. Proximity to the bronchial origin
would make successful surgical resection questionable.

I held on to the last four words of the report, "successful surgical resection questionable," and stared into the tumor, replaying Dr. Able's impartial, abbreviated account of a nomadic dog. I found the name Helen unusual and endearing (far preferable, in my opinion, to the easy Lucky or Chance) for a stray dog who had been welcomed into a family prepared to foot enormous medical expenses to give this virtual canine stranger a chance of experiencing something as ephemeral as a walk on a beach. I remembered this owner, Eileen, having performed surgery on her other dog, a huge Newfoundland called Didi, cursed with bad knees. Eileen had been wonderful to work with but our interaction had been brief. I had failed to appreciate how her love of animals went far beyond the role of attentive and responsible pet owner. How many of us would rescue a geriatric dog and welcome her so quickly and so deeply into our hearts that we would do whatever it took to give her a glimpse of canine bliss? It doesn't necessitate a remarkable dog. It necessitates a remarkable person to see a remarkable dog.

Despite the fact that Helen's problem lay at the limits of my and any other surgeon's capabilities, everything about this case, this hapless drifter of a dog, began to fall into place for me. I thought about Cleo, loving the fact that these two dogs could not have been more different. Helen was a sporting breed, Cleo a toy. Helen was in her dotage; Cleo had been little more than a pup. Helen would be cursed with the weighty, odiferous ears of her lineage, Cleo blessed with the attentive, pricked ears of hers. Based on the X-rays and the depth of back fat overlying her spine, Helen obviously liked to eat, whereas Cleo had been a lean and muscular machine. As far as I was concerned there was absolutely no overlap between the two of them, but I found myself becoming convinced that Helen might be exactly the kind of underdog that, according to Sandi, Cleo would have been rooting for. This dog had found her way to me. This wasn't a random pickup through emergency. I didn't happen upon Helen's story after the fact. I didn't seek her out because I was keeping track of heart-wrenching cases in need of surgery. There was nothing contrived about our encounter. *Helen* collided with *me*, for whatever reason, and all I can tell you is that as soon as she did, it became apparent that this was how I would fulfill my promise to Sandi Rasmussen.

Lulled by the peaceful darkness of the reading room I thought about what Sandi had said.

Take Cleo's spirit on a journey . . . realize all the wonderful qualities she embodied . . . pour all the skill, effort, and talent you had intended for Cleo into the lives and health of other unfortunate animals.

This promise, hastily but sincerely made in a flitting moment of supreme emotional susceptibility, suggested that I somehow knew how to take the spirit of a deceased dog on a sterile expedition into an operating room. Of course, I didn't. This scenario didn't come with a set of instructions as to how to proceed. To make this happen my scientific rigor would have to embrace intuition. To my way of thinking, Sandi wanted me to think of Cleo as a clinical touchstone, there if I, or some other animal, needed her. And it was clear if any dog did, it was Helen. I was facing a very tricky surgery trying to rid Helen of a cancer that had snuggled up to her heart, a location many of us consider to be the emotional and physical core of our being. Everything about this scenario required that I make an enormous leap of faith. So why not jump? These animals seemed like kindred souls. If anyone could guide me on this endeavor it would be Cleo.

Many clinicians (far wiser clinicians than I) might prefer to ignore, refute, or circumvent the concept of an animal possessing a soul. For the most part I had fallen into the latter category, but for my promise to be more than convenient lip service, I forced myself to dig deep, to consider some tough questions, to wander down ignored, forgotten, or neglected pathways and try to justify why this commitment seemed reasonable.

Much to my parents' chagrin, as a pimply teenage boy I rejected Church of England Sunday school and its ecclesiastical arguments for life after death, and that left the scientist in me succumbing to the sway of cynicism. Okay, so the law of thermodynamics, the one claiming energy can change from one state to another although the total amount of energy remains the same, gave me pause, but I found it a stretch to believe that some nineteenth-century German physicist had actually intended to engineer a scientific proof of a metaphysical afterlife. In fact, I would go so far as to say it wasn't until I became a father, with children of my own, that I came to realize there was so much more to life than could be grasped by mere mortals.

When my youngest daughter, Emily, was three years old she claimed to see dead people. One day we were in the car and she was strapped into her car seat, watching the road, singing along to another stirring riff by a purple dinosaur, when we were overtaken by an eighteen-wheeler and from nowhere she announced, "I remember when one of those took my skin off."

I glanced in the rearview mirror looking for Bruce Willis, waiting for the green vomit and a Linda Blair cranium spin, but Emily sat there smiling back at Daddy, totally unfazed.

"What do you mean?" I asked.

"My doll was in the road," she said. "I ran out to get it and it hit me."

This sixth sense reappeared some days later when I was tucking her into bed. Instead of sleeping in the middle of her twin bed, she made a point of setting up her pillows, stuffed toys, and blanket off to one side.

"Aren't you worried about falling out of bed?" I asked.

Again, with a weary look that she would later perfect as a teenager, she said, "This is where Grandma Ann sleeps."

I'm certain the hairs on the back of my neck plumped up like gooseflesh.

"But you've never met Grandma Ann," I said.

My wife's mother died four years before my youngest daughter was born.

"Yes I have," she said. "We met in heaven."

Coming from an older child, I might have blamed this on a vivid imagination, attention seeking, inappropriate channel surfing on the TV, or the rehearsed lines of a practical joke. But Emily was so young and she seemed so innocent, so sincere.

Only when a dog trainer came to the house to teach our Jack Russell terrier, Sophie, some tricks (or was it the other way round?) did we have an explanation (of sorts) for this unsettling phenomenon. I remember the guy clearly—late forties, transparent skin, baby-bird features, wispy hair of the postchemotherapy patient. Despite his frailty he was upbeat about his remission from leukemia. He worked with Sophie for about an hour, happy to have my daughter join him in the session. As he was leaving he told me he was a practicing Buddhist, but as I braced for the literature and awkward invitation to join him and his friends for coffee, he said, "Emily's a messenger. You need to listen to her."

Sadly, my understanding of Buddhism was restricted to shaved heads, orange monk suits, a reluctance to kill creepy crawlies, and the concept of reincarnation. I asked for clarification.

"Sometimes children get caught between two lives. They can remember their past. They may or may not be able to verbalize what they remember but for most of them that do, this window into their past closes by the time they are about four years old."

We never saw the cancer-survivor dog trainer again. I don't remember why exactly, because all of us liked him very much. Perhaps it was Sophie's fault for being too smart, too easy to train. Not that it mattered. What he said was absolutely true. Well, at least the closing window part. From time to time Emily would regale us with snippets of information that seemed as disturbing as they were impossible to contrive, and shortly after she blew out four candles on a birthday cake, her echoes from a past life faded away and were gone, forever.

I know what you're thinking—not exactly proof of a great hereafter—but please, bear with me. Leaning back in a comfy chair, hypnotized by Helen's X-rays, I realized this trip down memory lane was not a quest for definitive answers. I was just hoping to unearth some kind of vindication for my pact with Sandi. And again, I found a connection through my daughter.

Although Emily entered our world as a beautiful blue-eyed blond, her outward perfection was belied by her DNA. In an unwitting roll of the hereditary dice, my wife and I had beaten the one-in-four odds of a crafty Austrian monk by the name of Mendel, and passed on a defective pair of recessive genes. Our invisible, enduring gift to our daughter would be the number-one genetic killer of children and young adults, a disease called cystic fibrosis, or CF.

I won't go into the details of bringing up a child with a chronic disease for which there is no cure, apart from saying that such an experience has a funny way of changing your outlook on both life and death. As I stated earlier, in my opinion none of us are spared suffering of some description. Perhaps suffering is simply part of the plan. We might flail and thrash, cry out for help, make a lot of noise and smother anyone who comes to our rescue, but ultimately our choice to survive our personal form of suffering must come from within. Briefly, during my own battle, I considered quitting veterinary medicine. How could I justify working on pets when my own child needed me to find a cure? I should go back to school, become an MD, a researcher, and make a real difference in her life. Though the chaos and fear never subsides entirely, eventually I had a breakthrough. They call it *acceptance*, and with it came an appreciation of how lucky I was, how blessed simply to have this child in my life.

There's something to be said for the certainty of death and our absolute incapacity to control when our number will come up. Despite the prospect of a bony grim reaper finger tap-tapping on your shoulder at any time, it seems as though we only appreciate the dogma of living every day as though it were our last when our doctor drops his eyes and shakes his head. It doesn't have to be this way. For me, it took a sick child to make me recognize the fragility of life and the need to enjoy the moment and to live in it, until the desire to squeeze all the joy out of it becomes overwhelming and, with a lot of effort, even possible. I believe Sandi Rasmussen found this kind of joy in Cleo. Of course it's simply not possible or healthy to live every day as though it were your last. We'd go out of our minds, permanently tortured in some sort of hellish wonderland at the bottom of a rabbit hole, striving toward a goal guaranteed for failure. But Sandi found a compromise, able to relish and bask in every wonderful memory of her little dog, and in doing so, even given the relatively short amount of time they had together, she realized how lucky she was. Somehow Cleo cast her spell and also managed to squeeze in a little wisdom and a whole lot of loyalty. Regardless of when or how we lose them, our pets are with us for such a short period of time. Through my daughter, I came to find a renewed empathy for my clients, the "pet parents" whose fear of losing a loved one is no less heartfelt than mine. Sometimes I think this lesson helps me connect with people in ways that would have been unattainable before Emily.

Constant reminders of the possibility of loss can leave you vulnerable to the notion of what lies beyond the logistics of physiological death. And what's so bad about that? If it gives me comfort to believe in a spiritual afterlife then so be it. I promise to keep it to myself, no one's going to bill me for wasting my own time, and I seriously doubt that one day I will find myself standing alone in that silent black abyss, ridiculed by a James Earl Jones voice-over for being such a misguided loser. Why not extend the same courtesy to pet owners? Should the animals in our lives be any different? Think about your own pets, the ones who are no longer with you, and the ease with which you can conjure up their presence. They linger in our memories with remarkable clarity. Nearly forty years later I can still see my first dog, a formidable German shepherd named Patch, accidentally released into our backyard, chasing down a bunch of my childhood friends like he was tracking down escaped convicts. I call his name and he's turning to face me now, right now I can clearly see him, ignoring thrilled kindergarten screams, his enormous pink tongue flopping out the side of his mouth, offering me a look that says, "What? I'm just funning with them."

Then there's my first cat, Reginald, a tough ear-torn barn cat adopted as a stray. Reggie never backed down from a fight. It didn't matter if you were a Pomeranian or a Great Dane, he would shock his hair, arch his spine, and stand his ground. Right now, a decade after his death, I can still feel the weight of him as I pulled him out from his favorite shelf in the linen closet, still feel the barbs of his scratchy licks across the back of my hand, see the contentment in his closed eyes, his body warmed by a carefully selected band of sunlight, empty paws making muffins as he slept. How can these animals from so long ago be so close, so tangible in our minds, so able to vividly conjure all the sensations of what it meant to have them in my life? Perhaps it goes back to the purity of our relationships with our pets. What is shared is plain and simple, uncomplicated by disapproval, resentment, or conflict. Their attributes remain clear and easy to retrieve and can be relied upon just the same after they are gone. How far away can our pets be if they are with us faster than a pickup on the first ring? Sometimes they are so close they may as well be calling us.

Having come this far, exposed and candid, perhaps I can find sanctuary behind one incontestable truth pervading operating rooms across the country—the reality of everyday miracles. From time to time the inexplicable and the impossible happen. Behind a paper mask and under artificial lights I get to perform surgery on an unconscious body, the physical part of what we think of as a pet. Essentially I'm working construction. I'm the guy splicing wires, welding pipes, shoring up support beams, and generally renovating the house. All the other stuff, the important stuff, I cannot influence. These are the intangibles, the memories, the history, the bonds, the things that make the difference between a house and a home, the things that make the difference between a body covered in scales or feathers or fur and our pet. It is this everything else that eludes me. This everything else is the spirit of the animal. Under anesthesia, it might move out for a while, but when the surgery is done and the gas turned off, it comes back. In our worst-case scenario, regardless of whether it returns or not, it doesn't cease to exist. Anesthesia is just a training run for the soul.

In relative terms, I could argue that Sandi Rasmussen's request was actually quite pedestrian in comparison to that of a client I met several years ago, a fellow I shall call Mr. Prestone. Mr. Prestone was forcibly dragged into my examination room by his sturdy Akita, Phoenix, in the manner of a fabled Saint Bernard from the Austrian Alps on a life-or-death rescue mission. Having delivered his master at the appropriate destination, the dog glanced my way, calculated that I was as worthless as an empty food bowl, and found a perfect patch of cool flooring on which to lie down. Subjectively Phoenix appeared to be a picture of health, unlike his master, for Mr. Prestone was a young man prematurely aged by his weight, tired eyes lost in socket shadows and hound-dog cheeks hiding behind a lackluster attempt at facial fur. He was probably in his early twenties but I felt certain that he had not been carded in a bar for some time.

After introductions I rummaged with my paperwork, trying to glimpse the name of the referring veterinary hospital and the reason for this consultation. But no practice was listed and the dog's problem described only as "second opinion." Such a vague justification for our meeting was most unusual.

"So, I see here that Phoenix is nine years old. He looks great. What seems to be the problem?"

Mr. Prestone sucked back an enormous breath and let it out through his nostrils.

"Nothing," he said, a smile seeping into the corners of his lips, as he obviously savored my confusion. "At least, not until he's dead."

I nodded, trying to act casual, forcing a trite "uh-huh."

"Do you think he is going to die? Is that why you are here?" I said realizing too late that each word had come out loud and well spaced, as though I might be trying to grab the attention of someone in the waiting room who could rescue me.

He blinked several times and leaned forward as if to confide.

"I need the expertise of a surgeon when the time comes to put Phoenix to sleep."

I assured him that, flattered as I was by his thinking of me, technically any veterinarian could perform the procedure.

My response garnered another snappy sniff and forced exhalation.

"I'm talking about cryonics," he said, a tetchy edge creeping into his words. "I imagined, incorrectly it seems, that you would be sensitive to the timing and requisite needs of this delicate procedure."

Involuntarily muscles around my eyes must have betrayed confusion or trepidation. Mr. Prestone pressed on.

"See, I need a surgeon who can be on call 24/7 as the time

approaches, available to perform the act of euthanasia, flush the vascular system with heparin, and initiate the cooling process prior to exsanguination and the administration of cryoprotectant solution."

I looked over at Phoenix sleeping at his master's feet. I looked around the room hunting for the hidden camera. Nothing. Mr. Prestone was still talking, rambling on about details beyond my understanding—neuropreservation versus whole body, nanotechnology, vitrification, and ice crystal formation. It was obvious that he had done his research and was prepared to invest tens of thousands of dollars in the possibility that Phoenix could rise from the frozen tundra at some point in the distant and, in my opinion, extremely remote and scary future.

Now I understood his reason for being here, this second opinion: Dr. First Opinion had probably run from him screaming.

Yes, this was a most unusual end-of-life discussion, but still, diplomacy and respect were in order. I assured him that when Phoenix died our hospital staff would do their utmost to accommodate his wishes within the realms of safe and ethical medical practice.

But I still found one question irresistible.

"Mr. Prestone. Pardon me, but why?"

I was rewarded with a grin. Perhaps he was relieved that someone had finally taken the time to ask the obvious.

"Because I am going to be cryonically preserved myself. I want to come back, and if I have a future after my death, I want it to be with Phoenix. If I'm riding this lifeboat into the future, there had best be room for my dog."

His grin was contagious. He would get no argument from me.

THE beeping pager on my hip finally shattered the introspection—a liquid crystal summons to surgery for my next case. I returned Helen's X-rays to their folder and headed over to the prep area, where my patient lay ready and waiting. I put on a pair of sterile surgical gloves and sidled into position. I couldn't help but notice that both of my colleagues appeared to have been injured, making me wonder about the savagery of this particular beast.

"What's his name?" I asked, looking down upon this architect of mayhem.

"Pikachu," said the technician, adjusting the face mask feeding anesthesia and oxygen into a ferocious snout.

"And how much does he weigh?"

No one answered, the technician all business, shaving a patch of fur, hunting for a heartbeat with a goopy Doppler probe.

"Fifty-nine grams," said Dr. Hurley, the intern on the case after consulting her record. "But don't let his size fool you."

She held up her hand, the tips of her index and fourth fingers crudely wrapped in Band-Aids, blood seeping beyond their sticky margins. The technician joined in with her own pair, worn like the matching rings of people inducted into some kind of clandestine society.

"Perhaps it's time to put a 'caution, will bite' warning in his record," I said, draping off the back leg of this demon masquerading as a little white mouse. "How many people has he bitten?"

"Five," said the technician, speaking over the amplified whoop-whoop heart sounds reminiscent of a Chinook helicopter banking over Saigon. "He's a sneaky little bugger. Sucks you in, all cute and twitchy and before you know it, bang, he's feasting on your fingertip."

I was only half listening now, concentrating on my bit of micro-surgery. Unbeknownst to his owner, Pikachu had broken both bones in his shin, severing the delicate blood supply to his foot. All the tissue below the break was dead, black, and shrunken. My mission was to remove the dead tissue, clean up the wound, and get out as fast as possible.

As I was placing the last of my impossibly fine stitches, I said, "What's this I hear about a paralyzed tree frog?"

I glanced up at the technician, caught her smile, and went straight back to my needle. I was referring to a bizarre rumor swirling around the hospital, a rumor I had caught in snippets and one that deserved my attention.

"What have you heard?" she said, and I didn't need to look up to know she was enjoying her advantage.

"Can I have some skin glue, please?"

Dr. Hurley disappeared in search of sterile glue. Leaving stitches in the skin of rodents is asking for trouble. Talented incisors will have them out and your work ruined as soon as they wake up.

"Someone told me one of your clients wears a tree frog in her cleavage?"

"It's true," she said. "Right here." She slapped a palm against the V of her scrub top. "A young girl, acts like and dresses like Paris Hilton, but instead of a Chihuahua or a Yorkshire terrier she prefers to accessorize with an aqua-blue tree frog."

I dug deep for a look that said, "Doesn't everybody!"

"The poor thing was acting all floppy on its back legs. She wanted to know if it had been poisoned."

I know nothing about pet frogs but I was curious why the owner would leap to this conclusion.

"Amphibians easily absorb chemicals through their skin," said the tech, "and when we found out how she likes to show him off in public, poisoning seemed like the most likely cause."

"Poisoning," I said. "From what?"

The technician nodded, fighting to keep a straight face.

"Victoria's Secret Breast Firming Cream."

Her delivery was perfect, her pause just long enough for me to see the connection.

Dr. Hurley reappeared with my bottle of skin glue.

"The owner confessed to recently using this particular product in an attempt to enhance the contours of her cleavage. Naturally we wanted to find out exactly what chemicals give this magical cream its firming powers and that's when we hit a wall, the hospital's Internet firewall. For some reason the IT department didn't believe us when we told them we needed to surf the Web pages of a popular lingerie company in search of potential toxins."

I placed a few blue drops on the skin edges and pinched them together, extricating myself from Pikachu and this medical-grade Super Glue before I became his first postoperative snack.

I was about to selflessly volunteer my services for the greater good of cleavage-riding tree frogs everywhere by thoroughly researching the hazardous Victoria's Secret Web site, when Dr. Able appeared at my side.

"Have a chance to look at your schedule?" he asked. "Squeeze in my spaniel with the lung mass?"

I tried to remember what was lined up over the next few days but now that I had made up my mind it no longer seemed to matter. Any inconvenience would be mine because I needed to make this happen.

"Were you planning a CAT scan first?"

"I wish," he said, "but the owner just wants us to go get it if we can."

I paused, wondering if this would come back to bite me on the bottom, and said, "Tell Helen's owner I'll do the surgery."

"Great. But when?"

"Tomorrow," I said. "Let's do this first thing tomorrow morning."

My meeting with Helen the following morning only affirmed my decision to expose her to Cleo's magic. She was in a holding cage outside the anesthetic induction area and after checking the labeled band around her neck to confirm her identity, I made my introduction. The first thing that struck me was her independent spirit. Sure, I got a friendly little tail wag but there was no submissive roll over and pee. She was clearly not the kind of dog willing to flirt indiscriminately.

In fact she seemed distracted, like someone you meet at a party who abruptly ends a conversation as soon as someone more important comes along. I imagined that someone more important was the person who dropped her off—Eileen.

Though it may seem like a strange confession, I was also pleased by her physical imperfections. Like a cheeky street urchin, she had something of the Artful Dodger about her—the literal "warts and all" texture to her skin, the chartreuse barnacles of dental plaque, the heady bouquet of old sneakers wafting from her ears—which only served to enhance her appeal, her vital authenticity. It further fueled my affection for Helen's owner, making me respect her motivation even more. This had to be true love.

But as I listened to her heart and lungs with my stethoscope, I began to imagine what some people might think about my mission. Not surprisingly, there will be those who claim I was simply airbrushing my guilt for what had happened to Cleo, that I was finding a solution in order to realize a conviction. And maybe they were right. We all want to feel better about our mistakes. However, now that I was about to take Helen into the bright, sterile world of surgery, it wasn't my commitment or determination that gave me pause, it was the spiritual basis of the promise that made me uneasy. I mean, aren't miraculous clinical outcomes the kind of phenomena usually unmasked in retrospect, with hindsight and a vivid imagination, by joining dots, seeing patterns, and discovering a bigger picture? I didn't want this endeavor to feel too forced, too contrived. I hardly knew Cleo. It wasn't as though I had much to draw upon. Could I involve Cleo in a prayer I might chant over Helen's sleeping body? Would that do the trick?

Part of me wished I had something belonging to Cleo with me, like a collar or even a rabies tag, something I could leave in the breast pocket of my scrubs while I performed Helen's surgery. Years ago a client called Mr. Hartman gave me a cheap religious figurine, supposedly a replica of St. Sergius, the Russian patron saint of animals. I was supposed to take it with me into surgery as a good-luck charm while I worked on his sick dog, a remarkable German shepherd named Sage. Against the odds, Sage pulled through, and though I can't be sure how much was due to the preternatural powers of a plastic statue (to this day I remain convinced that it was actually a miniature statue of St. Francis of Assisi), St. Sergius has been my secret copilot on several tricky missions. Although his pointy plastic right hind is sharp and uncomfortable, poking my skin when I am mummified inside my sterile surgical gown, at least I am aware of his physical presence with me in surgery. If Cleo was to be my talisman for Helen's surgery, how would I know she was there?

ALONE at the scrub sink, working the antiseptic froth, I decided to think about the Cleo I had met and the Cleo I went on to hear about from Sandi. I tried to imagine the dog in her stories, the one who comforted a sick child at an airport, the one who befriended a frightened sheltie at a doggy day care. It didn't feel like much of anything, hardly enough to get a sense of her let alone to summon her spirit, but it was all I had and, best of all, this retrospective didn't leave me feeling like a fraud.

As soon as I stepped away from the laser beam, the hollow patter of water on stainless-steel sinks came to an end, the silence ushering in a new phase in the proceedings. By the time I walked through the swinging doors into the OR, dripping hands and arms held out and up in front of me like I was about to show off my robot dance moves, I was all the way back with Helen. I was thinking positive thoughts— "surgical resection questionable" turning out to be "surgical resection easier than anticipated." Like most surgeons, I don't get a pep talk from a fired-up coach, so I usually rely on optimism. If I didn't think there was every chance I could get this tumor out, believe me, I wouldn't even have tried.

From here on out, if my memories of Cleo and all she embodied chose to follow me, they would have to do so without help from me. I had a commitment to a spaniel in surgical suite seven, the one lying with her right side down on the table, the entire left side of her rib cage shaved, iodine brown, bracing for the opening slice of my scalpel.

15   TOUGH CALL

THORACIC surgery necessitates a major violation of basic physiology. Break the airtight seal of the chest and the lungs fail to expand, meaning you breathe for your patient or your patient doesn't breathe. Like the rhythmic background noise in a Jacques Cousteau underwater documentary, the audible hiss and sigh of a ventilator had to accompany me throughout the nitty-gritty of Helen's difficult procedure.

First, I counted her ribs. Unlike humans, who have twelve, dogs possess thirteen ribs, and knowing which is which is critical. Based on a correct identification, the surgeon will commit to opening a specific window into the chest. Pick the right window and you get the prize—great view, easy access, simple surgery. Pick the wrong window and you pay the price—restricted view, limited access, difficult surgery. It's the difference between a free ticket for a private balcony or a seat in the nosebleed section.

Here Helen proved to be less than helpful. Her baby backs were a little too fatty for my liking. My gloved fingers had hoped to find the discrete bony bars of her ribcage, not a series of questionable undulations. My latex fingers puppet walked forward from number thirteen, walked backward from number one. I did it once more to be sure. I pressed scalpel to skin between ribs five and six.

"Cutting," I said, informing the anesthesia technician that the show was about to begin, forging a six-inch rent down and into the chest cavity. Looking like a medieval torture device, a stainless-steel rib retractor was squeezed into the fissure I had created, its metallic dazzle dancing in my eyes.

The leading edge of an adjacent lung lobe licked the opening like a salacious, foamy pink tongue before slithering out of sight, and for a second I wondered if I had selected the wrong window. Then I got a glimpse of what lay beneath, an apple-sized mass bobbing in a purple bruise of deflated lung. Despite my optimal location I instantly recognized my dilemma. The treasure was big, cumbersome, and buried deep. Its rhythm was all wrong, ignoring the easy to and fro of the mechanical ventilator, preferring to dance to the faster beat of the heart and great vessels.

If ever there was a time for Cleo to have crossed my mind, this was it, as my fingers probed the very essence of this animal—her heart. My professionalism required complete mental focus on the task at hand, but I have no doubt that my subconscious was pursuing its own agenda, detouring through a maze of conversations and promises and images that conspired to buoy me through the difficult task ahead. While there was no conscious act, there was an awareness, something vague and unfocused, lost in the details of more pressing matters, and this was fine by me. If something remarkable was going to happen, it would never be conceived in premeditated thought. Like I said, we can't make the dots appear, we can only choose to connect them with hindsight. Fate is a retrospective gift.

Most likely my thoughts were overshadowed by a hankering for a smaller hand size or a larger breed of patient. This was going to be tight—one-handed bomb disposal down a rabbit hole. This close to a beating heart, cutting the wrong connection or failing to cut it clean could be fatal.

"I'll take a TA stapler with two V3 cartridges, if you please."

If my request for a stapler made you think about your office Swingline then you're not far off the mark. TA stands for "thoraco-abdominal," and in a manner similar to punching a metal clip through two sheets of paper, this particular stapling device fires three rows of staggered sterile titanium clips across the base of living tissue. With a single and enormously satisfying squeeze of a trigger, its tiny staples compress and seal arteries, veins, and small airways, demarcating a border between what can be safely left behind and what needs to be cut out. However, all my attempts to position the device exposed my single biggest fear--the tumor extended from the very origin of the lung, the root of the large cartilaginous airways and the even larger blood vessels. If this wasn't inoperable, it was pretty damn close.

Cancer surgery is more than all or nothing. Taking the tumor alone is not enough. The surgeon demands a margin of normal healthy tissue beyond the visible limits of the tumor, just in case the sneaky little bastard decides to extend its microscopic reach. For Helen, here was my biggest problem. Sneaking just one extra centimeter of margin would have compromised the major vessels carrying blood back to the heart. It wasn't a viable option.

Minutes of surgical indecision passed as I tried to make the call. Perhaps the best way I can describe what I was feeling is to think of the surgeon as a mountaineer, caught in bad weather on the way to the summit. I may have come a long way but up to this point I really haven't achieved anything. *I* might be fine, but by pressing forward I am putting the only other member of my team at serious risk. Turn back or keep going. Succumb to resignation and failure or embrace the one certainty that brought us to this point—the need for success. As I wavered over Helen's beating heart I believe I made the right decision, in other words, one that I could live with.

"I'll take some suture material, please."

The technician's paper mask failed to conceal her confusion, laced with a hint of disappointment. I smiled back, seeing where she had gone wrong.

"No, no, I'm not quitting, I'm not closing. I just need to go old school. Half these vessels are the size of a porky index finger. I'm hoping that if I can tie a few of them off by hand, it might give me enough space to squeeze in the stapler."

I risked one more crank on the rib spreader, trying to get as much room for my hands as I dared, fearing I might break a rib by going too far. But the crack of a fracture never came and I set to work, forceps teasing through tissue planes, nudged by the heart, jostled by the lungs, passing suture and cinching down knots. Tie, cut, and do it again, and again, and suddenly the tumor was becoming undone, mobile, and to my way of thinking, vulnerable. I went back to the TA stapler and this time there was enough of a gap for me to squeeze it into normal-looking tissue, fire my staples, and be rid of this thing once and for all.

With the tumor out of the chest I pressed the release mechanism on the device and the pretty little staple line bounced free. No arterial spurt. No red gusher. There was one more test to perform.

"Can I get a couple of liters of sterile saline, please?"

Here, the premise behind my surgical technique is identical to that of a cyclist trying to repair the rubber inner tube of a flat tire. Pour enough warm fluid into the chest to fill it with liquid and submerge the lungs. Wait as the ventilator moves air in and out of the lungs. Observe the staple line for a stream of leaking silver bubbles. I watched and I waited. No bubbles. No bubbles means no leaks, means a perfect, airtight repair.

I placed a chest tube to evacuate the residual air and blocked some nerves adjacent to my incision with local anesthetic, and then this time I really did begin to close.

Stitch by stitch, layer by layer, Helen's heart receded from view and disappeared. Once she was all zipped up, I placed a comfortable bandage around her chest, gave her a final pat on the head, and she was gone, shipped off to recovery and from there to critical care, destined to go on a happy drug bender for the next few hours. And why not? She had earned it. Under anesthesia Helen had never skipped a beat, literally, her heart rate maintaining a steady rhythm, her blood pressure more in keeping with that of a two-year-old than a teenager. A little indulgence and pampering at Angell's famous Spa Narcotica would do her a world of good.

This left me alone with the enemy, drowned and lifeless, pickling in its toxic vat of formalin. I held the transparent plastic container up to the light, rotated it back and forth in my hand, and studied the tumor. I liked what I saw. To my naked eye, the margin looked good, the tumor removed in its entirety. But almost as soon as I acknowledged my optimism, I became doubtful, fearing professional complacency. Sometimes the cure is a done deal but this was not one of those times. As I always tell my clients, my eyes are not microscopes. I forced myself to rein in the celebrations until the final written report came back from the pathologists. And as I watched Helen disappearing on a gurney I was forced to wonder whether the dead creature in my hand was destined to have the last laugh.

| 16 | **THE BOTTOM LINE** |

WHENEVER I watch animals recover from a major surgery I am struck by their tolerance of what must be a terrifying awakening—trapped in the now, unable to anticipate the benefits of what they must endure. You might think the panic and disorientation would be overwhelming, akin to waking up in a cheap hotel room with blood on the sheets, a gash next to your spine, and only one kidney. Yet, for the most part, our pets edge their way back into a familiar world of human touch and soothing words. We can console, even though we cannot explain. Chemicals may alleviate the pain, but we still rely upon our most fundamental and effective method of communication with our animals, our presence and physical attentiveness to their needs.

Helen's recovery went well. She didn't vocalize, flail, or fight. Though her hearing was shot, she could still register the hands stroking her head, tucking her into a blanket, getting her body temperature back into the normal range. Within minutes of her return to full consciousness she was riding a gurney from the recovery area to her new home in the critical care unit.

Unlike hospitalized children, hospitalized pets are not the lucky beneficiaries of mechanically operated beds, a neck-straining television bolted to the ceiling, bad chocolate pudding, and inopportune visits by scary clowns. Somehow they still manage to thrive as they recover from our interventions. Helen was no exception. She remained under Dr. Able's care and every time I checked in on her she was making remarkable and speedy progress. There was nothing frail or distressed about our ragamuffin spaniel. Though her compact pod in critical care afforded her space to lie down and move around freely, she was often to be found standing at the door to her cage. She would give me a cursory once-over with her eyes as I approached, but I was still the recipient of a curt wiggle of her tail rather than an exuberant wag, as though she were bound more by convention than genuine affection for the man who had reached into her chest and plucked a tumor away from her heart. She sensed my good intentions but I never got the impression she needed to be friends. Ours was a strictly professional relationship and I could understand why. With our greeting over, she would return to checking out the scene, a convict pacing nervously behind the bars, as though waiting for her moment to ask "Do I get out of here today? Did someone post bail?"

Helen's chest tube was removed the day after surgery. She was going for walks unassisted. A good appetite and drinking on her own meant that her catheter and intravenous fluids could also be discontinued. Her tether to the hospital was stretching and fraying one filament at a time until, just two days after the surgery, it snapped, and she was free to go home, receiving no more special care in the hospital than she could receive from Eileen and Ben. For all the talent of our nursing staff, we know when we are beat, unable to compete with the healing power of familiar surroundings, unwavering attention, and unconditional love.

THE power of Helen's recuperative prowess was intoxicating. How many of us would be trotting out of the hospital so soon after major thoracic surgery? It wasn't as though we were strapped for spare beds, cutting costs and corners by turning over cases as fast as we dared. Helen was home because she was feeling good and I wanted to believe that this was partly because the tumor was gone. So what if I was a victim of overconfidence and no small measure of hope? Sometimes this job has more than its fair share of bad news. Why not allow myself to bask in the simplicity and humanity of Eileen's dream for this dog? I had tried to create the impossible and wanted to believe I succeeded.

Carried along by this wave of optimism, I carved out some time to finally share the news with Sandi. I decided to write her a letter, to tell her about Helen and about Eileen's motivation for the surgery. Of course there was a hidden agenda to my urgency. In part, it was prompted by a fear of things going wrong. Helen was making a fabulous recovery but what if things changed? Surely it was better to capture the feel-good factor while it was still strong? And if I'm being honest, there was also an element of catharsis, the relief of dispatching a written version of events and fulfilling my obligation. I wasn't sure how much good it would do, but I had made a promise to a woman who wanted to give back when all she held dear had been taken from her.

Alone in my office, I sat in front of my computer, opened a new file in Microsoft Word, and tried to imagine the spaniel's first trip to the beach. I've never been to Prince Edward Island and I have never seen Helen together with Didi the Newfoundland, but thanks to Google Earth and to having met both dogs separately, I believed I had a pretty good idea of how this might play out. Naturally I pictured a balmy summer evening and generic golden sand, west-facing dunes and gentle breakers—their reward for the sixteen-hour car ride from Massachusetts.

Didi, the veteran summer beach bum, would be in an expectant frenzy as soon as she caught her first whiff of briny Nova Scotia air. The car pulls over, the passenger door swings open, and Didi is gone, a bouncing ebullient shadow on a mission, never looking back once to see if her adopted sister is in the chase.

Helen remains on her blanket on the backseat, the breeze rustling her hair, and she is trembling. Perhaps it has all been too much, this final leg of her final journey, but Eileen comes around, scoops her up, and lowers her to the ground. Helen's elbows and knees lock in stubborn extension, turning her into a canine piñata. Her paws slowly sink into the sand as she maintains her defiant rigidity, head pointed out to sea, carefully aligned so as to make watching Didi's aquatic antics unavoidable.

At first nothing happens. Space, big sky, and the simplicity of horizontal lines appear to overwhelm Helen. But then, off in the distance, Didi breaks free of the surf and prances in her direction, dropping down on her front legs, delighting in taunting her. Lip-reading is not necessary. Even at this range there is no mistaking the mischief in Didi's big brown eyes.

Helen sniffs the air between them, raising her nose, hoping to catch a scent or hoping to appear aloof. Eventually she loosens up, giving her body a good shake all over before setting off at a slow, indifferent walk.

Didi holds her ground, thrilled to have a showdown. She shimmies left, fakes right, maintaining eye contact, neck outstretched, her bark deep and booming, until the gap between them shrinks to a couple of yards of paw-print-laden sand and Helen comes to a stop on the precipice of the lapping surf.

Maybe she's afraid of the water? Maybe she's afraid of the black monster lurking in its depths? No matter, because Didi reads her hesitation and all the meaning in how far her little sister has come and she knows she must act. The gentle giant wades back into the shallows, close enough to offer a quieter word of encouragement, close enough to put Helen in the splash zone as she shakes herself down and unleashes a tropical downpour. And just as Didi hoped, the little black cocker spaniel takes her cue and with a short retaliatory bark, leaps into warm foam for the first time ever.

I huffed and smiled to myself. Why shouldn't it end like that—dusk on a secluded beach on PEI, a filthy, abandoned, insecure little dog getting the chance to play in the sea and sand. I could believe in it. I could slap on my rose-colored glasses and make Helen's future look pretty sweet because Eileen's hope for her dog was that simple. And shouldn't the best dreams be kept simple if they are to stand any chance of coming true?

SUDDENLY the glare from the monitor snapped me out of my reverie, and I realized its brightness was caused by the relative darkness of the room, an angry thunderhead overwhelming the daylight outside my window. Electrically charged and roiling heavens prepared to unload their wrath on downtown Boston. April showers becoming April monsoon—welcome to the unpredictable joys of New England weather. I turned back to my desk and as I did a message popped up in the bottom righthand corner of the computer screen. It was a Microsoft Outlook announcement—Helen's pathology report was in my e-mail in-box.

Hand to mouse, mouse to icon, double-click, double-click, window expanding to fill the screen, I took in the report, eyes scrolling faster than my hand, my mind playing catch-up as I read the language of pathologist-speak.

. . . partially encapsulated neoplasm . . .

Translation: "Yes, it's a tumor!"

The mitotic index is highly variable . . .

Translation: "Don't tell me you've forgotten basic pathology! 'Highly variable' means indiscriminate and unpredictable, two of the trademarks of a malignant tumor." (Mitotic index is a measure of the rate at which cells are dividing. The higher the index, the more rapid the division, the more aggressive the tumor.)

The tumor is locally extensively necrotic . . .

Translation: "Your dog's tumor had gotten so big, so greedy, it had outgrown its own blood supply and parts of it were starting to die." I couldn't stand it anymore. I scrolled down to the end.

"Diagnosis: Left caudal lung lobe—papillary adenocarcinoma of bronchoalveolar origin."

Translation: lung cancer.

No surprise here. However, the last sentence of the entire report hit me like a sucker punch to the gut:

"Comment: The malignant tumor extends to the margins of the surgical excision at the level of the hilus, thus complete surgical excision of the neoplasm cannot be confirmed."

I read it again—the words of a detached pathologist reminding me of my fallibility.

. . . cannot be confirmed.

Translation: "You didn't get it all. You came close and you might have thought you did, but you didn't. Your margin was at best questionable, at worst, contaminated with cancer. I'm happy to give you the diagnosis. Too bad about the cure."

Of course there was nothing mean spirited in the report itself. This was me twisting the sentiment, interpreting the abrupt and cold, but necessary, addendum as the authoritative proclamation of what felt like failure. I rocked back in my chair, letting the weight of my head snap my neck, and sighed. Close but no cigar. Was it going to be enough? Could I justify all that I had put Helen through? If tumor cells remained, how long before they grew back? Would there be time to fulfill Eileen's dream? Could I have done something more, something different, something better, to have stood a chance of getting every last cancer cell out of Helen's body?

The "letting down" thing became contagious. Not only was there Helen and Eileen to consider, but, by association, also Cleo and Sandi. Of course I recognized the stupidity of my naive and selfish desire for a happy ending, but I couldn't help feeling like this had been my shot at some measure of redemption and I had missed. Helen's had been a unique, challenging, and laudable case, and best of all, she had found me, not the other way round. But suddenly I saw how ridiculous and self-serving this venture had been, my conceit ruined by a pathologist's conclusion. How could the spirit of a dead dog become my talisman? Who did I think I was? It had taken the objectivity of written truth—dependable, scientific, and entirely void of emotion—to bring me back. So obvious now, the way I had fashioned a fairy tale. Driven by guilt and vanity. I had searched for salvation, and all that remained was the unfairness of Helen's cancer and the certainty of Cleo's tragic death.

I knew that inside another digitized envelope, inside another computer in another part of the hospital, there was another copy of Helen's pathology report, waiting to be read by Dr. Able. He was, after all, the primary clinician on the case and as such, normal protocol would require him to make the difficult phone call to Eileen, to inform her of the diagnosis of cancer and the likelihood that tumor cells had been left behind. He would be the one fielding the "whys" and the "why nots," the "how long?" and the "when will we know?" But why should he? It wasn't his fault, it was mine. Dr. Able wasn't even there. They say, "Don't do the crime if you can't do the time." Who was more responsible than me for Eileen's inevitable questions? Even though I didn't have all the answers, at that moment I felt like the least I could do was to be the one to field them.

I found Eileen's contact numbers from the computer record, picked up my phone, and decided to try her cell.

"Hello."

Only one word, but it came out fast, with unmistakable stress, and as I made my introduction I could hear the beat of windshield wipers trying to keep up with the steady booming percussion of rain on glass. I imagined her trapped inside her vehicle, caught in the storm that had eclipsed my office, only she was in the torrential downpour phase, cell phone squeezed between a shoulder and an ear, white knuckles on the steering wheel, negotiating rush-hour traffic and pooled floodwater on the highway. This was hardly the time to receive bad news.

"Did the biopsy come back?" she said.

Hanging up or claiming the call got dropped didn't seem right. And so I told her. I told her Helen had lung cancer and I read the pathologist's final comment verbatim.

"What does that mean, 'cannot be confirmed'?" she said.

"To me it means there's a good chance I left microscopic tumor behind."

After a pause she said, "Okay," sounding anything but.

I kept going, veering away from technical excuses, apologizing for my failure, insisting she call me anytime if she had more questions, if there was anything more I could do.

Throughout our conversation, Eileen kept her responses abbreviated, interspersing the occasional "uh-huh," "I see," "right," and "okay." Much later she would apologize to me for sounding dismissive and unmoved by my news. She had been petrified, juggling the call with horrendous driving conditions. In fact, my interpretation of her response was anything but indifference. The panic I'd heard in her voice made sense, laced as it was with the kind of flat tenor born of prophecy, of having braced for this confirmation for some time.

When I hung up I felt empty and restless and angry at my self-pity. Any sense of relief at having done what I had to do was tarnished by a feeling of deceit, as though I had taken advantage of her distraction, delivered my lines, fulfilled my obligation, and gotten off too lightly. I had decided not to mention Cleo and my assignment from Sandi. This hadn't seemed like the time to tell her. Thinking about what might happen to Helen over the next few months made me wonder if there would ever be a good time.

Surgery isn't meant to be like a game of weekend T-ball. There are no trophies for participation. Not every case will be a winner and it was time to get over my pathetic validation issues. And so I thought about what would have happened to Helen if Eileen had not come along. The lung cancer would have borne down on her just the same. Would the chef and wait staff at the restaurant have noticed her absence? Would she have slowed down, running no longer an option as her lung capacity rapidly declined, reduced to a trot, easy pickings for a hungry coyote, vulnerable to a speeding car, clipped as she misjudged how fast to cross the highway? Would anyone have noticed her niggling cough, her disinterest in food, how much weight she was losing? Would anyone even have noticed when she never came home?

Perspective changes nothing and changes everything. Half full or half empty, take your pick. It's like one of those optical illusions, the ones where there are two pictures in one, teasing your perception, asking whether you see the young girl or the old hag. It was time to adjust the light, squint a little, and choose the right perspective. There was still much to celebrate.

I called down to surgery.

"How are we doing with my golden?"

"She's just got back from radiology," said Jez, one of the anesthesia supervisors, "and about to get her epidural."

"Great," I said, hanging up, grateful for all that copious golden fur and the certainly that I had at least twenty minutes before my next patient was inside the OR.

There probably wasn't enough time but I knew it was the right moment to get back to my letter to Sandi. I pulled up Cleo's file on the computer and straightaway I saw that I had a problem. There was only one contact name and address—Sonja Rasmussen, Sandi's daughter living in Bermuda. I had forgotten to get her mother's address in Canada. I would have to ask Sonja to forward the letter to her mother. I hoped this would not be problem.

In part I wrote,

My encounter with your family proved to be an extremely moving and profound moment in my career. I was in awe of your mother's composure, compassion, and love for Cleo.

And with regard to Helen and Eileen,

Here was an animal finally having a chance at a good life with an owner who truly cared and wanted to give her the possibility to live what time she had to the fullest. Here was a dog who Cleo would have befriended, a dog she would have helped come out of her shell.

I made a point of sharing Eileen's beach dream for Helen (though I spared her my version of the event) and then finished with

Thanks again, for all I have learned from a little dog that, sadly, I hardly knew.

I could have worked on it some more, fluffed it up a bit, but sometimes stream of consciousness feels right. The biopsy report had brought me back into the real world of veterinary medicine, denying me the certainty of a cancer-free fairy-tale ending. Who knew what lay ahead for Helen, but I did my best to fulfill my promise to Cleo and I could only hope that even if it wasn't good enough to save Helen, it would be good enough to bring Sandi some measure of comfort and closure.

I printed it out, signed it, and stuffed it in an envelope. I took it down to the mail room knowing it would be on its way before day's end.

17 | WAITING GAME

NEW England meteorologists love to throw out their overworked truism "if you don't like the weather around here, wait a minute." The same could be said of veterinary medicine, and thank goodness for that because it doesn't matter if you're riding success or rebounding from failure, pets will keep walking through the front door in need of a doctor who can put aside his or her ego and grapple with what counts—making a sick animal feel better again.

In the year following Cleo's death and my attempt to surgically cure Helen, cases came and went, but two in particular caught me off guard, receptive in a way I might not have been before.

I am often intrigued by the coupling between pet and human. What was it about this particular cat? Why a mouse and not a gerbil? What did this puppy do that stopped you in your tracks and made you say, "Come home with me"? Unlike choosing a human partner, pet owners aren't usually set up by well-meaning friends. They haven't filled out a detailed online survey that ascertains compatibility. Rather, they rely on instant attraction and trust a gut feeling, an intangible instinct that more often than not ends up being exactly right. This fundamental connection, this palpable dynamic is usually obvious, but when Blue, a neutered nine-year-old husky mix and his owner, Mary Pizzachino, walked into my examination room, I realized the limitations of my superficial assessment of their or any other human–animal bond.

Some degree of mutual love and affection was a given, though Blue had that whole chilly arctic reception thing going for him—big sighs of indifference, content to lie down, cross paws, and pretend to sleep so he didn't have to engage the guy trying to wrestle with his bum knee. And all the while, Mary was animated and effusive, drawling over Blue with her strong Missouri accent.

"I've had him since he was five, rescued from an abusive home by a female police officer here in Boston. She was moving apartments and couldn't keep him so my boyfriend, Danny, brought him home."

This made sense to me. Mary and Blue seemed like a bit of an odd couple because Blue was actually the boyfriend's dog. Mary was carefully put together—obviously a regular at an Estée Lauder makeup counter, meticulously coiffed hair—whereas Blue was more of a Nascar addict, NFL tailgating kind of guy's dog. My mind was jumping ahead to "Why didn't Danny come to this appointment? Has he disappeared and left you to look after his dog?" I kept these questions to myself and focused on discussing the torn cruciate ligament in Blue's right knee.

"So what will he be able to do when he recovers from the surgery?" Mary asked, suddenly all business.

"Well, I'm hopeful Blue will be able to run and play and go for walks and be pain free."

Mary huffed and said, "I don't care so much about any of that crap, what I need to know is will he be able to jump on my bed?"

Not exactly a typical demand about my postoperative expectations. Occasionally owners are looking to get their dogs back into flyball, agility training, field trial work, or cadaver rescue. This was the first time my goal was to get my patient back into bed.

"I'd say yes, I'm hopeful that Blue will be able to jump into

bed . . ." The relief in her eyes stopped me from adding "with you."
Her smile cracked and then she let me have it.

"See, Danny died." The words came out and then she laughed, defending against the tears poised to ruin her mascara. "I was with
him for eighteen years. He was Danny's dog, but Danny knew I stole
Blue's heart as much as Blue stole mine. This dog hasn't just
changed my life, this dog *saved* my life."

Her voice began to falter as she added, "Blue is my last connection
to him. If this dog ever dies I die."

She let the statement hang between us, making sure I felt its
intensity.

"You have to understand, I am the last person in the world who
needed a dog." Suddenly the bravado was back in her voice. "I mean
I was one heartless bitch before Blue. There'd be girls at work crying
'cause their stupid dog was sick and I'd be all 'get over it and get back
to work' or I'd go over to my girlfriend's house and there'd be piles of
dog hair all over the place and I'd say, 'How d'you live in all this shit?'
And now look at me, wearing black pants, covered in white fur, and
lovin' it! You have dogs yourself?"

"Yeah, I have a Labrador and a Jack Russell terrier."

She shook her head, getting down on the floor with Blue.

"I mean, just look at that face. Isn't it perfect?"

Blue's tail found a rhythm as they found each other's eyes. I nodded because of course it was true. The owner is always right when it
comes to the innate beauty of a pet.

"It must be tough for you," she said, stifling her smile, "having to
live with inferior dogs! Poor Dr. Trout."

And Blue managed to regard me with a pitying look as though he
too was genuinely sorry.

"I mean I've not taken jobs for this dog because I won't leave him
alone all day. He sleeps in a blanket I bought him from Harrods of
London. And you don't even need to tell me how much this knee surgery is going to cost because I'll give up my retirement, get a second

mortgage, sell my car, do whatever it takes, whatever it costs, to make him happy."

I nodded, feeling Mary taking her read on me. She had felt compelled to put that out there like a test, to see how receptive I was to their needs.

"So I'm guessing Danny and Blue had a pretty special bond together?"

"No shit," she said, "a good friend of ours still comes by to walk Blue and he does it because he feels like Danny is walking with them."

With the consultation over and a date scheduled for surgery, I showed Mary and Blue back to the reception area to check out. Mary turned to me and said, "Tell me, what's your first name?"

"Nick," I said. "I mean Nicholas, but the only person who gets to call me Nicholas is my mother, and then only when she is angry at me."

"Then I will call you Nicky," she said, gaving me a hug, and she and Blue were on their way.

Let me make it clear, as I have to Mary on many occasions, the name "Nicky" does not work for me. She is the only client who gets to use this name and she does it to make me laugh and rile me up. I tolerate it for only one reason—it reminds me that I passed her test, that I didn't question her motives, and that I understood how certain connections between animals and humans are priceless.

BEFORE I get to the second case during this, my year of provocative thinking, I have to pose a big question—what's with chocolate Labradors? Okay, so I should preface my mischievous reservation with a declaration of love for the breed as a whole, plenty of experience living with the breed, and current ownership of the breed (my daughter wanted yellow, seconded by my wife as a preferable color to blend in with our couch). Perhaps a better question would be, where do chocolate Labs hide their stash of speed? Are the names Java and Mocha chosen because of color or caffeine content? When do these dogs calm down enough to merit the relatively tranquil label "hyperactive"?

Don't get me wrong, I am not a Labrador racist, but clearly I am not alone in my opinion that these dogs tend toward—how shall I put it best?—exuberance. I distinctly remember a five-year-old female chocolate Lab named Sonny who presented to me with a long-standing lameness problem. From the moment I met her I knew other sinister forces were at play. She sat quietly by her owner's side while I took her history. Her examination was not accompanied by frantic panting, relentless squirming, or vociferous barking. She was calm, cooperative, and perfectly polite.

"Is she always this well behaved?" I asked, trying not to appear rude.

"Yes," said Sonny's owner. "She's definitely become quieter over the past six months. I thought it might have something to do with her lameness."

My point is Sonny did not appear to be unwell, she appeared to be normal, and this observation of canine normalcy for this particular type of dog made me suspicious that she was actually far from normal. I decided to test her for hypothyroidism, a disease causing a deficiency of thyroid hormone that can make dogs appear sluggish and prone to packing on the pounds (sadly not a universal excuse for Labs). It turned out Sonny's thyroid levels were through the floor, hardly registering in her blood. Fortunately I was able to cure her lameness and provide a daily pill to correct her hormonal imbalance, restoring her to the kind of full-fledged chocolate recalcitrance we all know and love.

And if you still don't believe me, consider this observation from a lifelong lover of chocolate Labs. When he brought in his fourteen-year-old dog for an airway evaluation, I couldn't help but comment about the puppylike chaos that unfolded in my examination room.

"I thought you said he was fourteen?"

The owner considered me with a "d'you get out much?" glare.

"He is," he said. "If you think this is crazy, you should have met my last chocolate. He made it to sixteen and I swear he didn't slow down until three months after he was dead!"

But I digress. The case I need to discuss concerns a chocolate Lab named Theo, a dog proud to conform to what I jokingly consider to be his breed's stereotype—and I'll try to be politically correct here—curious, vibrant, talkative, and happy. Theo's owner, Frances Cardullo, however, could not have been more different. She had me from the moment we shook hands, a handshake that stopped me in my tracks, a handshake that told me, "There are things you think you know, things you might suspect, but listen to my story because you know nothing about what I fear."

I took note of her hands, which were too big, the nail polish enhancing, even affirming, their masculinity. I noticed her voice was too deep, a tendency toward a breathy whisper unable to mask the baritone muscle in her vocal cords. I saw the contour of her neck, the wattle of loose skin hanging from the gallows of her Adam's apple all wrong, as was the pale shadowing across her powdered cheeks. But mainly what I absorbed was the coerced smile, driven into sallow cheeks by sincerity and the willpower to override her pain.

I suspected this woman's life had been a battle but that she had found a measure of happiness, contentment, and unconditional love from the dog leaving paw prints across my freshly laundered shirt. I would like to point out that I fully appreciated my role in our triangular relationship. I have been commissioned to attend to the animal's health, not to profile, psychoanalyze, or, worse still, second-guess the owner's private life, but what concerned me most as I shook Frances Cardullo's hand was the aura of dread and fear hanging in the air around her. I could sense she had much to share, not because she needed a shoulder to cry on but because it was integral to what mattered most, the future well-being of her beloved Lab.

I began by gesturing to my examination room, letting Frances be guided by Theo. Unfortunately her frailty and his excitement were a dangerous combination. Frances was painfully thin, pale skin shrink-wrapped around her neck and the bones of her sternum, like that of an aging movie star determined to contend for leading roles. She probably weighed about the same as Theo but was no match for his strength as he acted like the lead dog in the Iditarod.

"Let me take him," I said to her relief, thankful for the braking action of my rubber soles on linoleum to slow him down.

Once in the room, I gestured for Frances to have a seat.

"I'll take his leash off," I said. "Let him wander around."

By "wander" I usually mean "let the dog have a casual roam about, get used to the strange smells, and start to relax." Theo's interpretation was more along the lines of an Olympic gymnast performing floor exercises, compelled to cover every possible square inch of space while demonstrating his gift for tumbles, jumps, and leaps. Just in case we weren't paying attention, he decided to add in his own soundtrack.

"Theo! Stop it! Be a good boy, Theo! I'm sorry," said Frances and every few seconds Theo would break his routine and circle back to her, aligning his head with her bony fingers, offering a cautious, healing lick to the tributary of bruised veins beyond the knuckles of her hand, meeting her eyes with the look of a guilty boy who knew what it would take to melt her heart and get away with murder.

They were like a comedy duo: Theo was the funny guy—loud, up front, in-your-face—playing it for every laugh he could get, whereas Frances was—and I dare say it because I know she would not be offended—the straight guy, apologetic, working her rueful brows as if she had any to work, keeping a smile at bay.

Between barks Theo sniffed the air, his neck extended, flaring his nostrils, and I could tell that he knew I had some dog treats to hand, invisible from his low vantage point, but emitting just enough of a fragrance for him to sense an opportunity to eat.

"I think he can smell my low-cal dog treats," I said. "Can he have one?"

I know, I know, this tactic will have the trainers and behaviorists shaking their heads in dismay. Oral bribery will only reinforce bad manners but if I was going to find out what was wrong with Theo, I needed to be able to hear Frances talk. Besides, my little bone-shaped treats are so tasteless, I knew exactly how this trick would play out. Theo bit the treat in two and worked it around his mouth for a moment before letting it fall to the floor, covered in saliva but essentially untouched. (Only my own Labrador will devour these dry, unpalatable morsels but then she would find the lint from the inside of my pocket to be mighty tasty!) Discovering the only food on offer inedible, Theo decided to quietly focus on sniffing the floor, my shoes, my socks, my pants, and back to the floor again. Frances saw an opportunity to tell her story.

"Theo has a tumor in his chest. He's had a CAT scan and a biopsy taken and I'm led to believe that there's a good chance that it's benign, that it can be successfully treated by surgery alone."

I noticed how the fear in her reedy voice seemed disproportionate to the words she was saying.

"I've seen the images from the scan," I said, "and I've seen the biopsy report. Theo has what is called a thymoma, a benign glandular tumor, and with any luck, if it hasn't invaded the surrounding tissues, he'll do great with surgery. And even if it is invasive, Theo should still have a good long-term outcome."

For a second I thought I saw her acknowledge my attempt at optimism, but any hint of gratitude was quickly overwhelmed by something resembling a physical ache, written on her face. She drew her clasped hands into her body, making me feel as though my statement had only made matters worse.

Frances Cardullo hung her head and then came back to me with an uneasy, affected smile that cut me like a razor.

"Life is meant to be full of surprises," she said, her delivery flat. "But no one said whether they would be pleasant or not." She waited a beat, thought about it, and added, "I'm battling stage four colon cancer, stage four meaning it has already spread to several other organs in my abdomen."

"I'm so sorry," I said, feeling the absurdity and futility of my polite response.

Frances kept going, as though she didn't want to linger on any awkwardness I might be feeling. I took note of her concern and it only made what followed all the more difficult.

"I came here today to talk about the surgery, to find out what will happen to Theo during his hospital stay and what I will have to do to care for him afterwards. But more importantly, I need to share two major concerns that worry me more than anything else about Theo."

"Sure," I said, noting how Theo had finally tired of sniffing the room for other mammalian life forms, contraband, or explosives and settled at Frances's feet.

"First of all I will need to organize all of this around *my* chemotherapy. They're going to be pumping me full of chemicals for the next ten months, so I'll let you know my schedule and we'll do this so that with luck he's home recovering during some of my good days."

I reassured her that I thought we could make the schedule work and that Theo would make a great patient, certain to bounce back, with that buoyant, no-nonsense optimism so characteristic of his breed. I didn't push for the second problem. The slow welling up and overflow of a single tear from her left eye let me know she was about to tell me in her own time.

"My other fear is what will happen to him when I am gone. I know he's a handful and he's not for everyone, but he's a great dog and I love him. Who will be there to look after him?"

I didn't know what to say. Most pet owners fear the end of their relationship with an animal, the letting go and the acceptance of loss.
Frances Cardullo's candor and foresight left me speechless. This
woman had the presence of mind and more than enough love to see
beyond her own mortality, able to understand that in all likelihood
she would be outlived by her dog. She made her own needs seem relatively trivial next to Theo's long-term security and happiness.

Parents frequently proclaim their children will be the death of
them. Do they mean more than the frustration and challenges of
guiding them to adulthood? Or are they really referring to the pain
they might inflict, the desolation they will leave in their wake, if they
are lost before their time? As the parent of a sick child, I would say
yes. But of course, the reverse is also true. The idea that I might leave
my daughter in this world, that she might need my help, that I might
fail to protect her is just as excruciating to consider, and I saw that
exact same fear trapped inside Frances when it came to caring
for Theo.

"Don't worry," I said, beckoning to Theo, rewarded with a sloppy
grin and a body slam from across the room, "if laughter is the best
medicine I have a feeling that you two are going to be together for a
long time to come."

Frances succumbed to a smile and once again, from out of
nowhere, I was being reminded of Sandi Rasmussen, another woman
blessed with clarity in the midst of so much pain. Do we need these
dark hours to discover who we really are? For those open to discovery, is it possible that in every crisis, every struggle or tragedy,
another truth exists? Perhaps the only real challenge is whether or
not we have what it takes to acknowledge this truth and speak it
out loud.

AND that's how the next twelve months went by, memories of Cleo
and Helen paying me a visit, usually when I least expected it. For

Cleo, it might have been a minor anesthetic hiccup with one of my cases, some David Blaine dog who found it amusing to temporarily hold his breath. The topic of anesthetic risk kept finding its way into my preoperative discussions with my clients, and though Cleo had so much more to offer, I began to fear that this might be her greatest legacy. Her mark was a scar guaranteed to last a professional lifetime. Though it was beginning to fade, I recognized that I still felt the need to show it off.

For Helen, the flashback might have flickered when a lung tumor popped out of a dog's chest like a jack-in-the-box, clean margins an absolute certainty. And then, every so often, when the pathologist patted me on the back with those magic words "excision complete," I could see that refugee spaniel and wondered what became of her.

I had thought my letter to Sonja Rasmussen and her mother, Sandi, might garner a reply. But as the months passed without further correspondence, I decided they were probably trying to get over their ordeal, and distancing themselves from me was probably good medicine.

When it came to Helen my approach was completely different. To be honest, my philosophy was more along the lines of "don't go looking under rocks if you are afraid of what you might find!" Eileen never called me back after I called her with the pathology report, and so I took the easy way out, capitulating to the adage "no news is good news." I could have picked up the phone. And it wasn't that I didn't think about it. I simply chose not to place the call. The summer, Helen's beach summer, had come and gone. I clung to the belief that she must have made it, had her moment in the sun and the sand. Then again, there had been no postcard. No photograph documenting this incredible accomplishment. Wouldn't Eileen have shared the celebration if it had actually happened?

Then, one Saturday afternoon, more than a year after I operated on Helen, everything changed. My appointments over, the operating rooms uncharacteristically empty and silent, I was ready to call it a day, but Dr. Fisk had other ideas.

"What do you think of these?" she said, accosting me in the surgical prep area, presenting me with a series of chest X-rays.

I held them up to the overhead fluorescent strip lighting, unsure as to what I was looking for.

"Do I get to hear a story or is that part of the challenge?"

Dr. Fisk, one of nine critical care residents on staff, grinned, clearly enjoying her advantage. I don't know how these young emergency doctors do it. Hooked on the buzz of fast-paced medicine, addicted to the everyday life-and-death tug-of-war, they constantly deal with people and pets at their worst. More often than not, their clients are in a state of shock, unprepared emotionally and financially for a crisis involving those essential nonhuman members of their family. Arguably, emergency medicine offers the most chances to actually save an animal's life and sadly, at the same time, the most chances to be the recipient of harsh words and complaints from owners unable to handle or to afford an emergency affecting their pet. Despite this inescapable yin and yang, Dr. Fisk defied the gloomy gray of her department's scrubs with a contagious excitement for what she did so well.

"He's a four-month-old male boxer puppy. Presented half an hour ago in severe respiratory distress. Check out his trachea."

I did as I was told, moving through the series of films and back again, seeing the abnormality with the surprise of a head-turning double take.

"It's an acorn," she said. "Or at least I think it is."

The boxer's name was Tyson and like most puppies, he embodied all the pleasures and foibles of any four-month-old dog. He was fawn with instant curb appeal drawing curious onlookers; a clumsy, adorable flirt, effortlessly charming his entourage. He did, however, possess that most dangerous trait common to all of puppydom—relentless curiosity. Sometimes smart dogs like boxers discover their environment in a relatively harmless lesson of action and consequence. Wayward backyard toads may be fun to play with, but they make my mouth all foamy and I want to throw up (though my five-year-old Labrador has been held back in remedial amphibious studies). That brown stuff that fell out of my bottom doesn't taste nearly as good as the little brown nuggets of kibble sitting in my dog bowl (unfortunately, from time to time, my Labrador will still graze the lawn looking for "seconds"). Occasionally, however, an unlucky puppy can fall victim to a small, forgettable, seemingly innocuous object, and as they say back in England, "come a cropper."

For Tyson it started with a sudden-onset hacking cough, a visit to his local vet, and an X-ray confirming the presence of a round object about the diameter of a dime stuck in his trachea. Under anesthesia a thin, flexible endoscope was snaked down the widest part of his windpipe, fiber-optic images revealing a pink cartilaginous tunnel trailing off into darkness, the intruder nowhere to be found. However, when they passed the scope down his esophagus, the camera popped into his stomach, and up on the video monitor, nestled in a corrugated pink lining, lay half a dozen acorns.

It was assumed that young Tyson had managed to cough up the straggler and swallowed it whole so it could join its nutty siblings for a short burst of gastric indigestion. Temporarily, the cough appeared to improve, but twenty-four hours later, Tyson was rushed into the Angell ER foaming at the mouth, his tongue and lips a stormy blue, his head and neck stretched out in full extension, hungering for air.

Dr. Fisk narrated this story while I continued to stare at the X-rays, nodding my appreciation of her theory as to why the previous vet had been fooled. The acorn had to have been acting like a ball valve. The X-rays were snapshots in time, one showing the object fired halfway down the neck in a cannonball cough, another taken while it was sucked deep inside the chest to a point called the carina, the anatomical location where the trachea separates into the smaller branches that supply each individual lung. When the acorn rattled around in the wide bore of the neck it would be irritating and induce a mild cough, but Tyson would be able to breathe around it. Lodged in the narrow carina, the obstruction would prove devastating, inducing suffocation, panic, and a coughing frenzy. Presumably the vet had been unable or reluctant to root so far down the trachea and besides, the evidence in the stomach suggested the acorn had already found an alternative route back to terra firma.

"Makes sense to me," I said. "Not that it makes it any easier to get out."

"What do you mean?" she said, obviously slighted by my pessimism. "I figured we could just grab it."

I flashed back to a previous experience with an object trapped in a trachea. When I was a veterinary student, we had a case of a three-year-old German shepherd who was performing retrieval exercises when he aspirated a six-inch-long metal wrench. Fortunately the wrench was removed, and the dog made a full and uneventful recovery and was working again within two weeks. What astounded me was the use of a wrench as a training aid, and the ability of a dog to generate enough physical force to inhale such a weighty metal object into his chest.

Regardless of the offending object, these can be particularly difficult cases. Under anesthesia, even with a tube in the airway, it can be impossible for the patient to breathe if something is obstructing the carina. Oxygen simply cannot get to the lungs.

"I hope you're right," I said, pretending to walk away.

"Whoa! Whoa! You'll be around to help us, right?"

I handed her X-rays back.

"Of course," I said and I watched her expression of consternation melt away as she registered my smile. "I'll be in my office doing paperwork. Just give me a call." But mischief got the better of me, and over my shoulder I couldn't help but add, "Assuming you need me."

Less than an hour later I got the call requesting my presence in radiology and as soon as I arrived I noticed the presence of an ominous addition to the assembled anesthetic equipment. Off to one side of Tyson, amid all the various monitoring devices, sat what is universally referred to as a "crash cart." It was like a big, mobile Sears toolbox teeming full of drugs to be used in the event of a cardiac or respiratory arrest. Clearly someone had seen fit to have the crash cart near at hand and that could only mean things were not going well.

There was no "told you so" moment, no pleasure in being right. The concern written all over Dr. Fisk's face informed me the adrenaline junky had enjoyed her fix but now she was ready to come down.

"This case is a royal pain in my ass," she said.

"The scope was too much?" I said.

Dr. Fisk nodded.

"It was one more thing jamming up his airway. Poor guy was blue enough when we started, let alone when we tried to grab the fruits of the forest. That acorn is one slippery little fella, and you just don't have time to grab it before his oxygen saturation levels begin to plummet to dangerously low levels."

I glanced over at the pulse oximeter monitor. In room air most humans would register 98 to 100 percent. Right then, on pure oxygen, young Tyson was hovering around 82 percent. His color was awful. No wonder the crash cart was waiting in the wings.

Then I noticed the unorthodox configuration of the tubing arching from the anesthetic machine to the dog. Normally the tube would enter directly through the mouth. Tyson's tube entered though his neck.

"So you moved on to a tracheostomy?" I said.

Once more Dr. Fisk nodded, the whites of her eyes inclined toward the heavens.

"I thought I was being quite clever. We took an X-ray which confirmed that the acorn was sitting slap bang in the middle of his neck—primo location. Instead of having a tube down his throat and into his airway, I said, why not put the tube directly into his trachea *below* the acorn. This way Tyson gets to breathe, the acorn can't go back down to the carina, and now we should be able to grab it easy."

My summons and Tyson's oxygen saturation level told me all I needed to know. Dr. Fisk handed over an X-ray for final confirmation. Yes, there was a tracheostomy tube in the appropriate location. Unfortunately, our wayward acorn had become trapped on its wrong side, now all but wedged into the carina.

"Do you think it's time to open his chest, to go in there and pull it out surgically?" asked Dr. Fisk.

I considered the logistics of what she was asking me to do. Technically, opening up the windpipe in the chest is relatively straightforward. The problem remained the delivery of adequate oxygen to Tyson's lungs. As soon as I cut a hole into the trachea to make a grab for the acorn, the biggest beneficiary of all those soporific anesthetic gases would be me. There was little chance that I would swoon into my incision but there was a good chance Tyson might succumb to fatal oxygen deprivation.

"I'd like to try one more thing," I said, as we all headed back to the nonsterile prep area in surgery.

It wasn't much of a plan but it was the only one that came to mind. Under anesthesia animals no longer possess a cough reflex, which meant the acorn's erratic movement back and forth in the windpipe had to have been driven by three primary forces—breathing in, breathing out, and gravity. If I could take advantage of these three forces, I might stand a chance of keeping this dog out of the OR.

"Let's get him lying on his sternum, head toward me."

Tyson was placed on a table that stood about waist height. Two strong women stood on either side of him as I dropped to my knees as though praying to the gods of the mighty oaks for divine intervention.

"You ready?"

They were, and on the count of three they hoisted Tyson's body and back legs into the air, head stretched out between his front feet like he was about to dive into a swimming pool. I pulled the tracheostomy tube out of his windpipe and introduced a pair of steel forceps into the opening left behind, forcing the serrated tips as wide open as they would go, waiting for that willful little acorn to "come to papa."

"Give him a tap on his chest," I said.

They began slapping either side of his rib cage, beating out a burst of hollow, resonant applause. This was when I expected something to fly into the waiting forceps sticking into his windpipe, but nothing happened.

"How about shaking him up a bit?"

The two of them looked at each other before synchronizing their contempt and aiming death glares at the presumptuous reprobate kneeling in front of them, the one happily giving out the orders, the one doing absolutely nothing while they carried all the puppy's dead weight between them. Consequently Tyson's jiggle was a little lackluster. I was hoping for a major upheaval, something akin to a full-blown grand mal seizure. What I received was more of a Jell-O wobble, a quiver, little more than a nervous twitch.

From my genuflected angle, I couldn't tell if their ruddy complexions and toothy grimaces signaled physical exertion or anger toward me. Shrewdly I opted not to criticize their efforts.

"His oxygen saturation is starting to fall," said Dr. Fisk. "He's dropped into the seventies."

I looked up at the monitor flashing scary numbers directly at me. 77 . . . 76 . . . 75.

Tyson wasn't breathing and his heart rate was beginning to slow.

And then, riding on the back of a bored schoolboy sigh, Tyson finally exhaled as though he meant it, and I sensed something had struck the tips of my instrument. Regardless of whether it was real or not I knew I had to stop. Tyson was in big trouble and I needed to replace his tracheostomy tube. Just in case, I squeezed the forceps together and felt them grab hold of something, which I plucked from the wound in a dramatic flourish. Uncertainty kept me from destroying the moment by proclaiming "voilà!" but even before I looked, the whoops and screams all around me told me what had happened. It wasn't Jack Horner's plum and it certainly wasn't Excalibur, but right then, I reckoned the fetid, slimy brown acorn in my hot little hand felt just as good.

Tyson was one of those cases veterinarians relish. His was the complete package—nothing magical, nothing heroic, just the right mix of drama, fear, instant gratification, and best of all, a certain if creative cure. The technicians and doctors who kept Tyson alive long enough for me to take my turn were the real talent in this case. I may have been the one who pulled out the acorn, but no one gives the kid in the stands who catches the ball the credit for hitting the home run.

Heady with success, I bounced upstairs to my office, intent on switching off my computer before taking off for the evening. Over the years I have learned to quietly bask in the clinical victories, however small, whenever they come my way, because the flip side, the daily struggle of medicine, lurks around every corner, whistling a bleak and insistent tune determined to worm its way inside your head. I figured Tyson would tide me over for quite a while, and that was why I was caught off balance when I saw it, a pop-up message from the hospital's communication center, my heart sinking before the words vanished from the screen, before they could crawl into my in-box and dare me, no, demand that I take a closer look. Finally, after more than a year of waiting, news about Helen had arrived.

"Eileen called. Says it's urgent. Needs you to call her back. ASAP!"

18	**THE RIGHT SIDE OF THE CURVE**

DIALED the number, nervously thinking this was like catching up with an old friend from high school, your association, your common ground, tied up in a brief period of history, trapped in a bygone era, outdated, disconcerting, and left behind for good reason. How could our conversation be anything but awkward? Too much time had passed. Any discussion at this point only served to highlight my apparent indifference to Helen's recovery.

To my surprise Eileen sounded upbeat, shocked by my prompt reply, not expecting a call back until Monday. It was all the push I needed. I resolved to hide the fear in my voice, step into the spotlight, face the demons in a critical audience of my own making. Finding an optimistic, almost nonchalant, tone, I asked, "So, how is Helen doing?"

I heard the tense I had used—"How *is* Helen doing"—pleased I had managed to speak in the present, making a show of hope and optimism.

"What?" said Eileen, obviously confused by my question.

The silent pause stretched between us, time enough for guilt to jump in, interpret her surprise as incredulity, the impossible notion

that I had not learned of Helen's demise, that I could be so insensi-
tive as to ask such a question about their beloved and deceased dog.

"No, no, no," she said, "you've got it wrong."

Wrong. Of course I got it wrong. I never got it right. I never got it
all, for starters. I left some of Helen's cancer behind. Too much and
just enough. Survival for four more months had been a pipe dream.
She would have been lucky to see the end of the spring let alone the
middle of summer. God, I hope she didn't suffer. I hope they did the
right thing and let her go with her dignity intact.

"This is about Didi," said Eileen.

Of course it is. Your Newfoundland—the other dog in the family.
But what about Helen, I wondered, even if I was also a little relieved
at the subject change.

"She's injured her opposite knee. Oh, and by the way, Helen's
doing great."

Sometimes I can be slow on the uptake, especially when the words
playing out in my ears contradict the certainty playing out in my
mind. I don't know how long the next pause lasted, but I do know it
was long enough to negate any attempt to hide my surprise, or my
relief. I didn't care, so I didn't even try.

"She is? That's wonderful. I mean that's incredible. I can't believe
it. I can't tell you how many times I've thought about her, and
what she went through, and the wonderful thing you were trying to
do for her. And to be honest, I was afraid to know how things
turned out."

Suddenly, my voice was in a hurry to catch up to real time, and I
heard myself rambling on like some schoolkid desperate to tell the
teacher his version of the story before his friends ratted him out with
the truth.

"Well, I can't say it's been easy," said Eileen. "But she's a remarkable dog."

"She's got to be," I said, and I couldn't have cared less that I
sounded all punchy and that I was drifting way off track from the

real purpose of this phone call. This was incredible. Helen was alive and well and she wasn't playing by anybody else's rules but her own. I heard the voice of the scientist in me wanting to pooh-pooh my promise to Sandi Rasmussen as the only reason Helen continued to thrive, seeing the claim as no better than one of those anecdotal advertising testimonials touting a veterinary product of dubious merit simply because "Mrs. Smith of La Jolla, California" said it worked wonders for her pet. But then the image of a boisterous Min Pin puppy popped into my head and my inner scientist was speechless.

And so, over the next twenty minutes, Eileen and I played catch-up, starting from the moment Helen left the hospital.

"I couldn't believe how fast she bounced back from your surgery. I picked her up and brought her home and she gave one little whimper when she was riding in the car, just the once, and that was it. And Didi was really sweet—very gentle and cautious around her, as if she understood what Helen must have been through."

Oftentimes other pets in a household can be less than sympathetic when one of their own is recuperating from an operation. That fresh incision cross-hatched by stitches or staples deserves more than a cursory sniff, and hey, with an Elizabethan collar impeding good grooming habits, it's the least they can do to offer complimentary lick-and-chew service. And what's with that big bald patch and bad comb-over job? What's with lying around all day? What's with all the attention? Isn't it time we caught up on a little roughhousing or are you going all soft on me?

"And I have to apologize," Eileen said, "for the phone call where you told me about the dirty margins, about leaving tumor cells behind. I didn't want you to think I was being indifferent. Truth be told I was just trying to stay alive. The rain was ridiculous and traffic was crazy and I couldn't believe I didn't get into a crash while I had you on the phone."

I reassured her I had thought no such thing, and she went on to tell me that my news persuaded them to go for two courses of chemotherapy, not least because Helen seemed to be doing so well.

"What a mistake," she said, but didn't linger. "Thankfully we got her teeth sorted out first. Dr. Able didn't want to risk the possibility of her getting an infection that originated in her mouth when her immune system was being knocked out by the chemo."

It made perfect sense to me. No amount of Listerine was going to defeat Helen's bevy of oral bacteria. But what went wrong with the chemotherapy?

"She had to lose a lot of teeth and so what if she had a crooked smile, she was doing great. So we started out with intravenous carbo-platin and I guess she did okay. But the doxorubicin . . . that was another story. It hit her really hard. She wouldn't eat. She would drink but she couldn't keep it down, throwing up over and over again. Eventually she fell over in her own pool of vomit and I didn't know whether she had lost her balance, fainted, or was having a seizure. I rushed her right back to Angell, where she stayed in the critical care unit for a week."

How had I not known about this? It must have happened when I was away on summer vacation, and for some reason, Dr. Able had failed to pass on this update during my absence. Maybe he had wanted to spare me the bad news, knowing full well how it feels to return to work, cheerful and revitalized, only to be crushed by a dis-passionate e-mail documenting the travails of one of your patients while you were relaxing in the sun.

I tried to imagine how much second-guessing played out between Eileen and her husband, Ben, during what must have been a long and difficult week in June. Their anguish at having agreed to poison their dog, for all the right reasons, but without the dog's understand-ing or consent. Dr. Able would have explained all the risks of chemo-therapy, the potential for complications, and reiterated that the odds of recalcitrant side effects were slim. Even so, and even though

Helen clearly pulled through and emerged on the other side, I could hear the remorse and distress in Eileen's every word.

"It was so hard to visit her, to see her constantly licking her lips from the nausea, and even though the chemo had stopped, its damage was already done. Her white blood-cell count plummeted and I know the nurses did a wonderful job of caring for her and keeping her clean, but I can still see the discoloration of the fur on the feet of her back legs from where it had been stained by her endless bouts with diarrhea."

The recollection caught Eileen in its net, and for a moment she was lost to me, swept away, dragged backwards through a painful quagmire of betrayal over her misguided enterprise. I couldn't deny her this introspection. In fact I would encourage all owners to take this journey *before* they send their pet into battle against a determined and despicable enemy. Consider the darkest hours if things go wrong, what you might be asking your animal to endure, and be aware and accepting of this possibility and how you might feel if they get dealt an ugly hand. If, for you, the rewards still outweigh the risks, then sleep easy at night, because regardless of the outcome you have made the right decision. But if you hesitate, remain uncertain, or uncomfortable with the potential for predictable remorse and heartbreak, then be the friend brave enough to intervene, to ward off denial and assure gentle mercy.

Helen had proved herself to be, and clearly still was, a fighter, a tough dog who made her own luck, scavenging for food, avoiding coyotes, cars, and freezing to death during the throes of a New England winter. After all she had been through she wasn't going to succumb to some chemically induced toxic conflict. She had surpassed her four months and so much more. Her summer had come and gone, and suddenly, though I realized I was ruining the chronology of Eileen's account, I had an overwhelming desire to find out how a dream about a sick spaniel playing on a beach up in Prince Edward Island finally turned into a reality.

OF course it was nothing like I had imagined.

"To be honest," I said, "I had this image of Didi bouncing around in the surf, goading Helen into taking her first dip in the ocean."

Eileen laughed, because what transpired was far less predictable and, as a result, far more wonderful.

"Didi happens to be one of the few members of her breed who refuses to swim," she said. "She might have the webbed feet and water-resistant coat, but she never goes in beyond her elbows and knees."

"So what happened?" I asked.

"Oh, Helen never really swam in the ocean. I guess I'd describe it as more of a civilized saltwater foot massage, whenever she felt like it."

Too funny, I thought. The only thing I had right was the only thing I could have guaranteed as soon as Helen crossed the Confederation Bridge from Nova Scotia to the island—the welling up of pride and wonder in Eileen and Ben at the accomplishment of a canine cancer survivor used to fighting for everything in her life. I didn't have to ask. I could hear it in Eileen's voice as she talked about their vacation. It didn't negate all the fears and the perpetual uncertainty and I imagine it never felt like vindication for the tough choices Eileen had to make. I'm certain the reward came packaged in that moment, shared liberally between them, all-consuming, humbling, and unforgettable.

In truth, my Hallmark version of Helen's happiness being so very wrong is one of the greatest pleasures I take in her achievement. How can any of us impose our version of happiness on others, let alone the animals in our lives? I asked Eileen if Helen had been happy playing on a beach for the first time, and as soon as the question got away from me, I realized it was futile. Can we take a reading from the canine wag-o-meter and determine a dog's degree of ecstasy? Do the volume and frequency of your cat's purrs crank up to eleven when she is approaching feline nirvana? Thankfully our pet's version of happiness exists in a one-of-a-kind language, something far more subtle than what we read about in books on animal communication, something explored, cultivated, and gradually understood by those who take the time to learn. All they have to do is observe and they just know. It might have been clear from a certain look from Helen's upturned eyes, the intensity in her concentration during her hours of crab herding, the ferocity of her newfound appetite, or the ease with which she slept, utterly exhausted every night. However she managed to convey her message, it was obvious Eileen and Ben saw it, over and over again, as plain as if Helen herself had written "having a wonderful time" on a tacky tourist postcard.

I COULD try to make excuses for what came next, claim I got caught up in a moment of euphoria, the romantic in me shirking objectivity and scientific reason, but I felt compelled to share what I had kept to myself for all this time.

"I have a confession to make," I said, rewarded with a predictable moment of silence signaling Eileen's confusion or unease at being privy to some awkward, unanticipated declaration. "I need to tell you about a little miniature pinscher called Cleo and her owner, Sandi, and where they fit into my version of Helen's success story."

I hadn't confided in Eileen sooner because, well, to be honest, it felt ridiculous, even unprofessional, asserting that the spirit of a deceased dog somehow played a part in Helen's extended survival. There had always been something appealing in Cleo's role, if you could call it that, as a secret benefactor, working her magic from afar, generous and anonymous. But as I heard Eileen's good news, part of me understood Cleo and Sandi deserved some of the credit for how well everything had turned out. Regardless of whether or not you believe they had any influence on the course of Helen's disease, one thing is for certain, they had a profound influence on me when I set about fighting it.

Eileen listened attentively, a kindred spirit, instantly bonding to a mother, a daughter, and a dog lost to tragedy. She got it, like I knew she would, because, like Sandi, Eileen has also been cursed and blessed by an affinity for stray animals, animals who need her help. Two women, two dogs, one life ending as another was allowed to begin. A painful symmetry between strangers whose lives unwittingly entwined to become a testament to the power of letting go and the possibility of a better future.

In this new era of cancer treatment, we hesitate to use the word *cured* (perhaps for fear of jinxing ourselves). We are confused by the word *remission* because how can we be keeping cancer at bay if the disease appears to have gone away and we are no longer pursuing treatment? That leaves us with the concept of cancer as a chronic disease we need to manage over what time remains. This makes the "big C" sound more like bladder stones, eczema, or constipation. It is *time* that is the crucial variable here. In humans we used to think of five years in remission as a cure. In dogs and cats, especially teenage dogs and cats, five years might not be within their grasp even if they are perfectly healthy. I am not an oncology specialist, but sometimes when I discuss expected survival times for certain canine cancers with owners, I find it helpful to consider the future in *dog years*. Relative to their life expectancies, an extra dog year of quality living might equate to seven years cancer free for you or me. Of course this is hardly scientific, but, for some people, thinking in these terms can be helpful. Once upon a time the options for an animal succumbing to cancer were pretty much limited to a fatal overdose of a barbiturate. The owner had the comfort of knowing he or she had sought treatment, but veterinary medicine offered little more than an alleviation of pain and suffering through humane euthanasia. In the twenty-first century, veterinarians have smacked the ball deep into the pet owner's court, bombarding him or her with detailed medical information, a huge variety of therapeutic alternatives, and, not least, the fiscal challenge of how to pay for it. Maybe, when faced with the inevitable and tough decisions in your pet's health care, the vagaries of survival, and what you and I may think of as relatively small packets of time, a consideration of longevity in terms of animal years might not seem so ridiculous. And bear in mind, with all our advances, fifteen is the new eleven for dogs and twenty-two is the new fifteen for cats!

Not long after my conversation with Eileen, I hit the hospital library, trying to get a handle on the magnitude of Helen's achievement. The scientist in me had a flashback to high school statistics, could see a bell-shaped curve on a graph, the one in which the majority, the average, stand in the middle, leaving smaller numbers of individual stragglers on either side. How far was Helen hanging out to the right side of the curve? After all, cancer is an accomplished and perverse killer. Clearly Helen had dodged a quick, vicious attack, and based on Eileen's description, she did not appear to be the victim of a slow torture, taking its time and savoring an inexorable demise. Helen was beating all the odds, but she was still vulnerable to what some consider a most disturbing and heartbreaking assailant—cancer as a faceless assassin who catches you off guard, with your defenses down, stepping out of the shadows when you least expect him.

Wading through textbooks and scientific journals, given the particulars of Helen's case, I concluded that Dr. Able's estimate of four months had been reasonable, doable, that eight months might be a stretch but not implausible, and that twelve months deserved a little more credit than merely remarkable and might even be working its way toward the loaded "M" word—*miracle*. By now, Helen had been alive for well over a year.

Scientific indoctrination makes most medical professionals reluctant to describe a clinical outcome as a miracle. It feels theatrical, affected, even conceited. As I perused my pile of data, I imagined it would be possible to decipher the minutiae and language of Helen's pathology report, trace the line of the appropriate Kaplan-Meier survival curve, calculate her percentile in terms of disease-free interval, and manage to come up with a perfectly logical explanation for why she was still alive. And then I stepped back from the numbers and charts and dry, detached statistics and thought about a filthy, foul-smelling black spaniel greeting a stranger in a parking lot on a cold November night—a dog harboring a cancer, a stranger who would do whatever it took to give an innocent animal a shot at life. Following Helen's journey from then to now, with everything in between, it is hard not to be staggered by her change in fortune and those who brought it to bear.

I closed the books and pushed the papers aside, smiling, the sentimental part of my brain telling me to lighten up, to live in the moment, demanding I surrender to the spirit of victory. Helen's story may be as good a candidate as any for the term *miracle*. And besides, if I may bastardize the words of the legendary writer Cormac McCarthy, "If it ain't, it will do until another one comes along."

19 EVERYTHING IS CONNECTED

FOR better or for worse, thinking about Helen inevitably and appropriately led me straight back to Cleo, and given this unexpected and marvelous update, I was eager to share Eileen's news with Sandi Rasmussen and her family.

Over a year had passed since I wrote to Sandi via her daughter Sonja, who lived on the island of Bermuda. During that time I had received no response. I had suspected that they were not ready to revisit the wounds, had moved on, but surely they would welcome this amazing news.

For over two weeks I waited patiently for a reply, happy to impugn the inadequacies and tardiness of international snail mail until my second letter to the Rasmussens sailed all the way back into my mailbox at work, branded with the discouraging label "Return to Sender, Address Unknown."

Puzzled and a little perturbed I went back to the computer record and managed to discover Sonja's work phone number. Calling her during office hours, stirring up what were still likely to be painful memories in the presence of her colleagues, was less than ideal, but remembering my promise to her mother, believing there might be a measure of comfort in my news and left with no alternative, I dialed the number.

The dial tone gave way to an automated phone system at an insurance company (no surprise there, given Bermuda's prowess in the business). I was guided to a staff directory based on the first three letters of the last name and I punched in R-A-S.

"I'm sorry. We are unable to locate an employee by that name."

"Hum," I thought. "I wonder if she's using her maiden name or married name."

Though my disappointment was offset by the charm of the preset British accent, managing to make my dismissal sound polite but authoritative, I dialed again and bided my time until I could speak directly to a company operator, who informed me I should call back on Friday, after four thirty local time, and speak to a supervisor. This I did, only to be informed that Sonja Rasmussen no longer worked for their company and had left no forwarding address.

Running into this brick wall was a double whammy. Not only was I unable to get in touch with Sandi, but now there was an even greater probability that my first letter, fulfilling my promise to report on a deserving case, missed its mark, my silence interpreted as a dismissal. For days, whenever I had a spare moment between cases, I went online, hunting for leads, trying to track down mother or daughter, coming up confused and empty-handed.

In the end I printed out Cleo's entire medical record. Thankfully it included the paperwork put through our financial department, and there, scratched in curly female cursive, I discovered Sonja had provided an e-mail address.

I didn't hold out much hope. People change their e-mail addresses all the time. If she was no longer living in Bermuda there was a good chance she had changed her Internet provider. And this was when a troubling thought crossed my mind. What might have prompted Sonja to leave Bermuda in the first place? Did this have anything to do with the death of Cleo?

I copied and pasted this second letter into the body of an e-mail, added an apology that once again I was directing this communication to Sonja and not her mother, Sandi, and hit "Send."

IT ALL happened so fast—I arrived at work the next morning to find replies in my in-box and messages on my voice mail. There was a time when sadness and trepidation might have given me pause before picking up a phone and calling Sandi Rasmussen, but not now, not with what I wanted to share. And there was something else that made it easier, woven into her written and spoken words, sentiments that touched and pained my heart—delight and gratitude.

"I've written you so many letters and never mailed them," said Sandi. "You have no idea how much impact you had on all our lives."

"Oh, God," I thought. "This can't be good."

"I will never forget the day I walked out of your hospital, how much I ached for Cleo, how much I appreciated our time together, that you hadn't rushed me, that you were genuinely interested in what I had to say. You remember Sonja, my daughter?"

"Of course."

"I love her with all my heart, but she and I have always had a tough relationship."

Sandi touched on her childhood, her emotional estrangement with her mother, her emotional fulfillment through the animals in her life.

"It's taken me a long time to realize that Sonja is not like me. She never will be. She never should be. And the only reason I finally came to this understanding was through Cleo. I'm sorry, do you have time to hear this?"

"Please," I said, and even though she was calling me from thousands of miles away in Canada, I could remember and feel her aura, the resonance and power of her attitude, her understated, selfless interpretation of life's vagaries and conceits. I was all ears, hanging on every word.

"Heading home to Canada from Boston I had plenty of time to think. Plenty of time to think about Cleo. And I found myself remembering this one time when we were in Bermuda visiting Sonja, her husband, Dave, and their Min Pin, Odin. I think I told you how Cleo and I were always together, I mean always."

"She traveled with you on business. Loved airports," I said.

"That's right. Good memory."

I said nothing. Given the sad circumstances and my concern about our confrontation, there wasn't much about our meeting that I was likely to forget.

"Cleo doted on Odin, loved him to pieces, and during the second week of our stay, she suddenly decided that she would rather spend her nights sleeping with Sonja and Dave and Odin than with me. At the time I was devastated. I couldn't believe that Cleo would abandon me. Every night for the next two weeks she would say goodnight and trot off down the hall to sleep where she preferred, with someone other than me. All I could do was watch her go. And every morning she and Odin would come bounding onto my bed, happy to wake me up and thinking nothing about it.

"Then it hit me. It wasn't that Cleo didn't want to sleep with me. It wasn't that she was making a conscious choice or demonstrating a preference. She just loved being around Odin. Simple as that. She wanted to spend time with him. And I started to realize where we go so wrong with love. We waste so much time imagining, idealizing how we think love should look and how it should feel. We miss out on all the good stuff, the subtle stuff which is what it's all about. If it is real love, all we have to do is focus on making the people or animals we love happy, giving them what they need, and you can guarantee it will come full circle. The first time there was a thunderstorm, it was under *my* sweater where Cleo wanted to hide. When she got a thorn stuck in her pad, she hobbled over to *me* for help and nobody else."

"Long before I got home that day I came to believe Cleo was trying to teach me a lesson. I think Cleo wanted me to understand that if you really love something, true love, be it for a dog or a daughter, show them by loving them the way *they* need to be loved."

Okay, I thought, I liked the sentiment but what about all those lopsided, futile relationships, with one partner doing all the work for little in return. Maybe that was why she used the phrase "true love," a reciprocal love. Or maybe her conviction was better suited to the unembellished, uncomplicated love of an animal.

"After Cleo died, Sonja flew back to Bermuda, devastated. She felt like she had let me down. She desperately wanted to make my pain go away and she didn't know where to begin. I didn't push her or try to get her to open up. To this day I still don't know exactly how all this happened, how Cleo got injured. And what difference would it make? Would Sonja have been in any less pain? My daughter is an extremely private person. She's not like me. She keeps her feelings bottled up inside."

She waited a beat, collecting her thoughts, coming back on track.

"And that was when Cleo's lesson hit me. I needed to learn to love Sonja the way she needed to be loved. I have wasted too much time expecting her to love me my way. What makes my way right? Just because Sonja uses a different emotional vocabulary doesn't mean I can't learn to speak her language."

I was beginning to wonder where all this was leading. It seemed so personal.

"In the end it was your letter that brought us together, closer than we have ever been before."

"My first letter?" I asked, thrilled that she actually received it and stunned by its apparent impact.

"Yes. I still carry it with me. It's all dog-eared, and I've folded it so many times it's held together with Scotch tape."

"I don't understand," I said. "I just wrote to tell you about Helen. To let you know I took my promise to you and Cleo seriously. I didn't know if it would make any difference, but I did know Helen was a dog who deserved a chance, the perfect underdog, precisely the kind of dog Cleo would have rooted for."

"I agree," said Sandi, "but because you didn't have my address the letter went via Sonja. It was addressed to her and naturally she read it. When she did, your message caused something about her to change."

I was lost. I didn't remember being particularly eloquent or poetic. What on earth had I done?

"You wrote so many nice things about me and Cleo, and when Sonja read them, it was as though she was able to see me for the first time through another person's eyes. Don't get me wrong, she's always loved me, but she loved me on her terms. You gave her another, different perspective, as though it had been hidden in plain sight, and now she knew exactly where to look. It has changed everything."

"For the better, I hope."

I made the appeal in my voice pretty obvious but she didn't answer.

"Even before Cleo's passing, Sonja had been struggling to save her marriage. She wanted me to be angry at her, to blame her, and in turn, she ended up blaming Dave. It was the final straw. She left him, filed for divorce, and moved back to Canada."

Somehow I kept the "Oh, my God" to myself. This was why I had been unable to reach her in Bermuda. I had created a butterfly effect. Because of me a dog dies under anesthesia, and it ruins a marriage and drives an irreparable wedge between a mother and daughter.

"Don't worry," she said, as if divining my anxiety from the static between us, "they're back together and better than ever. In fact not long ago we had an incredible reunion. It was the first time I had seen Dave since Cleo's passing. I wanted him to know that this was nobody's fault, that there was no blame to assign, but he was so sad and so sorry, the three of us ended up hugging each other and crying."

And then Sandi returned to the way her daughter had rediscovered the importance of her marriage.

"I'm not saying it wasn't touch and go for a while, but ultimately Cleo's death awakened something inside both Sonja and Dave. They both realized they were making a classic mistake, living their lives only appreciating what they had when it was taken from them. This little dog may have been gone, but ultimately her absence alone was powerful enough to salvage a marriage."

I was already speechless and in need of a handkerchief, but Sandi Rasmussen decided to finish me off with the kind of philosophy and celestial insight guaranteed to pierce the armor of even the most hardhearted cynic.

"So you see everything happens for a reason. Everything is connected. Cleo lived a wonderful life and even in death she reached out and changed lives. She changed your awareness of, and attitude toward, a dog named Helen. She rescued a failing marriage. And she forever changed the relationship between a mother and a daughter. As painful as Cleo's passing was, I cherished every moment we were together, and when you can see it in this context, the amount of actual time is irrelevant because the intensity of the moment is guaranteed to last. I could have lost a child, a dog, a cat, or an elephant. It doesn't matter, because what remains, and what can never be lost, is a spirit. And besides, she was never really *my* dog. I just had the privilege of sharing fourteen months of my life with her."

| 20 | **LETTING GO** |

N OT so long ago, over at a friend's house for dinner, I was introduced to a man who had just celebrated his ninety-first birthday. His name was Jim, and though the years had stolen a few inches from his spine and his tidy white hair had reverted to the fineness of the newborn, he was sharp and witty and full of life. Call me sentimental, but when I get a chance to talk to someone who's done a whole lot of living you can be sure I'm looking to learn a thing or two.

I made a point of sitting next to him, and over our meal Jim discovered what I did for a living and leaned into me.

"A word of advice," he whispered, as though this pearl was for my ears only.

I stopped eating, my knife and fork drifting from mouth to plate.

"Never breathe your soul into a dog."

His milky blue eyes tried hard to focus in on mine as though this was the best way for the old man to give his point extra weight.

I swallowed and began chewing his sentence over in my mind, wondering if I should have heard the phrase before, if it was a quotation, something Jim had picked up along the way or plagiarized to fit his needs.

"What do you mean?" I asked.

For a moment, he worked his cracked lips, taking his thoughts for a test drive, as though he were trying to remember the lines he had rehearsed. Then he said, "A dog is just a dog. You would do well to remember that."

His tone was warm, more fatherly advice than disciplinary action. Even so I just stared back, letting him know I was waiting for more.

It took another beat before he capitulated.

"I've had dogs all my life," he said. "Beagles. Best dogs in the world. Over the years I've had eighteen of them."

Funny, I thought to myself, the way we never forget the animals in our lives. It's like asking a mother who has lost a child how many children she has. No mother ever does mental subtraction before she replies. The number is a constant, homage to the memory. And for so many pet owners, a similar logic applies.

"Every one of my beagles lived outside in a dog pen I built special. Every one of them," he paused, "except for Bee-bee."

"What was so special about Bee-bee?" I said.

And he smiled the smile of someone who doesn't have the time or the talent to put it all into words, but a smile that says it all. I smiled back.

"You let her in, didn't you?" I said. "You let her into your house and you let her into your heart."

He said nothing.

"When you say that," I said, "when you say 'never breathe your soul into a dog,' it sounds like you're defending yourself against the pain of having lost something special."

I saw a glint of something in his eyes, perhaps a memory of this dog, his favorite, abiding dog, talented and relentless, scenting a rabbit, barreling through the woods; or maybe it was a simple recollection of his late wife seated in front of the TV, Bee-bee, the lucky conscript, curled into a ball at her feet. And then he was back, pretending not to have heard what I said, quickly changing the subject to safer, less tender territory.

So here's the thing. How many of us can share our lives with animals and *not* become attached, involved, committed, or even, for some pet owners, infatuated? I'm not talking about turning cats, dogs, rabbits, or ferrets into so-called fur babies. I'm talking about the normal, natural, unavoidable, inevitable, and wonderful attachment that develops through time spent doing what it takes to properly care for an animal. Even Jim, old-school, hardnosed dog lover that he was, couldn't resist, broke down, and became infected by the love of a dog, and, at ninety-one years of age, he was still paying the price.

Perhaps Jim had it the wrong way round and what he should have said was "never let an animal breathe their soul into you," for once we become smitten, true love will always come at a price. For all the smiles, the laughter, the simplicity, certainty, and ease of sharing each other's company, at some point in the relationship, the price that must be paid will take the form of emotional pain.

Okay, so maybe love and pain are not conjoined twins, but frequently they are inextricably linked, an unwanted twofer, and sometimes it can be hard to tell where one ends and the other begins.

Pain will come for us when we are parted from our loved ones, cheated by our loved ones, face the fear of losing our loved ones. Sometimes it is this awareness of pain that makes us realize we must be in love, pain that signifies a love worth fighting for. It can make you wince, buckle, and scream. It could be a niggling ache, a stab of cold steel to the gut, or a heavy, intransigent weight, impossible to crawl out from under.

While I was trying to straighten this out in my head, hoping to divine the power of Sandi's take on life when it came to losing Cleo, I received a letter from a woman whose sister has cystic fibrosis like my daughter Emily. It struck a chord, perfectly tuned in to the heart of Sandi's philosophy:

"The doctor told my mother (a widow at the time) that she should tell my twelve-year-old sister that she will die. My mother said, 'Doctor, you are going to die, I am going to die, we are all going to die. I will not tell her she will die because right now she's too busy *living!*'"

And isn't this what it's all about? It doesn't matter whether you're talking about time spent with a child or an animal, the message is clear—savor the moment, big or small, and get busy with the joy of living.

The letter concluded with the kind of told-you-so statement parents of sick children live for.

"Paulette is now forty-six years old with two children of her own."

B**EYOND** living in the moment, I wish I knew how to defend against the pain, how to make it bearable, make it possible to love and not get hurt. In these last twenty years of working with sick animals, Sandi Rasmussen has arguably come the closest to offering me an answer because she was able to see what lies beyond the pain. She appreciated that loss is a part of life—not an end of life. She *chose* not to dwell on the unfairness of losing Cleo. She *chose* not to let it become the catalyst for anger, resentment, or self-pity. She never saw Cleo or her daughter or herself as a victim. There was no "poor me," no "poor Sonja," no "why did it have to be my dog?" She had every right to harbor resentment, to feel aggrieved, to want to avenge her loss. Cleo had died on my watch and inadvertently, indirectly, and unceremoniously I had compelled Sandi to react. She could have gone either way, and most of us would recognize anger as the natural, reasonable response. But Sandi opted for something far more difficult. I don't know how she did it, how she had the strength to resist its allure, but somehow she saw anger for what it was—an all-too-familiar siren, its rewards transient and hollow. Perhaps the answer lies rooted in her childhood, in the lessons she learned from the stray and abandoned animals that more than paid her back for her kindness and devotion. For whatever reason, Sandi chose to surrender to the pain, to say "I will not be defined by the events of my life, by what happens and is beyond my control." She didn't fight her loss, she accepted her loss, she saw that the loss had a purpose, a purity, an impact, and a lesson from which many might learn. In essence, Sandi Rasmussen let go, and as she already knew, letting go can be a powerful thing. The pain became tolerable and, for those of us who witnessed it, even inspirational.

I WISH I could tell you that Helen was still with us, but some twenty months after I performed her thoracic surgery, her cancer returned and she passed on, at her home with Eileen and Ben by her side. For a while I succumbed to sadness, but only for a while because every recollection I had of this dog brought me right back to her greatest attribute—Helen was a survivor. She had already achieved the medical holy grail of "miraculous." What did I expect, "everlasting"? This was cancer after all. There are no rules of fair play. Cancer wants to have the last word but I won't let it. You can look at this story from all sorts of different angles but I choose success and a remarkable victory. Thanks to veterinary advances, dedicated owners, and a whole lot of love, Helen got to enjoy more than two years as part of a family who doted on and adored her. Somehow this crafty, determined little dog had beaten the odds but eventually her luck had run out. Our pets will never be with us for long enough, at least not physically, but when they have been blessed with opportunity and been able to live a full life, how can we respond with anything less than pride and celebration?

One of the things that struck me about Helen's story was her wonderfully agreeable temporal distance from the physical and chemical intrusion of our veterinary medicine. This far out from surgery, from the bouts of chemotherapy, her survival had become all about her.

We may have played our part, but ours was only ever a cameo perfor-mance. Helen had been the one beating cancer, and she and her family were the ones who deserved the credit.

If you are still curious about the final pathology report on Cleo's postmortem, no specific cause of death was ever defined. I wasn't surprised or relieved. I didn't know whether Sandi would feel any differently if she had an answer, if she had someone or something to blame. Given my read on her, I imagine it no longer mattered. Per-haps it never did, pointing fingers was not her style. Truth is, more often than not, unexpected or accidental death fails to leave a calling card. In my experience speculation and inference rarely coincide with the pathological equivalent of a smoking gun. Maybe the ele-ment of mystery in life's disasters and miracles packs a bigger punch. When we are left to wonder, uncertainty becomes a clinical terrorist, a permanent threat meant to keep us vigilant.

I F writers of crime fiction are to be believed, detectives are sensitive to, and leery of, coincidence. Too many connections, mutual friends, and chance encounters, and suspicious minds become aroused. But for those of us traveling through life's more mundane destinies, when does coincidence become fate? What were the chances that Cleo and I were destined to cross paths? Looking back over the events leading to our encounter I began to realize the odds were far shorter than I first imagined.

Cleo's leg could just as easily have fractured for the third time in Canada rather than Bermuda but this particular Min Pin had a pen-chant for living the island life. If such an injury were to occur, there was a fair chance it might transpire in a land of quaint shorts and gauche socks.

Bermuda lies about seven hundred miles from Boston and there are many direct flights to closer veterinary referral clinics capa-ble of performing her surgery along the East Coast. Sonja could have picked the Carolinas, Virginia, or New York. However, the island's pet population is served by two major veterinary practices, both of which regularly refer their tricky surgical cases to yours truly. Of course I don't have a monopoly on Bermuda's surgical referrals, but the odds favor me.

This leaves the minute probability of anesthetic risk mentioned earlier, small but not nearly as small as all of us would prefer. When I tally these variables, consider my and Cleo's flight path, the choices made, the chances that things would turn out the way they did, the odds are long, but nowhere near as long as picking a Powerball winner. Clearly, not everything that impacts our lives will be good or pleasant, but if we are open to learning from our experiences, regardless of their nature, they can at least be meaningful. Cleo's clinical outcome may be the epitomy of failure and yet for me, thanks to Sandi, her legacy has been powerful and far reaching. Call it coincidence, fate, or whatever, sometimes it feels as though we live our lives like an iPod Shuffle—we may think that everything comes at us in a random fashion but every so often a particular sequence feels just right because, when you get right down to it, we are the ones programming the tunes!

THE only question that remains is, what part, if any, did Cleo play in Helen's recovery? I know what you're thinking: here he goes again, cooking the emotional books, contriving a transcendent connection for his happy ending. If I am, then let me argue my point with the story of a much-loved German shepherd called Lucy. Lucy and I had met several times over the years—two knees, numerous lumps and bumps—and so a phone call from Lucy's owner, Ava, to schedule an appointment so I could examine a troubling growth on Lucy's lower eyelid came as no surprise.

"I have something to ask you," said Ava when we met, "and please, feel free to tell me if I'm being stupid." She hesitated, letting the tears catch up, injecting a tremor into every word. "But, my father died recently. He had a pacemaker, you see. The battery pack was brand new and he had insisted it be removed before he was cremated. I can't tell you how much he loved Lucy, how important she was to him."

She smiled into the pain, trying to master it, failing dismally. I took my cue.

"You don't have to tell me," I said. "A lot of grandparents make soft targets for dogs in search of treats and table scraps. I can guess where most of Lucy's nutritional love came from!"

She laughed, intoxicated by that familiar unashamed cocktail of truth and the memory of what she had lost.

"You're right. Dad was awful and no matter how much I tried to tell him, Lucy could always win him over when it came to food."

She waited a beat and went on.

"One of his dying wishes, and like I say, it could be silly, was to see if some animal could use his pacemaker. It would have meant the world to him to think his loss could be another creature's gain."

People never cease to amaze me. Talk about giving from the heart. Once again I was floored by human generosity when it comes to the animals in our lives. Without hesitation I applauded what her father had done, and his intent, and promised I would look into the plausibility of what he wanted to achieve after his death.

If I really was guilty of fashioning a fairy-tale ending, we all know who should have been the lucky beneficiary of the pacemaker. Lucy may have become a gourmand Alsatian but fortunately her heart was in perfect working order. In fact, after consulting with several cardiologists, I discovered that relative to the price tag of pacemaker implantation, the cost of the battery pack itself is a relatively trivial fee. Most owners would prefer a brand-new battery at a cost of $150, rather than settle for a used version.

When I contacted Ava to share my disappointing news, part of me still hoped a needy case might come along, perhaps a shelter dog, a

stray, a creature abandoned by someone for whom $150 may as well
have been $150 million. And part of me still does, only now I realize
there was something far more important to learn from Ava's father's
request.

After my experience with Cleo and Helen, I can see it doesn't
really matter whether we get to use the pacemaker or not, because
what does matter and what will never be lost, is the spirit of the offer.
The act of generosity is set in stone. It will never wear out, fade, or go
away. And to me, the exact same generosity exists between Cleo and
Helen. It doesn't matter one iota whether it made a difference or not.
The intent was positive. The outcome for Helen was wonderful but
essentially superfluous. The reward comes from what was let go and
not from what we got back.

It's probably fair to say we all want to leave some sort of mark,
some sort of legacy from our time spent on this earth. I'm not talking about an entry in *The Guinness Book of World Records* or a Pulitzer
prize or an Oscar or summiting a mountain high enough to require
supplemental oxygen. I'm talking about what counts, what sets certain people apart, like Ava's dad and his pacemaker, a regular guy
whose succinct, humble, whispered appeal still resonates loud and
clear. I'm talking about the poise and understanding of Sandi Rasmussen in the immediate aftermath of losing Cleo. I'm talking
about the selfless desire of Eileen and Ben to give an abandoned dog
a chance. These marks are real. These are the marks that count. On
the crowded beach of my years of clinical experience, these are some
of the people who have left permanent footprints in the sand.

And then there are those who left paw prints.

Acknowledgments

ONE of this would have been possible without the cooperation, honesty, and trust of Sandi Rasmussen and Eileen Aronson. I am sure there were certain details and nuances of their stories that I failed to convey. Realistically, I could only ever hope to capture a fraction of what it meant to know Cleo and Helen. For any discrepancies or mistakes I made in trying to achieve this goal, I am sorry. My thanks go out to their husbands, Jan and Ben, whose roles and importance in what transpired was undoubtedly far greater than I portrayed. And, of course, I cannot forget Sonja and Dave. Sonja's quiet understanding and forgiveness at such a difficult time still astounds me. I tried to be respectful of her relationship with Dave, to intimate tension while leaving the rest to imagination. I wish them both all the best.

In no particular order I should like to acknowledge Nick Glynn, Neil Burnie, Allen Sisson, Sherry Nadworny, Lisa Moses, Leah Myrbeck, Kara and Grace Dunne, Mary Pizzachino, Frances Cardullo, Lois Wetmore, Meaghan Tracey, Ava McGarr, Peter Demosthenes Raft, and James McDonough. Thanks to my agent, Kristin Lindstrom, and all the fabulous folks at Broadway Books. I owe them a huge debt of gratitude and in particular, my editor, Christine Pride.

Once again, Christine performed magic as she polished, refined, and enhanced. I am truly fortunate to have her on my side.

Finally, working a full-time job and playing make-believe as a writer can only come about through the love and support of my family. Whitney, bless you for your tireless optimism and confidence in my success; Emily, you are the angel who changed my life, opened my eyes, and made all of this possible; and Kathy, my wife, best friend, and trusted confidante, you are our heart and soul.

Ever By My Side

The Definition
of Different

I wish I could tell you I have enjoyed the company of a dog or a cat every day of my life, but it's simply not true. In fact, my earliest appreciation of pets in any form did not occur until I was four and, even then, was limited to my grandmothers' dogs.

My mother's mother possessed a white male toy poodle named Marty. From the start, Marty made it abundantly clear that he had no patience for small curious hands, except perhaps as chew toys. Venture into his territory, that is, anywhere within an invisible fifty-yard perimeter of my grandma's house, and he would come at you, bouncing forward as if his legs were little pogo sticks, emitting a bark that could crack bullet-proof glass, before scurrying away to safety behind Grandma's ankle, only to repeat the process over and over again until he finally ascended into her arms. From this lofty position he could look down at me with an expression that said "if you bother me, I will make you pay in blood and tears."

Marty was not even a year old and his presence had already negated what few pleasures there were after a two-hour car drive to visit my grandma.

"Sit you down while I put the kettle on," Gran would say as everyone rushed for a vacant seat in a game of musical chairs that invariably left me with the sofa where Marty had settled. Curled up on the middle cushion, Marty would emit a throaty, malicious grumble if I so much as inched toward the ends of the couch.

There was also the smell. The entire house reeked of the only food Marty deigned to consume—sausages! I never once saw him eat regular dog food. And I'm not talking about classic British bangers. Marty's delicate mouth and discriminating palate preferred, no, insisted upon, a small, handcrafted breakfast sausage from a local butcher that had to be fried, allowed to cool, and then carefully chopped into congealed mouth-size pieces. At some point during every visit Gran would excuse herself, go to the kitchen, take up a position next to the stove, and disappear into an oily cloud as she seared sheathed meat that crackled and spat in her direction. I would look over at her and she would smile the smile of old people everywhere, content to check off another comforting chore in her daily routine. Meanwhile Marty might squirm a little on his throne and sigh, not out of boredom, but approval, pleased the hired help was doing his bidding.

Neither my grandma nor my parents ever suggested Marty and I become acquainted or that Marty become socialized around children or that he be reprimanded for his bad manners. Perhaps I couldn't be trusted not to pinch, yank, rip, or snap as I did with most of my toys. Perhaps they didn't want to take any chances. Whatever the reason, I kept my distance, painfully curious to discover the feel of his hypoallergenic, steel-wool fur but convinced he would practically explode if I so much as touched him. After a while, I lost all interest in Marty. What was the point? How could I have a relationship with an animal who might as well have been behind bars in a zoo? I couldn't understand what anyone saw in a pet you couldn't, well, pet.

On the other hand, my grandmother on my father's side had a placid female Dalmatian named Cleo and to my delight (and no doubt to the delight of my mother), they occupied a small bungalow next door to our house. In contrast to Marty, Cleo could be completely trusted around children. She was tolerant and forgiving and endowed with seal-pup insulation that possessed a certain . . . give, similar to a Tempur-Pedic foam mattress. Cleo never tired of me petting her, happy to relinquish her short, fine hairs to my sticky palms, which would soon resemble a pair of black and white mittens. I could fall over her or fall into her and she would either lie there and take it, indifferent to the contact, or rise quickly to her feet and find somewhere else to lie down, as though she was sorry for getting under foot rather than angry at being disturbed. At the time, my little sister, Fiona, was too small to play with me, so I was thrilled to share our backyard with a big old spotty dog who never once regarded me as though I were a tasty hors d'oeuvre.

To fully appreciate the bond that formed between me and Cleo, you have to understand our shared interest in swallowing inanimate objects and to help you to do so I must mention a chilling yet formative recollection from my childhood.

Late one night, barefoot and immersed in oversized cotton pajamas, this four-year-old boy stood alone in the kitchen having snuck out of bed in search of a snack and a glass of milk. I have always been partial to yogurt, methodically working my way to the bottom of the carton, scraping every last pink glob of strawberry-colored additives off the plastic and onto my spoon. Even now I can recall the feel of that particular spoon, cool and smooth and small, like a silver christening spoon, satisfyingly tinkly on my deciduous teeth and almost weightless in my mouth. With the yogurt gone and my mind in a dull and dreamy state, I began playing with the spoon in the back of my mouth, appreciating the metallic sensation way back on my tongue and how it was possible to push it a little farther and induce gagging, a sharp and forceful contraction deep in my belly—until somewhere just beyond this point, the reflex of actual swallowing took over, involuntary, and to my horror, completely irreversible. I felt the tiny handle leaving my fingertips and slipping from my grasp, and suddenly, like the yogurt, the spoon was gone, disappearing deep inside my body.

When I felt it go there was no pain or discomfort, only the rush of fear that I had done something very wrong and, perhaps more importantly, impossible to justify. I mean you don't just swallow a spoon by accident. What was I going to tell my mum and dad? I fell on a spoon while my mouth was open! I was so hungry I ate my yogurt, spoon and all!

I waited for a few minutes and nothing happened. I had a drink of milk and nothing happened. I didn't feel any different. If I jumped up and down nothing rattled inside my body, nothing tickled or poked through my skin. In the end, instead of confessing my sin to my parents, I decided to wait and see what, if anything, happened and besides, I was tired, so I went back to bed.

At this early stage of my life, I'm not entirely sure I could make any connection between what went into my mouth and what came out the other end. All I knew was that by the next morning I still felt fine. No one seemed to have noticed there was anything missing from the cutlery drawer and so I decided to keep my acquisition of a foreign body a secret, comfortable with the notion that the little spoon was lost inside me, hidden somewhere dark and warm and safe, not causing me any harm, inert and happy to simply hang out. It was not until I was thirteen years old, and clearly not much wiser, that I feared my secret would be revealed.

In trying to define my early teenage stature, some might use the word lean out of kindness. Truth be told, I was a scrawny whippet of a boy. I was, however, blessed with a semblance of speed, a characteristic that did not go unnoticed by our school sports teacher, Mr. French.

"All you have to do is catch the ball and run for the line."

Sounded simple enough, but his synopsis of what would be required of me as a winger on our school rugby team failed to do justice to the rough and tumble of what the game meant to boys with far more muscle, spite, and testosterone.

I like to remember the critical moment in terms of the dying seconds of a crucial game, perhaps a grudge match against local rivals or a match to claim a league championship title, with time running out, and one more try needed to win—me making an impossible catch, a shimmy left, a fake right, defenders falling at my feet as I charged for the line, rugby ball tucked tight and safe in my chest as I leapt over giants and landed for my winning points just as the final whistle blew. What actually transpired was that I caught a ball in the middle of the field and hesitated, and in a moment of panic half a dozen boys jumped on top of me, frozen mud on the right side of my body, hundreds of pounds of grunting, writhing, sweaty bodies on my left. Something had to give as a result of this mayhem and unfortunately that something happened to be my breastbone.

I'd be lying if I said there was an enormous crack akin to a shotgun blast. In fact I got up and carried on playing. All I noticed was an increased difficulty in breathing and by the end of the game it was obvious that this was more than a general lack of physical fitness on my part.

And so I found myself in an emergency room hearing a young doctor suggest that I get a chest X-ray and realizing that for the first time since swallowing that fateful spoon, I would be the recipient of a test that would surely unmask my embarrassing silverware secret.

"You know, Dad, I think I'm feeling better. It's probably nothing," I said to my father, convinced that after all these years the spoon was somehow still sitting in my stomach or casually leaning into the side of my esophagus, minding its own business.

When the doctor emerged with the images, I braced for the ramifications of their peculiar and unequivocal revelation.

"Well, guess what I found hidden in his chest?"

I knew it. The X-ray machine was just another type of camera and I knew how a camera never lies.

"See this dark line, here. That's a crack, a fracture. Your son has broken his sternum."

I looked at the black-and-white film for myself, not at the break, but all over the image, looking for something metallic, white, and vaguely spoon shaped. But there was nothing.

It wasn't until I studied biology in school and ultimately medicine at college that I realized the stupidity of worrying over a chest X-ray. They would have had to take an X-ray of my lower abdomen. I'm sure this is where that pesky spoon is still lurking to this day.

But let's get back to Cleo, to the two of us in our backyard, my green universe, playing endless rounds of fetch with her favorite ball.

For a while the game proceeded as expected—slimy ball, painfully short throws from an uncoordinated little pitching arm, patient softmouthed dog politely performing retrieval exercises. Then I noticed something long and thin and obviously amiss dangling from the base of Cleo's tail and trailing behind her. She took a time-out, intermittently squatting, straining, and dancing around as if she had a length of unshakable toilet paper stuck to her foot. She was visibly upset and unable to continue our game. If I had to put an emotional label on her behavior I would say she appeared to be embarrassed.

Concerned and curious, I ran to the house to fetch my father, insisting he come and check out Cleo.

"Look," I said, all business as I pointed toward the aberration. "There's something up her bum!"

Dad greeted Cleo with a pat to her head before shuffling around behind her, nodding his agreement.

"It's okay, son. It's one of Gran's old nylon stockings."

I was puzzled and a little upset.

"Why would Gran stick a stocking up Cleo's bum?" I asked.

"She didn't," said my father.

"Then who did?" I said.

My father hesitated, deliberated, and ultimately opted for a time-honored adult approach to my line of questioning, that is, he ignored it.

"Let's just give Cleo a few minutes in private. See if she sorts herself out."

Dad took me by the hand and we backed off, retreating several yards before he squatted down by my side and whispered, "We'll watch her from here."

"But why is it coming out of her bum?" I whispered back.

He considered me with what I would later recognize as a mixture of pride and frustration for being such a relentless little bugger when it came to my wanting to figure out the ways of the world.

"Because she swallowed it," he said, trying his best to tamp down the curt edge creeping into his voice. "Because Cleo likes to eat things she shouldn't. Things that aren't good for her. Things other than dog food. Things like Gran's underwear. But don't you worry, no matter what your Cleo eats it always comes out the other end."

Here was my first lesson in basic gastrointestinal physiology, that according to my father, what goes in, must come out. Of course I was potty trained and more than capable of taking myself off to our bathroom alone, but this was the first time I recall a clarification of the cause-and-effect relationship between ingestion and elimination. What I really needed to know was whether, during inappropriate dining, Cleo had ever swallowed a spoon. If her current discomfort was anything to go by, surely I would have noticed when a firm metallic object found its way out?

My father must have misread the confusion and anxiety playing across my face and tried to placate me by adding the word "Eventually."

It didn't work.

We waited for what felt like three hours but was probably more like three minutes and watched as Cleo spun around and around, scooting her rear along the grass in vain, clearly becoming more and more frustrated.

"I've got an idea," my father said, standing up and heading back toward Cleo. "Go grab her ball."

I did as I was told and reported for duty.

"Now, when I'm ready, I want you to throw Cleo's ball as far away as possible."

I didn't understand.

"Why?"

"You'll see," he said.

Another adult response all inquisitive children despise because obviously I didn't see and that was why I was asking the question in the first place.

"But I can't throw very far."

My father insisted that this wouldn't matter (alternatively, he may have said, "Just shut up and do as you're told") and stood a short distance behind Cleo after placing me and the ball in my hand at her head.

"Hold on a moment, son," he said, watching and waiting as Cleo forgot about her troubles, focused on the ball, and tried to anticipate which way it would go.

At the time I never noticed how my father was placing the sole of his shoe firmly down to the ground, pinning the trailing end of the wayward hosiery in place.

"Now," he shouted, and with concentration and enough fierce determination to produce a little grunt as I bit down on the tip of my tongue, I released the airy plastic ball from my hand like a shot put, and it landed about three feet away.

Not far but far enough for Cleo to pounce forward, retrieve the ball, and leave the stocking behind, lying on the ground.

Cleo acted as if nothing had happened and plunged right back into our game, dropping the ball at my feet, ready to go again. Just once, she glanced over her shoulder at my father and the stringy, discolored length of nylon before focusing on me, as if she seemed disturbed by what he was doing, as if she would rather he pick up whatever it was that had become stuck to his foot because it was disgusting.

Although I like to chalk this up as my first, if indirect, canine medical intervention, I should point out that this approach to treating Cleo's protruding foreign body may have seemed rational but was totally inappropriate. My father should have left well alone and sought veterinary advice. What if the stocking had been lodged in Cleo's small intestines? What if the nylon had cheese-wired through her guts? Fortunately, as it turned out she was lucky, perfectly fine, ready to graze her way through my grandmother's lingerie once again. It would be decades before I saw the error in our approach to her predicament.

All three of us walked away from the incident as though nothing much had happened. At no time did my father and I dwell on what we had done, on how our ploy had brought about Cleo's transition from anxious and uncomfortable to oblivious and happy to play. He never paused to ruminate on the moment when the seed of possibility was firmly planted, to recognize the first inkling of his son's interest in helping sick animals. Within seconds Cleo and I had returned to the carefree rhythm of fetch and my fickle attention had moved on, my pitching arm quick to tire, boredom setting in, and a more pressing question racing to the forefront of my mind.

"Mum," I shouted, "when will dinner be ready?"

* * *

Being around Cleo was great. She was the perfect playmate. I think the best way to describe our relationship would be to say that I was like a smitten grandparent with my first grandchild—I got to enjoy all the fun stuff, but at the end of the day I could walk away. And when I did tire of canine company, searching out other kids in the neighborhood, Cleo never complained or bore a grudge, happy to pick up wherever we left off on my timetable and not hers.

I should mention that this was England in the 1960s, an era when children led "under-scheduled" lives, kicked out of the house at eight o'clock in the morning, only allowed back in if there was no more daylight, you were suffering from clinical dehydration, or you had sustained an injury requiring nothing less than a blood transfusion or surgical removal of an appendage. Exiled kids, forced to use their imagination, tended to gravitate toward one another, mergers leading to friendships and the emergence of something we were all proud to be a part of—a gang.

Across our street and a few houses down lived Timmy and Keith Toenail. Timmy was a terrier of a boy: squat, scrappy, and determined, cursed with disobedient locks of tightly curled platinum blond hair, making him look a bit like Shirley Temple in *Heidi*. He and his older brother, Keith, demonstrated all the physical similarities of brothers like Prince Harry and Prince William, that is to say they were both male and that was about it. Keith's hair was jet black, overly conditioned to a greasy shine, and meticulously maintained in the style of a German World War II infantryman's helmet by his doting mother. Unlike his younger brother, Keith was prone to tears and a trembling lower lip, a feature accentuated by an overbite that would forever vex his orthodontist.

Across the street and one house up lived a girl several years my senior. Her name was Amanda Ravenscroft and she was my first crush (after the cartoon character of Daphne on *Scooby-Doo*, of course). Amanda was tall, blond, and muscular. She favored braided pigtails that made her look as though she had just stepped off a conquering Viking ship.

For the most part our playtime together was predictable, rotating between cops and robbers, cowboys and Indians (the term "PC" had yet to be coined), and of course, "war" (we always fought "the Germans," and not "the Nazis," since England lacked a significant Germanic component to its general population). Amanda's maturity made her leadership material and on the whole the rest of us were putty in her hands, as easy for her to manipulate as a group of dolls at a tea party. Strangely, every plot she concocted seemed to include a damsel in distress, Amanda happy to step into the role, living a little fantasy, no doubt enjoying the fierce competition among the three of us boys trying to come to her rescue.

When we tired of make-believe, we would break out our bicycles and tricycles and the four of us would prowl the nearby streets in search of adventure. On one memorable day, we hit pay dirt.

It was Amanda, leading our formation, who made the discovery, noticing something white and writhing tossed into the bottom of a hedgerow. I heard the squeal of her brakes as her bike clattered to the pavement and she dismounted, and watched as she retrieved what appeared to be a dirty old pillowcase.

"Look what I've found," she said, raising the bag in the air like a trophy.

And even before the rest of us had peeked inside, it was obvious what she had discovered given the chorus of muffled cries coming from inside the case.

"Kittens," Amanda proclaimed, as though the hapless threesome who finally caught up to her might need help identifying the four angry newborn mammals crawling over one another.

It was a good job there were four of them—one all black, one all white, one black with white patches on his paws and chest like a tuxedo, and one white with a black swatch under its nose like a mustache. We all knelt down, formed a circle, and passed them around between us, consistently changing our opinions as to which one was the best, the strongest, the runt, or our personal favorite.

I wasn't used to cats or, for that matter, any other life form that seemed so upset and vulnerable. Their pointy, triangular faces, their incessant mews, their perfect little paws and claws and plump bald bellies were so very different from what I knew because all I really knew was a dog named Cleo (to my way of thinking Marty the land shark didn't count).

"I'm calling this one Sugarplum," Amanda declared, cradling the all-white kitten in her cupped hands and rocking him or her back and forth.

"Then I'm calling this one . . ." Timmy hesitated, as if he had prematurely pressed his buzzer on *Jeopardy* and didn't really have an answer for Alex. "Um . . . um . . . Blackie," he said triumphantly.

At the time this seemed perfectly appropriate and original.

"I don't have a name for this one," said Keith, holding little Mr. Tux, his voice trailing off in a manner we all recognized as a potential preamble to tears.

"Me either," I said, gently stroking the one with the mustache. Secretly I was pleased with the way our game of "musical kittens" had worked out. In my opinion, Pancho Villa was the best, the runt and my favorite.

Suddenly Keith laid Mr. Tux on the ground and made a lunge for Timmy's kitten.

"I want Blackie. Who says he belongs to you? Give him to me, he's mine."

Timmy sprang to his feet, pulling Blackie into the security of his chest as he backed away.

"Get off me or I'm telling Mum."

Ordinarily, especially if there was nothing much going on, Amanda and I might have looked on as the two of them got into it, Keith bigger and stronger, Timmy tougher and more resilient, their fights guaranteed to end in tear-streaked dirty red cheeks all round. But on this occasion, Amanda's maturity and wisdom were their undoing.

"Do you really think your mum will let you keep him?" she asked.

I wasn't sure whether the question was directed at Keith or Timmy, but Keith latched onto this perspective, shaking his head.

"Not after you killed our goldfish."

"Did not," said Timmy but without conviction.

"I know my mum and dad won't let me have a kitten or a puppy," said Amanda, wistfully. "I ask them every birthday and Christmas and they always say no."

Though no one turned to look at me or ask me directly, I felt as though I was the kittens' last hope of finding a home. The thing was I'd never really considered why my parents didn't have a cat or dog of their own. They both seemed to like Cleo, so what was holding them back? Maybe all I had to do was ask.

"I know," said Amanda, briefly offering Sugarplum up to the heavens before planting a kiss on the kitten's pink nose. "We'll go ask the Cat Lady what to do."

This should have been my cue to raise an eyebrow and work a little apprehension into the reply "Cat Lady?" but Keith beat me to it.

"Do you know her?" he said, with the kind of veiled reverence normally reserved for celebrities.

"No, but I know where she lives and my dad's met her and I heard him telling my mum 'she's a little strange but well-meaning.'"

I had never heard of the so-called Cat Lady, making her no less mysterious than Bigfoot or the Wizard of Oz. And what did Amanda's dad mean by "strange but well-meaning"?

"Come on, it's just down the street," said Amanda, already ten yards ahead of us. "We can leave the bikes here."

So, armed with a kitten each, Keith still whining over being dealt Mr. Tux and the fact that none of us were prepared to swap, we marched off in the direction of a small cottage hidden behind a forest of vines and dense thorny vegetation. If we had celebrated American-style Halloween, this would have been the spooky house no kids in the neighborhood dared to hit up for trick or treat.

"What a pigsty," whispered Timmy as Amanda knocked on the dilapidated front door.

At a downstairs window a shredded lace curtain fluttered and then a tiny woman appeared at the doorstep looking as if she had just got out of bed in her mauve bathrobe and matching slippers, even though this was the middle of the afternoon. She was not much taller than Amanda but her skin was waxy and wrinkled, her gray hair stiff and lopsided, as if it had dried in a strong crosswind.

This is all the description I can offer because my eyes began to water, my vision blurred, and I had an overpowering desire to pinch my nose and run away, gasping for fresh air. The Cat Lady was careful to close the front door behind her, but she had already unleashed a pungent, toxic cloud of aerosolized feline urine into our environment.

To her credit and my surprise, Amanda managed to stay focused and told the story of how we found the four abandoned kittens in a pillowcase and how they seemed hungry and in need of food and shelter. In the meantime Keith looked like he might vomit, the nausea contorting his face fueling a giggling fit that his brother Timmy struggled to contain.

"We didn't know what to do," said Amanda, showing Sugarplum to the Cat Lady.

Now, some parents might be reading this and thinking an impromptu visit to a complete stranger with a local reputation for being a bit of a weirdo might not have been a particularly good idea. What if the Cat Lady invited us in and introduced us to her husband, the Big Bad Wolf? In fact, personal danger never crossed our minds. Helicopter parenting had yet to be invented and besides, the old woman's getup gave her a warm and cozy bedtime aura, as if she might break out the hot chocolate and tell us a story at any moment.

The Cat Lady kept her lips pursed, head angled slightly down, forcing her eyes to roll up as she considered the four of us through wispy gray eyebrows. We held our collective breath (primarily because of the overpowering aroma of cat pee), but she may have mistaken this for worry on our part over what she was going to do.

"Follow me," she said in a plummy voice that exuded military hustle, leading us down the side of the house—not through it—to a small backyard. There, inside a wooden shed (thankfully well ventilated), was a series of crates and cages containing a couple of older kittens and some adult cats. Everything was clean and orderly, plenty of newspaper and blankets to go around.

"Let's have a look at him," said the Cat Lady and held out her hand to Amanda, taking Sugarplum and inspecting his belly, his mouth, and his eyes. At the time I thought this was just another way of judging which one she would choose to be her favorite, but of course she was trying to get a sense of the kitten's age—whether it still had the dried and shriveled umbilical remnant of a kitten up to three days old; whether it had any nubbins of teeth coming in, suggesting a kitten about two weeks of age; whether, as was the case with our litter, the eyes were still shut.

"You can leave them with me," she said, "but I'm not promising anything, you understand. They're more than three days old but less than ten. A difficult age and a lot of work, but I'll give it a try. You never know."

One by one we said our goodbyes to the little creatures in our hands and entrusted them to the Cat Lady. We thanked her and headed back the way we came, ignoring any uncertainty about their futures. To our way of thinking, what could be so difficult? Don't you just give them food and water and watch them grow? The biggest dilemma was whether your mum or dad would let you do it at your house, not whether or not it could be done.

Looking back, I realize that no one earns the moniker Cat Lady by having one or two cats lounging around the homestead. How many cats does it take to go from cat lover to collector of cats? Six, a dozen, a hundred? When does devotion become obsession, become something compulsive, pathological, and terribly sad? All I can tell you is our Cat Lady may have benefited from opening a window or two, neutering all her male cats, and investing in a little Febreze, but from what I saw of her cat-rescue operation she was no hoarder of cats. The animals out back appeared to be in good health and well looked after. I simply had no point of reference for the smell of tomcat pee in confined spaces.

To fully appreciate how good we felt that day, you need to know that we were a generation of kids who loved to visit our local movie theater every Saturday morning, basking in the opportunity to throw candy at each other, to stomp our feet to the rhythm of every chase scene, to watch a cartoon, a serial, and a feature-length movie that always portrayed kids our age as would-be heroes who got themselves into, and out of, a tight spot, beating the bad guys and living to play another day. Well, that particular afternoon, we walked away from the Cat Lady's house with a certain swagger, heads held high and big smiles all around, because for the first time in our lives, albeit with a quartet of

abandoned kittens, and in spite of their uncertain future, we believed
we got to right a wrong, just like our idols on the big screen.

. . .

Time has a knack for distortion—fogging the images from the past,
making everything feel bigger than it really was, messing with the col-
lage of mental snapshots pinned to the corkboard of our memory. So I
have to believe the clarity with which I still see what took place on an
empty beach pounded by an angry Irish Sea as a reflection of its enduring influence on me.

Like most kids, I was blissfully ignorant of my family's financial and
social status. Now I don't want to give the impression we were *Angela's
Ashes* poor or anything, but I never saw a banana until I was twelve and
thought that trousers were meant to be worn above the ankles, and va-
cations were something you did for one day and always within driving
distance.

On this particular day trip our normal family dynamic was upset by
the addition of my grandma and more importantly, and to my dismay,
her four-legged escort, the infamous and menacing Marty. Quite why
we had to take the poodle with us on a car ride to a sleepy seaside town
in northern Wales I will never know. What I do know is the six of us
piled into our Morris Minor, Mum and Dad up front, Grandma in the
middle between me and my sister, Marty perched on her lap. Nobody
wore seat belts back then, so for several hours we were tossed back and
forth and side by side on winding country roads, my father impersonating a British Grand Prix driver as we sucked down his secondhand
cigarette smoke, wondering who would be first to claim car sickness.
All the while Marty kept vigil, staring me down, defending his personal
space, offering me the occasional snarl and wrinkle of his upper lip,
feigning innocence and doe-eyed stares every time I complained to
Grandma. There's a reason why I have always found poodles to be one
of the smartest breeds of dog.

When we got there we had a picnic on the beach, adults sipping
hot tea from a thermos in plastic cups and commenting on the gritty

sandwiches they had prepared, the ominous-looking clouds, and the threat of rain. There was the promise of ice cream later, but first my father had agreed to help Fiona build a sand castle. For some reason I was more interested in beachcombing, so my mum, Grandma, Marty, and I set off on a postprandial walk down to the water's edge.

This was autumn, off-season, chilly, and there were very few people out and about. The overcast sky blended into the ocean. We were wrapped up in sweaters and overcoats and the tide was way off in the distance, forcing us to head out across wet sandy flats if we wanted to get near the waves and the possibility of washed-up shells. Marty was off leash, having the time of his life, scampering around, quick and dainty, hopping from one tidal pool to the next. He didn't even mind that I was holding Grandma's hand.

At the water's edge it all happened so fast. The tide was still headed out, the surf crashing hard, frothy gray breakers with quite a pull washing over the sand. This was not swimming weather (in this part of Britain it rarely ever was). This was not even paddling weather, the water icy cold to the touch. So you can imagine our concern when one minute Marty was gaily dancing in and out of the lapping foam and the next he was gone, disappearing out to sea, swallowed by a wall of gray water, quickly ten, fifteen yards out and drifting still further away. He didn't bark—he probably couldn't from the cold shock stealing his breath—he just tried to paddle, head up, neck outstretched, looking in my direction.

There are several possibilities as to how this pivotal moment in my early life might have played out. For starters, I couldn't swim, so a selfless, heroic act in which I rescued a drowning dog as motivation for a career helping animals in need was never in the cards. Besides, I'm pretty sure my mother had not packed my inflatable rubber ring.

At this point you would be forgiven for gasping in horror if you feared the possibility that I was some sort of malicious Damien child, a furtive witness to poor Marty's exodus, seizing the opportunity to be rid of my nemesis and rival for Grandma's attention by squandering precious time pointing out a particularly fascinating variety of seaweed before offering an inquisitive but nonchalant "So, where's Marty?"